THE
ALTERNATIVE

THE
ALTERNATIVE

THE ALTERNATIVE

Politics for a Change

Edited by
Ben Pimlott, Anthony Wright
and Tony Flower

W H ALLEN & CO PLC

Each contribution is original to this book: the copyright is held by the individual author of each piece, dated 1990 (except John Mortimer's contribution which is copyrighted in the name of Advanpress Ltd., 1990)

First published in Great Britain by W H Allen and Co plc 1990

Printed and bound in Great Britain by
Butler & Tanner Ltd, Frome & London
for the publishers, W H Allen and Co plc,
26 Grand Union Centre
338 Ladbroke Grove
London W10 5AH

ISBN 1 85227 168 X

A CIP catalogue record for this book is available from the British Library

Preface

All contributions to this volume were specially commissioned for it and are published here for the first time. The book is intended for everybody who is interested in finding an alternative: it does not contain any exclusive point of view or prescription. Neither does it presuppose any set of attitudes in the reader.

The book is loosely divided into three sections. The first is about alternative political and governing principles; the second is about the changes an alternative government might put into effect; the third is about ways of getting there. Some chapters look closely at particular controversies. Others are shorter and more personal. The latter – the raisins in the cake – are distinguished by a bolder type.

We would like to thank the authors for the thought and care they have put into the project. We would also like to acknowledge the role of all those who have given support to *Samizdat*: Michael Young, who first had the idea for such a venture and helped bring it to fruition; the newsletter's steering group (several of whose members are contributors to this volume) for their encouragement; the many other excellent authors who have written for *Samizdat*; the Joseph Rowntree Social Service Trust for vital grants towards the running costs of the newsletter; Susanne McDadd, formerly of W. H. Allen, who suggested this book and guided it through its early stages; the anti-alternative journalists whose denunciations helped give *Samizdat* invaluable publicity at the outset; the remarkably large number of sympathetic commentators who have backed it; and, above all, *Samizdat*'s subscribers and supporters.

Finally, we should stress again that each opinion in *The Alternative* is individual to its author, and does not necessarily express the views of other contributors, the editors, or *Samizdat* itself – though all are part of the growing movement which we call the popular front of the mind.

Contents

POLITICS

Contents

Introduction

This is a book about a different future. Its point of origin is the newsletter *Samizdat*, launched in October 1988 to promote a 'popular front of the mind' against the present government. Written by *Samizdat* authors and sympathisers – members of several left-of-right parties and of none – it is a book not just for the new decade but, ambitiously, for Britain in the new millenium. It looks beyond the bloody, idealistic, hungry, prosperous, polluting, freedom-seeking, genocidal, sceptical, creative spirit of our own century to the doubtless equally bumpy next. But it is mainly about the present. Its premise is that Britain is governed badly, on the basis of dangerous principles and false assumptions and in the interests of the wrong people. It sees an opportunity for change, and its writers have the exhilarating sense of an approaching historic turning-point.

The opportunity is exciting because it is new. The most chilling slogan of the last decade was composed of four negative words: There Is No Alternative. With hindsight it is easy to understand their power, especially in the despairing early 1980s. They hypnotised because it was hard to argue that they were not true: the Labour Party did not look like any kind of alternative. For a time, there was another contender: but the dogged loyalty to Labour of many working-class voters in the poorer parts of the United Kingdom, together with the protective shield of the electoral system, prevented the Liberal-Social Democratic Alliance from breaking through. So the Conservatives went unchallenged. The non-existence of an effective opposition became a commonplace even among anti-government commentators, and has had no parallel since the 1930s, when right-wing administrations similarly ruled with big majorities and no need to bother about critics or voters.

It would be misleading to suggest that TINA (the slogan's harsh, feminine acronym) won the last two elections single-handed. Mrs Thatcher's uncompromising personality undoubtedly played a major part. The Prime Minister and TINA have, in a sense, worked hand in hand. The 1980s was not a time for bromides. If not the premier's castor oil, what? Would Labour's claim to be able to reduce unemployment without causing economic havoc have been realised? Would the Alliance have waved a magic wand over industry and the unions? Opinion polls revealed the depth of uncertainty that existed even among supporters of the opposition parties.

The turnaround in public opinion did not come until early in 1989. When it occurred, it seemed to reflect a revival of confidence in Labour (at the expense of the centre) more than an immediate rejection of the government, whose support remained comparatively stable. Changes within the Labour Party itself help account for new attitudes. An influential factor was the shelving of electorally unpopular commitments. As important has been the restoration of the power of leader, executive and whips. Like many of his predecessors (especially those who have suffered an election defeat), Neil Kinnock has been strongly criticised: yet (as John Lloyd points out, p. 185) much of the improvement in Labour's fortunes must be counted as the Opposition Leader's personal achievement.

One major triumph was the policy review statement *Meet the Challenge, Make the Change*, promised by Kinnock after the 1987 election. This carefully-constructed edifice of detailed proposals has served its political purpose well: burying in a soft molehill of Walworth Road prose any surviving accusation of Labour extremism. However, it was not intended to be – and emphatically is not – an innovative or inspirational document. It strives much harder to avoid hostages to fortune than to be bold.

Perhaps, at the time of its preparation, that was wise. Unfortunately the temptation between now and the election may be to draw the wrong conclusion from its tactical effectiveness and conclude that radicalism must be excluded at all cost. By this interpretation, Herbert Morrison's famous dictum about socialism being what a Labour government does, gives way to a *fin de siècle* principle that socialism is what the public doesn't object to.

It might not fail. Parties have won elections with unremarkable policy packages before, and a sobriety-based formula may be enough to catch a tide that appears to be flowing Labour's way in any case. Perhaps, once the new Labour Prime Minister is in office, his enthusiastic team (like its Tory predecessor in 1979) will develop its own distinctive approach, which will soon be called 'Kinnockism' by the pundits and become the subject of analytic books. Quite apart, however, from the question of whether blandness is the best electioneering strategy, there is the point that Labour can scarcely hope for the luxury of a 1979-size majority in order to work out its ideas in office. So far the Labour Party has *never* obtained a substantial working majority at an election fought with the Conservatives still holding power, except in the unique conditions of 1945. If Labour gets in by a whisker or without an outright majority the opportunity for distinctiveness will have to be seized swiftly, or not at all.

Assuming that the economy goes on getting worse (the most likely basis for a Labour win), then good-natured, mildly inflationary moderation will not solve the difficulties an incoming administration is sure to face. 'The economic agenda of the next government will be dominated by one overwhelming problem – the correction of the exceptionally large British balance of payments deficit,' writes Christopher Huhne (p. 107). The necessary response, he suggests, will be measures of 'Crippsian austerity' which will run counter to Labour's would-be image as a party of welfarism without tears. The more things change, the more they stay the same: it was under precisely such conditions that the ill-starred 1964 Labour administration came to power after a long period of Conservative rule. A new government in the early 1990s will have to be flexible, and even draconian, without apology. It should not constrain itself with over-optimistic promises, or it will soon be blown off course.

But it would be even worse not to have a course at all. There are many worthwhile proposals in Labour's programme, but they do not, as yet, add up to a vision of progress. The alternative, to be uplifting, has to be more than a compendium of plausible expedients. 'I miss the days when the thought of ousting Macmillan's Tories made the heart leap that something new, and something hopeful might happen,' writes Jenny Diski (p. 174). In the short time remaining before the next election, the task of those who sincerely want something better must be not merely to win the reluctant support of depressed ex-Tory voters, but to fire the nation's anger and its hope – and this time with good reason.

We may both feel frustrated, and rejoice, at symptoms of the government's senescence. In economics, it has boxed itself in with an interest-rate policy that fuels the inflation it is intended to check. In local government finance, its poll-tax commitment has come flapping home to roost. In the health service, all ranks – from doctors to drivers – have been alienated. In education, disillusioned teachers are leaving the profession in droves, while a disconsolate minister presses on with a plan for raising standards of pupils who are, because of government policy, frequently untaught.

Now that the hollowness of the Tory 'miracle' has become apparent even to many of those who once proclaimed it; now that the nasty equation of the acquisition of money with personal achievement has lost its gloss; now that it is not quite so fashionable to value bond-dealers more highly than headteachers or to regard bookies as more successful than nurses, it is possible to imagine ways in which the 'Me' decade can give way to a 'We' decade, linking the individual's understandable pursuit of self-interest with a wider social concern.

The increasing signs that the government is a busted flush render unnecessary yet another polemical indictment of the Conservatives: *The Alternative* takes the grubby inadequacy of the present administration for granted. Its primary aim is not to condemn the current regime but to expose TINA – whose indisputable sovereignty has lasted so long – as a naked empress. There has always been an alternative: what was lacking was the means to put it into effect. The means is now there and we need to shape as confident an alternative – in terms of its philosophy and political strategy, as well as its policies – as we can imagine.

The alternative starts with improving the economy which (as we have already indicated) may be the hardest thing to do. If we accept Huhne's near-disaster scenario for an incoming administration and the consequent need for measures to counteract the electioneering inaction of the outgoing regime, then the new government's public expenditure will be seriously limited. Hence it is best to think not only in terms of creating a bigger cake but also of how best to divide the existing one.

An early step will be to cut defence spending at least (as Huhne suggests) to the Nato average. It is too soon to be sure of the implications for this country of changes in Central and East Europe, but it is already clear that any surviving reason for Britain's exceptionally high level of expenditure on military commitments has been removed. Though there is a sense in which, like the poor, the problem of security will always be with us, future security (as Ken Booth argues, p. 167) is more likely to be guaranteed politically than militarily; and the Soviet threat, if it still exists at all, is greatly reduced for the foreseeable future.

Lower defence spending will not pay for a costly programme but it will ease wider difficulties, including those caused by declining oil revenue. At the same time there will need to be a re-ordering of priorities so as to increase investment and improve training, to protect the environment, to restore the morale and efficiency of hospitals, to increase the status and attractiveness of the teaching profession, and to reduce the need for cardboard shanty-towns in our cities. All these are important, directly or indirectly, for a confident economy and a proud nation. All involve traditional forms of state intervention. But there is also a wider problem concerning the role of the state which a true alternative will need to address.

This arises from an uneasy feeling, upon which the present administration has been able to capitalise, that state involvement can often be the problem rather than the solution. The night the Berlin Wall came down, one Moscow newspaper editor remarked: 'bureaucratic administrative socialism is dead'. He was proclaiming the end of tyrannical Marxism: yet it is not just communism that has had 'bureaucratic administrative' features. As the young Soviet sociologist Boris Kagarlit-sky has pointed out in his recent examination of socialist movements East and West (*The Dialectic of Change*) the 'bureaucratic' features of state socialism have been almost as much a brake on innovation in social-democratic parties as in Marxist-Leninist ones. Indeed, we may anticipate that the anti-authoritarianism sweeping in from across the former Iron Curtain will cause an increasing intolerance of forms of Western socialism that amount to little more than an extension of civil service activity.

Raymond Plant, Paul Hirst and Sarah Benton (pp. 33, 19 and 219) all consider the problem of providing a democratic socialism less dependent on state paternalism, and one which combines the aim of equality with the no less important socialist aims of liberty and fraternity and – as David Marquand reminds us (p. 3) – of community. Elsewhere (p. 97), Richard Holme makes a case for humanising government itself – whether Left or Right – through an extension of legal rights and constitutional change. The growing movement for constitutional reforms, including a change in the electoral system, undoubtedly deserves greater support than the Labour Party has so far been prepared to give it.

The erection of new structures, and the development of new kinds of political relationship, are a vital ingredient of an alternative that involves more than welfarism and economic tinkering. It is not, how-ever, the structures of socialism or social democracy but socialist and social democratic values that retain their hold on the public imagin-ation, and make the Left-Centre the 'natural' basis (as John Rentoul suggests, p. 211) for a British government. Historically, as Rentoul points out, it has been the Left's commitment to social justice, as well as its 'apologetic and confused egalitarianism' that have been closest to the values of the British people: and recent surveys show that this closeness is increasing.

Yet, with the effective abandonment of nationalisation and other traditional collectivist instruments (including state planning, a dog that conspicuously fails to bark in the policy review document), the Left does have a serious problem of identity. In the past, leftness was positional – defined by closeness to founding fathers and distance from the Right. It was also seen in relation to the open defenders of the *status quo*: in the 1960s Labour won votes as the party of modernity. Recently, however, the Right has seemed radical and earth-shifting and the Left has been driven to adopt postures of conservatism.

The answer must lie in a firm loyalty to values, combined with a restless promiscuity in relation to methods of implementing them. The Left should never be ashamed of what it believes to be important: yet it should always watch itself for confusing means and ends. The ends are clear. The Left is on the side of the underdog. The Left seeks the prosperity of everyone, but not just for its own sake. Where the natural alliance of the Right is with established authority and the better-off, the Left champions the economically average and below-average, the physically or mentally or socially disadvantaged, the educationally or medically underprivileged, and innocent victims of the law, capitalism, industrial effluence, racism, sexism and exploitation in all its forms. The Right may scoff at this shopping list of causes and call it do-gooding. The Left can reply that a politics that aims to do good is better than one without moral purpose at all.

The two main points about the list, however, are first that it is essentially doctrine-free: it sets the problem rather than (as in some forms of Marxism and liberalism) prescribing the remedy. If, for example, a market approach at a particular time seems best for helping the poor, the Left should eagerly embrace it. Second, that while many items on the list would be treated with derision by both the traditional and neo-liberal Right, a list of domestic priorities drawn up by radicals of the so-called Centre (and some of the Greens) would be very similar.

Here we come to another ingredient of the alternative and perhaps the most vital of all: the popular front of the mind.

Samizdat began with a call for ideas. Its first editorial declared a belief

> that the basis for a convincing and effective alternative exists, but that a quite new – and for some, uncomfortable – approach is needed to challenge the divisiveness of the government and the fear of the new of so many of its opponents.

The newsletter was launched by people with a variety of political ties and many differences of opinion, but one overriding point of agreement: their joint desire for an administration that would repair the social damage done by the government since 1979, and which looked for the best in people rather than the worst. It predicted that the Thatcherite fashion would play itself out – and it promised to launch a debate on the alternative.

It also announced its ecumenicism. As in religion, so in politics, this did not require a common belief: it meant an acceptance of some shared values – those that related to health, social services, education and the rights of citizens in particular – as the basis for discussion. It was specifically *opposed* to the then fashionable proposal for a Centre-Left electoral pact. Instead it favoured a loose and informal partnership, based on an acknowledgement of a common interest among the progressive parties, to break the taboo against inter-party dialogue and draw together the threads of what it argued was an already-existing anti-government consensus. Thus it described its vision of 'a popular front of the mind' against Mrs Thatcher's regime. Its objective, in sum, was

> to build a set of ideas around which the actual and potential opposition can join forces, in order to break the cobra's gaze of this administration. The Prime Minister has said that there is no such thing as society, only individuals. She must be stopped from proving herself right.

Since this was written, the cobra's gaze has to some extent been broken. Moreover, with Labour well ahead in the polls and centre party support apparently close to vanishing point, it may be argued that the case for 'partnership' has been removed, and Mr Kinnock can and should win the next election without help. Against this, however, it can be said first, that Labour's present happy position in the polls may not last and, indeed, a narrowing of the gap as polling day approaches is to be expected; second, that British elections are often won or lost by tiny margins, and Labour needs to consider anything that might increase its advantage; and third, that the 'popular front of the mind' is not about a crude aggregation of votes but about the creation of a more progressive climate, in which anti-government sentiment becomes the norm.

Now that Labour is almost within sight of victory, and need no longer fear the centre parties as rivals, the case (from Labour's point of view) for such a popular front is certainly strengthened. It should also be much easier to achieve than two years ago. A more confident Labour Party is less nervous about Centre–Left debate (a development to which *Samizdat* and like-minded pressure groups may have contributed), while the policy gap between Labour and the Centre has almost disappeared. Not only has Labour become enthusiastic about the possibilities offered by 'social' Europe; the biggest issue of contention – defence – no longer stands in the way of co-operation. Only Labour's relationship towards the trades unions remains as a serious cause for dispute, and even this may soon begin to alter. Meanwhile, any lingering sympathy for Mrs Thatcher in the Centre has now evaporated, along with centrist fantasies of independent power. The remaining differences between Labour and the Centre – in particular, over electoral reform – are important but are certainly not irreconcilable in the conditions of an informal, non-electoral, popular front.

Labour and the centre parties have little to gain from trying to pool their voting support: British voters are not troops to be dragooned. They can, and should, make their own tactical choices when the election comes. But if the leaders of the Centre were to begin to say more openly, and with fewer ritualistic insults, that the best option for the causes in which they believe is now a Labour or Labour-based government; if Labour politicians and policy-makers were to consider seriously aspects of their programme which could take centrist sensibilities into account; if a loosely structured, but regular, liaison could be established between Labour and one or more of its minor rivals – if some of these quite painless steps could begin to be taken, then the public would become aware of a new political reality: that of a Tory government isolated by its own narrow assumptions, and besieged by an electoral majority increasingly united in its desire for change.

The popular front of the mind is partly a matter of coming clean on the convergence of policies; partly a recognition of histories with much in common (a point made by Peter Clarke, p. 195); partly a pooling of intellectual resources (as Bryan Gould put it in *Samizdat* last year, such a popular front will meet a need 'for exploring common ground or indeed encouraging each other to advance into new territory'); and partly a means of mobilising public attitudes. Here we should not forget the constituency of the chattering classes: the journalists, writers, administrators and other professionals who help to shape opinion, whose support for the Left was a key factor in 1945 and 1964, and who were lost in the late 1970s.

This book is written in the spirit of such a popular front of the mind. It discusses ideas, proposals and tactics which all radically minded people can support. In so doing, it sets out a new framework for a modern social-democratic European state. Its search is for an approach that will overtake Thatcherism, and not trail reluctantly behind it. It offers, not a moral lecture or a manifesto, but a set of independent reflections. It looks – above all – to the day when hearts may leap and victory belong not just to politicians and parties but to the people.

Now is the time: the chance to fire the nation's imagination is there, as never before in thirty years. Hayekian dogma is dead, but so is stale statism. A triumphant post-Thatcher, post-Cold War, post-twentieth-century alternative must leave behind the facile panaceas of neo-liberalism and offer – in education, health, employment and leisure – the freedom of genuine equality of treatment and genuine equality of choice. It must offer a national liberation from the confines of party. It is a challenge far bigger than defeating the Tories. It is about winning – really winning – the election. Let us hope that there are leaders with the ambition to meet it.

PHILOSOPHY

A Language of Community

DAVID MARQUAND

At the beginning of the new decade, the public mood is rapidly shifting. 'Markets', 'enterprise', 'choice' – the bugle calls of the neo-liberal counter-revolution which seemed destined to carry all before it in the early 1980s – no longer stiffen many sinews or summon up much blood. Even among Conservative ministers the talk now is of 'citizenship', 'responsibility' and 'stewardship'. In the realm of policy, private interest still holds sway, but there is not much doubt that in the realm of feeling and aspiration, the pendulum is swinging back to public concern. Market failure once again looms larger in the public mind than government failure, and the erosion of community seems more alarming than the excesses of collectivism.

There is, of course, nothing new in a swing of this sort. Much the same thing happened in the early 1960s, when Jack Kennedy was elected to the Presidency of the United States on the ticket of more public intervention, and the Conservative Government of Harold Macmillan began the switch from arm's-length Keynesianism to indicative economic planning and tripartite consensus-building. In a well-known essay, *Shifting Involvements*, Albert Hirschman has even suggested that a continuing cycle whereby involvement repeatedly shifts from the public sphere to the private and back again is a built-in feature of human history[1]. Be that as it may, it is not difficult to see why the extreme neo-liberalism of the early and mid-1980s should have started to pall by the 1990s. Whatever else it may or may not have achieved, the neo-liberal experiment has not ended the century-long relative decline of the British economy. Meanwhile, its social costs have become more obvious and less tolerable. Above all, there is growing evidence that the threat of environmental catastrophe requires a huge, unprecedented change of attitudes and behaviour which cannot conceivably be accomplished through the market.

All this provides fertile soil for the opposition parties of the 1990s, just as Kenneth Galbraith's famous (and essentially similar) paradox of private affluence and public squalor provided fertile soil for the opposition parties of the early 1960s. But it would be a mistake for them to crow too loudly or too long. Hirschman's cycle may be shifting back from the private sphere to the public and therefore from neo-liberalism to interventionism, but it does not follow that it is bound to shift from the political Right to the political Left. Individualistic neo-liberalism is by no means the only strand in the Conservative inheritance, and not necessarily the most important. In its long history, the Conservative Party has been on different sides of more than one argument at different times. It has been for protection and for free trade; for imperialism and for little England; for the free market and for planning. That, of course, is why it is the oldest right-of-centre party in the world. Where its rivals have gone through agonies of introspective revisionism when circumstances changed, it has simply drawn on a different strand in its constantly evolving tradition. As the sacred names of Burke, Disraeli and Joseph Chamberlain remind us, there is plenty in that tradition to support a kind of Tory collectivism.

There are, in fact, no grounds for the widely-held assumption that the Left is, by definition, better fitted than the Right to work with the grain of what seems likely to be a neo-collectivist era. One of the reasons why the pendulum swung towards Thatcherite neo-liberalism in the first place was that the predominantly left or centre-left collectivism of the 1960s and 1970s collapsed in humiliation and acrimony. One of the reasons why it collapsed was that the Left was in certain important respects as individualistic in assumption and behaviour as the Right. It advocated public intervention, but as a means of satisfying private aspirations; it promised entitlements, but said little about responsibilities. Its trades-union allies represented the narrow, sectional interests of their own clienteles, and rarely acknowledged a wider social interest. Partly because of all this, it allowed the public sector to become a battleground for predatory private groups; as a result, its collectivist slogans came to seem hypocritical or even threatening. Indeed, one of the reasons why the 'Thatcherites' prevailed was that, by the end of the 1970s, they were more successful than the Left in mobilising such collectivist attitudes as loyalty to country and a willingness to put the common good ahead of individual appetites.

The moral quality and social impact of the approaching neo-collectivism of the nineties have yet to be determined. It can be authoritarian or participative; repressive or tolerant; High Tory or social-democratic. The project of the Centre-Left should be to ensure that the second of these sets of alternatives prevails over the first. If it is to succeed in this – if it is to win the argument against a Heseltinian or Hurdite Tory collectivism – it will have to examine, much more honestly than it has done so far, the reasons for its failure in the 1960s and 1970s. It will also have to learn the appropriate lessons.

Exit, Voice, Loyalty

A complete examination would have to range wide. It would have to explore the impact of such factors as the first-past-the-post electoral system, the fetish of 'free collective bargaining', the adversarial industrial culture and the class-based party system, to name but a few. The scope of this essay is more restricted. I shall be concerned primarily with ideas and assumptions, and only incidentally with policy and practice. I shall try to show that the origins of the practical failures I have just mentioned lie – at least in part – in certain strands in the intellectual and cultural inheritance which most of the British Left has shared with most of the British Right. More particularly, I shall argue that they lie in a set of attitudes about the relationship between the individual and society which makes it difficult for those who hold it to transcend the familiar dichotomy of state and market, and therefore to operate a mixed economy that depends on both. Finally, I shall speculate about the possibility of a different approach, centred on the notion of community.

I begin with another insight of Albert Hirschman's, the theme of his now classic study, *Exit, Voice and Loyalty*[2]. In that study, Hirschman suggested that there are two mechanisms with which consumers may control producers. One is Exit: taking one's custom elsewhere and ceasing to buy the product – the quintessential mechanism of the market. The other is Voice: nagging, argument, persuasion, education, complaint. And, says Hirschman, Voice goes with and depends upon Loyalty: upon ties of mutuality which endure through time. You will listen to me only if, in some sense or other, I am loyal to you. I will think it worthwhile trying to persuade you only if, in some sense or other, you are loyal to me. That insight, I believe, throws a vivid shaft of light on the confusions, evasions and failures of the centre-left collectivism of the 1960s and 1970s. The central project of the Left was to make the market the servant of democratic politics, instead of the master. In Hirschman's language, it sought more scope for Voice and less for Exit. Unfortunately, it did not see that Voice would be ineffective without Loyalty. In more familiar language, it sought equality, and made ritual genuflections towards liberty, but forgot about fraternity.

The reasons go deep. Occasional dissenters apart, the British Left has never managed to emancipate itself from an implicit model of man and of society – of the springs of human purpose and of the relationship

[5]

between individual purposes and social purposes – which has permeated the political philosophy and dominated the most influential social sciences of the English-speaking world for around two centuries, and which I shall call the model of reductionist individualism. For reasons which I will explain in a moment, that model can make sense of Exit and Voice. Loyalty, however, is alien to it.

Oversimplifying wildly, but not, I think, unfairly, its chief features may be described as follows. Central to it is the tacit assumption – which perhaps reflects the reductionist materialism of the eighteenth century – that, just as the world is made up of solid lumps of matter, so a society is made up of separate, sovereign, atomistic individuals. The obligations which these individuals owe to their society derive ultimately from the fact that it can be shown that it is to their advantage to belong to it. They follow their own purposes, which they choose for themselves. These purposes may be altruistic as well as egoistic, but in either case they are individual, not social; and even altruistic purposes are pursued in the same manner as egoistic ones. Firms, colleges or research institutes may have common purposes, but whole societies do not. The notion that politics is, or should be, a process through which a political community agrees its common purpose is therefore nonsensical. The community, in Jeremy Bentham's cutting phrase, is a 'fictitious body'. Politics is about reconciling conflicts between individually chosen purposes; it has no business with the choice of purposes. Indeed, in some versions of the intellectual tradition inspired by this model, the notion that politics might have something to do with the choice of purposes is at least incipiently tyrannical. Freedom means *my* freedom to choose *my* own purposes for myself, and to pursue them in my own way, provided only that I leave others free to choose and pursue their purposes in their ways. To allow others to take part in the process through which I choose my purposes would be to allow them to trespass on psychic space which belongs to me – space which it is my right to keep inviolate.

The intellectual tradition of which that model is the product has great achievements to its credit. It helped to liberate our ancestors from superstition and oppression. Its axioms still provide a basis (though not the only possible basis) for the demand for equal citizenship and equal rights. Unfortunately, however, its legacy has constricted the imagination as well as enriching it. Reductionist individualism can encompass only two ways of living together in society, and therefore only two conceptions of politics and political man and only two modes of co-ordinating the actions of men and women in society. One is the command mode and the other the exchange mode. Co-ordination may be imposed from the top down or it may emerge spontaneously from free exchanges of one kind or another. Society is either a kind of hierarchy, held together because those at the bottom obey those at the top, or it is a kind of market, held together by the calculating self-interest of its members. Thomas Hobbes, in some ways the greatest of all the thinkers in the reductionist tradition, painted a marvellously coherent, if chilling, picture of a society operating by the command mode. The seventeenth-century English Whigs and their eighteenth-century American intellectual descendants drove out their respective rulers in the name of the exchange mode.

Both modes are, of course, omnipresent in the real world. One reason why the reductionist-individualist model has been so influential is that both are easily recognised and readily understood. It would be hard to imagine a society in which neither played an important part, and no social theory which ignores them will get us very far. As a number of social scientists have recognised, however, they are not the only modes. The political scientist Charles Lindblom, for example, has distinguished between three kinds of social relationships – the exchange relations characteristic of markets; the authority relations characteristic of states; and what he calls 'preceptoral' relations, the relations of teachers to pupils, of advertisers to consumers, of indoctrinators to the indoctrinated[3]. Brian Barry, the political philosopher, has proposed a different, but in some respects complementary, triad. There are, he suggests, three 'models' of social collaboration. In what he calls the liberal model, A will do what B wants because B makes it worth A's while to do so. In the hierarchical model, A will do what B wants because B has authority over A. In the third model – the model of what Barry calls 'altruistic collaboration' – A does what B wants because A wants to help B[4]. More recently Wolfgang Streeck and Philippe Schmitter, theorists of corporatism, have distinguished between 'markets', characterised by 'dispersed competition'; 'states', characterised by 'hierarchical control'; and 'communities', characterised by 'spontaneous solidarity'[5].

These triads plainly differ from each other. Lindblom's preceptoral relations obviously have something in common with Barry's altruistic collaboration, but they are not identical. For its part, altruistic collaboration does not quite capture the flavour of Streeck and Schmitter's 'ideal community', in which 'chiefs, notables, leaders etc. desire the esteem of their followers, while the latter seek a sense of belonging to and participating in the group as such'. But the differences are less revealing than the similarities. All the writers I have mentioned emphasise that in the real world the forms of behaviour which their triads are designed to illuminate coexist with and shade into each other. Lindblom's authority, exchange and preceptoral relations; Barry's liberalism, hierarchy and altruistic collaboration; Streeck and Schmitter's market, state and community are not mutually exclusive. In real institutions and real societies, they are always mixed up together. Secondly, and more importantly, all these writers have become dissatisfied with the familiar dichotomies of exchange and command, market and state, around which so much political argument has revolved in the last two centuries. They all sense that alongside the command and exchange modes of co-ordinating the actions of people in society, there is a third, more elusive, 'fuzzier' mode, which is in some sense fraternal or communitarian: that we collaborate with our fellows, not only because we have been ordered to or because we calculate that it is in our interests to, but because we have learned to, because we believe that it is our duty to, because the ties of mutual obligation which derive from membership of a community impel us to.

On one level, no doubt, this is scarcely an epoch-making discovery. Though all of us can recognise the command and exchange modes when we see them, none of us really believes that they exhaust the repertoire available to political and social man. If we met someone whose behaviour appeared to be governed solely by these two modes, we would consider him a kind of monster. By the same token, many thinkers in the reductionist-individualist tradition have known perfectly well that the communitarian or fraternal mode exists, and some have tried to reconcile its manifestations with their model. The trouble is that the reconciliations have never been very convincing: it is worth making a short detour in the argument to see why.

I believe that the explanation lies in the extraordinarily tenacious, though frequently only half-acknowledged, psychological assumptions which underlie the reductionist-individualist model. In that model, as Brian Crowley brilliantly demonstrates, the 'permeable', three-dimensional self of the real world – the self which has been fashioned by constant interaction with other selves, in a structure of common traditions, interlocking histories and shared meanings – is replaced by an impermeable self, 'radically individuated and unencumbered'[6]. This impermeable, unencumbered, isolated and historyless self can command, or obey, or exploit, or trade with other selves, but it cannot engage with them. It is incapable of the relationships which enable members of a society to learn from each other and which lead them to define themselves as social creatures: of the relationships which teach us who we are and which enable us to become something other than we once were. But it is these relationships which make the fraternal or communitarian mode possible. That mode exists because they exist – because in the real world, the self *is* permeable; because real people in real societies *are* social creatures, genetically programmed for sociability; because, as Mary Midgley puts it, the state of nature of the social contract theorists 'would be fine for intelligent crocodiles if there were any. For people it is a baseless fantasy.'[7] For the same reason, people do not only command, obey and exchange one good for another, but also teach and learn and become different people in doing so. And because of all this, the mirror which the tradition of reductionist-individualism holds up to us reflects only part of our true natures.

But because almost all the exponents of the reductionist-individualist tradition have been trapped in the psychological assumptions which underpin it, they have taken the image in the mirror for reality. When they have been faced with manifestations of the communitarian mode, their instinctive reaction has been to explain them in other terms. Not all the consequences can be examined here, but one consequence is of great importance for my theme. This is the widespread confusion between community loyalty and altruism. Altruism exists, of course, but communitarian behaviour is not necessarily altruistic, while altruism is not necessarily communitarian. (The good Samaritan is an example; part of the point of the story is that he was motivated by something other than community loyalty.) Notoriously, societies often behave towards other societies in highly oppressive ways. Can it really make sense to say that it is altruism which inspires the members of a non-altruistic society to display loyalty to it and to each other? Were German soldiers in World War Two, who died for their country in a war fought to enslave allegedly inferior races, behaving *altruistically*? If they were, hasn't the notion of altruism become almost vacuous? But it would be absurd to say that they were acting out of calculating self-interest; and even coercion cannot provide a complete account of their behaviour. The truth, surely, is that they were motivated by a well-known form of communitarian loyalty called patriotism – a salutary reminder that the communitarian mode, like all manifestations of human nature, can serve evil purposes as well as good ones. But group loyalty is group loyalty, not altruism; and it is a classic example of reductionism to imagine that it can only be understood as a form of something else.

To put the point in another way, 'altruism' does not capture the full flavour of words like 'comradeship', 'loyalty' and 'duty' which lie at the heart of any notion of community. The dictionary definition of altruism is 'regard for others as a principle of action; unselfishness'. There is something a little watery about the concept, perhaps because it goes too wide and insufficiently deep. 'Regard for others': which others? 'Unselfish': but *is* it unselfish to discharge one's obligations to the community which has helped to make one's self what it is? Communitarian loyalty is both stronger and narrower than this. It implies loyalty to the other members of the community to which one belongs, not to everyone: and it carries with it a flavour of obligation which altruism lacks. Altruism is freely-chosen by the sovereign, atomistic, impermeable individual of the reductionist model; and what the sovereign individual can freely

[9]

choose he can freely un-choose when his mood changes. In a community, the individual is not sovereign, or not, at any rate, in the same way. A community is like home – the place where, 'when you have to go there, they have to take you in'. Membership of it is not altogether involuntary. You can, in Hirschman's language, 'exit' from it. But if you do, you deny or lose part of your nature.

The Attempt to Change Behaviour

Against that background, the failures of the 1960s and 1970s fall into place. The crucial point, I believe, is that the mechanisms on which the centre-left governments of the period depended in practice – the combination of public and private power which Andrew Shonfield described in *Modern Capitalism*; the combination of progressive taxation and high welfare spending which Anthony Crosland proposed in *The Future of Socialism* – were rarely justified by a convincing moral and political theory. Their advocates proposed them on the grounds that they delivered the goods, in particular, rapid growth and social stability; not on the grounds that they were morally right. That argument served its purpose in the boom years when the mechanisms concerned did work, but it carried much less conviction when the boom petered out. In the 1970s and 1980s, the revisionist 'social democracy' which had become the tacit governing philosophy of the entire Centre-Left therefore became increasingly vulnerable to the intellectual counterattack mounted upon it by the neo-liberal New Right.

The reasons go deeper than might appear at first sight. Croslandian revisionist social democrats and Shonfieldian technocratic 'planners' broke with the conclusions which the classical and neo-classical economists of a previous generation had drawn from reductionist-individualist premises, but they did not construct an alternative set of premises. In the political class and, for that matter, among the academic and quasi-academic technocracy on which the political class relied for advice, the individualist paradigm continued to hold the field – not on the level of everyday practice, of course, but on the level of principle and theory. While the practices worked, no problems ensued. When they started to run into trouble, however, the gap between practice and theory became increasingly obvious, and the practitioners found it increasingly difficult to justify their practices to themselves. That was only the beginning of the story. Neo-liberalism is much closer to the individualist paradigm than was revisionist social democracy, and the neo-liberals could therefore appeal much more convincingly to it than could the revisionist social democrats whom they were trying to displace. When social democracy stopped delivering the goods, it was therefore easy for the New Right to show that its intellectual foundations had always been shaky, and to capture the intellectual high ground from which its defenders were gradually dislodged.

All this applies to the plane of ideas and argument: to revisionist social democracy as a system of belief competing with other systems of belief. Even more damagingly, much the same was true of the practical plane: of social democracy as a guide to policy and action. The revisionist middle way depended on negotiation, power-sharing and mutual education – in other words, on the kinds of relationships which Lindblom calls preceptoral. To the extent that it depended on these, it also depended on the communitarian ties which make such relationships possible. But because they were trapped in the individualist paradigm, its intellectual defenders did not (perhaps could not) realise this; and because they did not realise it, there was a contradiction at the heart of their system. Central to that system was the notion of a mixed economy, in which resources are largely allocated by the market, but in which public power intervenes on a significant scale to supplement, constrain, manipulate or direct market forces for public ends. Public intervention, however, implies a public purpose. But how can there be a public purpose without some notion of the public good? And how can there be a genuinely public good if reductionist individualism is true?

That is putting it in a rather abstract fashion, but the consequences were all too concrete. Almost by definition, public intervention is designed to change behaviour; otherwise there would be no need for it. In order to change behaviour, the interventionists had to influence choices and purposes. In principle, there were two ways of doing this. They could influence them through a mixture of punishments and rewards – perhaps indirectly, by manipulating the punishments and rewards of the market, perhaps directly, by regulation and prohibition. But in order to persuade they would have had to appeal to a communitarian ethic of some kind, capable of generating a sense of mutual obligation and civic duty; and because they had never broken out of the reductionist-individualist framework, no such ethic was available to them. Only rewards and punishments were left.

The result was a paradox. Revisionist social democracy depended on communitarian ties, but it could not speak the language of community. All too often, it became a technocratic philosophy rather than a political one: a philosophy of social engineering rather than of argument, negotiation and persuasion. In Peter Clarke's terminology, its view of government and of the relationship between government and governed was 'mechanical', not 'moral', emphasising outward changes of structure and law rather than inner changes of value and belief[8]. In the halcyon days of the long postwar boom, that view provided an adequate basis for policy-making. When the economic climate began to turn cold, however, social engineering became more and more difficult; and governments had to turn to argument and persuasion after all. Since the changes they sought were often painful, moreover, they had to argue on non-hedonistic grounds: on grounds of fraternal solidarity or community loyalty. But their philosophy gave them no basis on which to develop arguments of that sort, and only the watery notion of altruism remained to them. It is not surprising that they became progressively more frustrated as time went on. The triumphant neo-liberals of the early 1980s were the legatees of their frustration.

Centre-Left Communitarians

These are harder sayings than they may sound at first hearing. If the argument set out above is right, the centre-left collectivism of the 1960s and 1970s collapsed because it could not generate or mobilise the communitarian loyalties without which its measures could not succeed. Voice failed because Loyalty was lacking. Neo-liberalism offered a way out of the impasse in which the Centre-Left was bogged down: Exit would replace Voice, and Loyalty would no longer be necessary. Now Exit is beginning to lose its charms and Voice is returning to favour. But in the opposition parties, at any rate, Loyalty remains a faint and ghostly presence on the margins of debate, a theme for uplifting perorations rather than a guide to action. The opposition parties all promise more public intervention, but with the possible exception of the Greens they still present it primarily as a means of extending private satisfactions. There is much talk of liberty, and a little of equality, but virtually nothing is said about fraternity. We hear a great deal of citizenship, but of the liberal-individualist notion of citizenship which sees it only as a guarantee of individual rights. The civic-republican notion that citizens also have duties, that citizenship brings with it an obligation to honour and defend the city, is rarely mentioned.

Yet the obvious implication of the argument set out here is that if the Centre-Left is to address the problems which will press on this country in the 1990s – if it is to repair the damage which the neo-liberals have done to the social infrastructure; if it is to halt, or even significantly to slow down, the spoliation of the environment; if it is to put the economy on a path of sustainable development in a world which puts an ever-higher premium on human capital – it will have to call on the third, communitarian mode of social co-ordination to redress the balance of the other two. It will, in other words, have to lay more emphasis on Lindblom's preceptoral relations, and less on the more familiar relations of command and exchange. It will have to do its best to restore the fraying bonds of community, to offset the omnipresent cultural and economic pressures which atomise the individual and fragment the ties that bind individuals to each other, to create spaces in which the habits of community can be learned and practised. Above all, it will have to find an idiom in which an ethic of fraternity and mutual obligation can resonate in a diverse, medium-sized, multicultural late-twentieth-century society in an increasingly interdependent world.

Almost by definition, no one can be certain how to do this. The Centre-Left got into the impasse in the first place because it lacked the intellectual and moral resources to transcend the command-exchange dichotomy, because its approach to man and society was saturated with assumptions which made communitarian relations incomprehensible, if not inconceivable. All the same, one or two points seem plain.

'We do not learn to read or write, to ride or swim, by being merely told how to do it,' wrote John Stuart Mill, that strange amalgam of civic republican and liberal individualist, 'but by doing it.'[9] We learn the habits of community by practising them; we become responsible by taking responsibility. Where High Tory communitarians see the community as a matter of blood, soil and inheritance, a centre-left communitarian would see it as a construct, made and re-made by the free and conscious decision of its members. The values of a centre-left communitarian would be civic republican values, the values of active citizenship, as opposed to passive subjecthood. But such values cannot be instilled from on high. They have to be learned; and they can be learned only in action. Centre-left communitarians will therefore seek the widest possible diffusion of responsibility and power – not only in what is conventionally thought of as the political sphere, but in what Mill called 'the business of life', at work, in the school system, in the health service, indeed wherever discussion and debate can help to determine collective purposes, and, in doing so, to give the participants a chance to experience the disciplines of collective choice.

Unlike the revisionist social democrats of the 1960s and 1970s, centre-left communitarians would not deploy public power only, or even mainly, through the central state. But where the neo-liberals tried to resolve the crisis of central-state social democracy by narrowing the scope of public power, centre-left communitarians would do so by widening access to it; and where neo-liberals draw in the frontiers of politics and citizenship, centre-left communitarians would extend them.

The Barbarians, Oscar Wilde and the Labour Front Bench

JOHN MORTIMER

Nothing is more disconcerting than the sudden disappearance of an enemy. The old cold warriors, Caspar Weinberger or Mr Heseltine for instance, suddenly find themselves confronted by an alarming absence of threats from Eastern Europe. Instead of rolling its tanks towards us, the Evil Empire seems to have folded its tents and departed. What can the old-style politician do, except murmur a few comforting and familiar phrases like 'we mustn't drop our guard'? There is a strong feeling that the old days were best: things were at least simple then. This dilemma has been well expressed in C. P. Cavafy's 'Expecting the Barbarians'. An entire country, you may remember, is kept going by the fear of barbarians at the gates, and then the terrible news comes from the frontier that the barbarians have apparently gone away, and Cavafy ends his poem with this chilling thought:

> And now what shall become of us without Barbarians?
> These people were a kind of solution.

Just as Foreign Secretaries and NATO generals may apply these disconcerting thoughts to the present withering away of communism, the Labour Party must have similar forebodings about the day, which cannot now be too long delayed, when Mrs Thatcher departs for Dulwich. The blessedly simple time when all that seemed necessary was to abuse the Prime Minister and plot her downfall will soon be over. In a way she was of great benefit to those on the Left, giving them, after a long period of aimless confusion, a simple cause in which we might feel comfortably united. When the Thatcherites are gone we may feel a distinct sense of loss, for these people were, after all, a kind of solution. When monetarism is no longer the current morality what shall replace it? The question may be of interest and indeed of importance because one of the strengths of the Conservatism of the 1980s was that it had a creed, and the present creed of the Labour

[15]

Party, should it exist, is coyly hidden under a number of businesslike breasts wearing dark blue suits and anonymous, not quite regimental, ties.

In the old days, socialism, mixed with a powerful dose of Methodist fervour, could stir the heart and thunder beguilingly in the speeches of Nye Bevan and Michael Foot. But socialism is rarely mentioned nowadays in polite Labour circles, and it's important to remember that the astonishing revolutions in Eastern Europe have not only discomforted the Pentagon but those who place too much faith in the complete control of an economy by government bureaucrats. So what are we left with in the department of burning faith, given the fact that many of this government's ideological acts, the sell-off of natural resources to millions of small shareholders and the destruction of a remarkably successful television system, for instance, may prove difficult or even impossible to reverse? Are we to accept that the days of great political ideals are over? Is a victory for the forces of progress to mean little more than some more government intervention in a restricted number of business enterprises and the greater availability of hip replacements? If this is so, the end of the Thatcher era may herald an age of great dullness, and we may live to miss even the colourful, hissable villains like Mr Tebbit, or Nicholas Ridley, who once provided us with some riveting melodrama.

It was with these thoughts in mind that I went back, not to Marx or even to Shaw, but to Oscar Wilde, who once wrote a long political essay, I dimly remembered, called 'The Soul Of Man Under Socialism'. He undertook this work in 1891, a year in which he published four books, wrote *Salome* and became a famous West End dramatist with *Lady Windermere's Fan*. As you would expect, his thoughts on politics are brilliant, paradoxical, based on aesthetic values and occasionally maddening. It's a piece of prose which I would like all those blue-suited and efficient characters on the Labour front bench to take home and read in bed. Strangely enough, when they put out their lights, they may start dreaming of a better world.

'The chief advantage that would result from the establishment of Socialism is undoubtedly the fact that Socialism would relieve us from that sordid necessity of living for others which, in the present condition of things, presses so hardly upon almost everybody . . . The majority of people spoil their lives by an unhealthy and exaggerated altruism – are forced indeed, so to spoil them.' What Wilde is saying is the reverse of Thatcherism: there is no virtue at all in feeling sorry for the poor, by flattering ourselves for our humane concern or doling out small sums in charity. It's an essential function of government to abolish the conditions which make such self-indulgence possible. The end of poverty, the proper provision of housing, the more equal distribution

[16]

of wealth, the organisation of health care and so on are the basic services which a government can perform. Once done, this will save us all from having to go round feeling sorry for each other, signing deeds of covenant or going on sponsored swims. But this is not an end in itself, it's merely an essential part of any decent government service. You could, if you wished, call it socialism, but socialism is not an end in itself. 'Socialism,' says Wilde, 'will be of value simply because it leads to Individualism.' And what is individualism? Simply the right of us all to make the most of our lives, to improve their quality and take full advantage of our powers of enjoyment. It is to have open to us whatever can widen our horizons, the consolations of religion, the stimulus of the arts, the right to a decent system of education and the enjoyment of a countryside rescued from the destructive deprivations of the last ten years.

Of course Wilde overstates his case, and puts it with all the theatricality of a man who lectured in a velvet coat, knee breeches and diamond-buckled shoes. But in a way, this essay, exaggerated as it is, provides a useful antidote to the new Tory idea of freedom. Government activity, so runs the Thatcherite creed, should be reduced to a minimum so we are all set free to make money. Government activity must be increased, says Wilde, to solve those basic problems which prevent us living fulfilled and satisfactory lives. And among those restrictions on complete and successful living he lists the pursuit of property and an obsession with personal enrichment. It's not only the rich who should be relieved of such concerns. 'There is only one class of the community', Wilde says in one of his better epigrams, 'that thinks more about money than the rich and that is the poor. The poor can think of nothing else. That is the misery of being poor.'

So, as they read these thoughts which are no doubt meant to shock the bourgeois, and even the left-wing bourgeois, two aims may present themselves to the thoughtful member of a new Labour government. They are two ideals which may well be unattainable, but there is nothing wrong with unattainable ideals if they lead to some small improvement in the state of the nation. The first is to remove the demeaning and soul-destroying results of social injustice. Let's get that cured, Wilde said, so at least we may not have to waste our lives feeling sorry for each other. And then, and always, let's aim for a rise in the standard of living, that standard to be judged not solely, or indeed at all, by money.

It's not too hard to begin on this task as we start from such a low base. Our schools, our universities, our theatres, museums and concert halls have been neglected in a way that would be inconceivable in France or Germany. Our broadcasting system, long the envy of the world, is about to be pulled apart for the sake of a political theory, or so that it may become the mindless money-spinner of detached million-aires. The countryside of southern England has been concreted over, its villages deprived of schools, its towns degutted to make way for chain stores, its cottages sold at the highest prices to bankers and stockbrokers, so that rural England, the source of a great deal of our pleasures and most of our literature, is in danger of disappearing into an endless suburb.

All these are issues on which the Left should be vocal: they would give it a cause in which it could believe, they could provide the basis for an alternative faith to the potent brew of Thatcherism. It cannot be said that the Labour Party has spoken of them with any stirring or inspired voice, or indeed with much voice at all. There is silence about any decent alternative to the government's broadcasting schemes, and although some good work is being done on the arts, no one seems to have addressed the problems of the countryside which can only be solved by low-cost housing and various sorts of rural industry to replace a declining agriculture. Thought on those matters is urgent. We who live in the country are already beginning to feel like a threatened species artifically preserved in a series of theme parks.

What is needed is a statement of faith by politicians who make clear that our, and I think the majority of electors', idea of the quality of life is not that of the regime now passing away. The time must go when the Conservatives could present themselves as belonging to the party with the strongest beliefs. We need men and women as truly radical as Wilde to state our ideals and not, as he wrote in *Lady Windermere's Fan* (not usually thought of as a politically committed work), politicians who 'think like a Tory and talk like a Radical, and that's so important nowadays'. Nowadays it's not.

From Statism to Pluralism

PAUL HIRST

The future of socialism is often debated as if socialism had a single past. In the 1980s the radical Right have tried to bury socialism. One of their best tactics in doing so has been to identify socialism with the authoritarian states and failing economies of the communist world. Western socialism can then be presented as a lesser version of this greater failure, but sharing essential features of authoritarian collectivism and economic stagnation. Socialism is defined by the Right in terms of the triad of collective ownership, state intervention and centralised planning, and it is still defended by some of its supporters in those terms.

The vast majority of socialists, however, recognise the need for a more libertarian political creed compatible with an open society. Some radical revisionists think it necessary to go outside the socialist tradition altogether in order to do so. They embrace the free market and redefine socialism in terms of liberal democratic theory. This is to behave as if there are no *socialist* sources for a libertarian socialism. In fact certain important socialist doctrines have been strongly anti-collectivist and opposed to centralised public ownership. They have also been strongly anti-statist, advocating reliance on the self-governing activities of freely associated individuals. Associational socialism is the most valuable alternative to the undiluted individualism of the free-market Right and to the centralist and authoritarian trends in modern society.

Associational Socialism

Associational socialism, which flourished between the 1840s and the early 1920s, was a third force in the history of socialism, distinct from both Bolshevism and social democracy. It embraced a variety of movements and ideas, including Proudhon and the mutualist and syndicalist traditions in France; William Morris and the Arts and Crafts movement; and G. D. H. Cole and the Guild Socialists in Britain.

[19]

Associational socialism often won the battle of ideas; only to lose out to other socialist movements which relied on the more effective means of either electoral or insurrectionary politics. In an era of world wars, big government and highly concentrated industry, associational socialism came to seem an irrelevancy. Its stress on self-government and local autonomy ran counter to a period in which there were strong imperatives to central control. Because it believed in the virtue of voluntary action in civil society, it neglected the forms of political action necessary to create a state sympathetic to such voluntary activity and also failed to compete with other political forces to influence the existing state. The associational socialists were pushed aside by the 1920s. Yet the view of the associational socialist tradition as utopian and unworldly is quite wrong. Associationalism was not inherently impractical, rather it required the right context in which it could become practical politics.

The major wars of this century promoted centralisation and bureaucratic control; tendencies inimical to the autonomy of self-governing associations. The wars also gave the political rivals of libertarian socialism the conditions in which to flourish. However, in the 1980s the international environment has changed radically – and perhaps irrevocably – with the end of the second Cold War. The transformation of East–West politics, the pace of reform in Eastern Europe, and the prospect of at least partial demilitarisation all weaken the imperatives for centralised and secretive state security institutions to dominate national politics. A movement that seemed naive in the 1920s can profit from the liberalisation of Great Power politics in the 1980s.

Associational socialism may also benefit from recent economic changes in the West. The imperatives towards the large scale in industrial organisation have been perceived to be closely connected with standardised mass production for homogeneous mass markets. However, since the OPEC oil price shock and the consequent world depression of the early 1970s, markets have both internationalised and differentiated. The reasons for this are ably explained by Michael Piore and Charles Sabel in *The Second Industrial Divide*[1]. Markets have become more volatile, product ranges have differentiated and firms have now to contend with changing demands for a more varied range of products across a series of national markets with specific characteristics. This undermines the relevance of 'economies of scale' and encourages firms to change their production methods to permit more flexible output.

In such an open international economy, in which the major industrial nations trade manufactured goods ever more intensively one with another, there is less scope for purely national regulation. The social democratic strategy of using Keynesian measures to boost national consumer demand and thereby sustaining mass markets has given way to more complex strategies for preserving the local manufacturing base, particularly at the regional level. In such a competitive and rapidly changing industrial environment the scope for a central state-directed industrial policy is much reduced, thus undercutting the traditional socialist advocacy of 'planning'. The two major forms of active state intervention, Keynesian macro-economic management and dirigiste planning, are thus both weakened as socialist answers to the problems of economic policy.

In this new environment both regional economic regulation and small-to-medium scale firms have grown in importance. But at the same time, other quite contradictory tendencies have developed and these are most marked in the USA and Britain. If the logic of *industrial* concentration based on economies of scale in production has weakened, the purely *financial* pressures towards concentration of ownership have accelerated. The divorce of financial operations from the direct investment in new industrial plant and processes, conjured up in the phrase 'casino capitalism', has led to the concentration of ownership of industry based almost solely on stockmarket opportunities. The acquisition and take-over of firms is often devoid of manufacturing or marketing logic. In this context, top management becomes ever more powerful and yet more remote and unaccountable. The operations of subsidiary firms will thus tend to suffer from such remote control. It can hardly be a matter of chance that it is Britain and the USA that have shown the greatest import penetration and consequent de-industrialisation. These countries have participated least in the recent changes towards flexible specialisation in production and the regional regulation of manufacturing sectors.

The financially-based conglomerate holding companies lack a *raison d'être* in economic necessity; they are not essential for the organisation of manufacturing. They are beyond the control of the formal machinery of shareholder representation and are unaccountable to their employees. Industrial concentration without economic rationality turns large-scale firms from a source of economic strength into a very real weakness. It represents a form of pure ownership increasingly divorced from managerial necessity. Traditional socialist remedies such as nationalisation do not offer an answer to such concentration, since the component parts of such conglomerate companies make little industrial or administrative sense when gathered together. Decentralisation and the promotion of economic self-government offer the best prospect of a form of industrial organisation in which the major contributing interests – the providers of capital, management expertise and labour – have an active interest in the continued manufacturing success of the firm.

This need for democratisation and decentralisation is where associational socialism becomes relevant; because it stresses above all that economic units should be co-operatively owned self-governing associations. The tradition undoubtedly needs to be modernised. It is also true that traditional associational socialism was highly workerist and emphasised manufacturing industry, and it could hardly cope with today's complex division of labour within the enterprise or with the increasing diversity of occupations in the wider society. However, G. D. H. Cole's stress on organising society on the basis of voluntarily formed self-governing associations was basically correct.

Battlefield

The Left has been mesmerised by statism. Even moderate democratic socialists have constantly advocated giving more and more tasks to the state. The result, when such advocacy is successful, is to give more power to the state and less to socialists, and this in turn drains socialism of creative energy as a *social* movement and diverts it from constructive enterprise in civil society. We have built socialism (or rather tried to) through the agency of the state and encouraged passivity in the recipients of state services. Yet we wonder why socialism is no longer a mass movement.

The more tasks that are given to the state, the greater is the stake in controlling it and the more the state can take away if control changes hands. We have learnt that lesson through our experience of Mrs Thatcher, but we have hardly adapted to the fact that we need to devolve activities from the state to civil society as far as is possible. Socialists in the West, just as in the East, have seen the need to 'capture' the state, to make certain changes in policy 'irreversible'. Yet such a vision is hardly compatible with a pluralist society, in which there are other groups and social projects than socialism. It rests on the belief that socialists have a natural majority in society and, therefore, a right to a monopoly of effective political power. This belief has been widely held by democratic socialists; it is not a peculiarity of the authoritarian Left. This belief is almost inevitable if the state does come to control more and more of the affairs of society. Democracy becomes a battlefield; the only issue, who shall control the levers of power?

As the state has directly provided more services, so the individual has enjoyed less and less liberty in determining *how* they are provided. The recipient of collectivised services administered by officials, the individual is also increasingly likely to work for a large private organisation in which she or he has little or no say. The growth of state activity has not checked the growth of big business: often it has actively promoted it. The result is to place much of the affairs of 'civil society' into the hands of unaccountable private governments that dwarf many pre-twentieth-century states in size.

If socialists could accept the idea of a state that facilitated the work of democratically run associations in providing work and welfare, then they might have some chance of finding a more secure future for socialism. Democratic socialists seek to encourage co-operation, mutual assistance, fellowship and the greatest measure of equality attainable. They are not necessarily tied to particular social institutions like state ownership or central planning in meeting these objectives. Understood in this wider sense socialism can co-exist with a society of plural organisations and differing objectives. It could build its institutions of co-operative work and mutual assistance alongside other active groups of citizens and their projects; religious groups, ethnic communities, lifestyle communities, etc. A socialism committed to a pluralist society and to concentrating on organising social life through self-governing associations in civil society would pose less of a threat to others than a statist socialism, and might therefore expect to command more support. In particular it would be more open to Green conceptions of social organisation and to coexisting with Green associations.

A challenge to statist socialism does not mean a return to the Marxist illusions of 'smashing' the state. On the contrary, even if as many social activities as possible are devolved to self-governing associations in civil society, there will still be a need for a public power to regulate the actions of these associations and to ensure that they have the resources to carry out their tasks. A pluralist society with diverse social projects needs a public power to ensure order, but that public power need not be a 'sovereign state'; that is, a state claiming the exclusive control of power, asserting its primacy in every social domain, and imposing itself through a single centralised hierarchy. A pluralist state – as conceived by such English political pluralists as J. N. Figgis, G. D. H. Cole and H. J. Laski – would be based on a quite different principle: that the state exists to protect and serve the self-governing associations. The state's powers would be limited by its function and such a state would recognise the inherently plural nature of all free social organisation. Pluralism requires that distinct locally and functionally specific domains of authority should have the autonomy necessary to carry out their tasks. This pluralist conception of the state is essential to a libertarian society, for 'decentralisation' and 'devolution' of power will accomplish little if all they do is to re-create centralised authorities at lower levels.

Traditional state socialists raise two major objections to such a society of self-administering associations. The first is that while self-governing firms may give employees more say within the workplace, the wider economy remains anarchic and at the mercy of the 'laws' of the market. This, however, is to treat the market economy as if it were a single self-sufficient system divorced from control by the wider society. There are no 'laws' of the market; rather there are specific markets with diverse social conditions and consequences. Markets are embedded in social relations, and it is these relations that play a major role in deciding how markets work. Moreover, there are other ways of organising an economy than centralised planning. Associational socialists like Cole always stressed the important role of voluntary co-ordination between associations at national, industry and local levels. Some of Cole's conceptions of how to accomplish such co-ordination were naive, but this does not diminish his general point. There is much evidence that those national and regional economies that achieve such patterns of co-ordination, that provide for the effective consultation of social interests and that support firms with a surrounding network of social institutions which provide essential services, are the ones that have been most successful under modern conditions of manufacturing competition. West Germany, Italy and Japan offer excellent examples of different patterns of such co-ordination. It is the most un-regulated 'free-market' economies in the West, Britain and the USA that have done least well.

Centralised state planning is, moreover, no answer to the supposed inherent anarchy of the market. Planning produces its own anarchy, its own distortions of economic behaviour and its own corruptions. This brings us to the second objection. This is the claim that a system which assigns most welfare tasks to voluntary associations must produce inequalities in provision, benefiting some households and localities at the expense of others. Yet this inequality is just the result that centralised bureaucratic welfare systems have managed to accomplish. Nothing, moreover, prevents the state in such an associationalist system from enforcing minimum standards on associations in receipt of public funds or from providing its own welfare safety net.

Cats' Homes

In such an associationalist society there would be public funds raised by taxes and there would be capital markets to provide investment resources for firms. Voluntary associations would not finance all social activity through flag days. The state could, for example, collect an 'associational tax' as a substantial percentage of total tax revenue, and allow taxpayers to nominate, say, about 25% of their associational tax payments to a limited number of organisations (perhaps five to ten). That would prevent all revenue going to cats' homes and the like. The state would then distribute the bulk of the remainder of the associational tax according to the registered membership of associations and retain a reserve for meeting shortfalls. Such a system would ensure funds would flow towards the more popular associations. Moreover, industrial finance would become a mutually owned sector. Firms would establish credit unions; pension funds, insurance companies, etc., would lend to industrial banks and buy industrial associations' bonds. Self-governing firms would thus have access to external sources of capital and would be subject to the disciplines of borrowing at interest on organised capital markets.

Such a society is administratively and organisationally feasible. It is not a utopia, nor does it – as most utopias do – make unwarranted assumptions about human stamina and motivation. Self-governing associations need not be participatory democracies nor need they be small-scale: representative elections and a professional management answerable to a democratic governing body may well be sufficient for most purposes. Many voluntary associations at present are of this nature, and providing they perform their tasks well enough, members are happy to subscribe and do no more than vote for the existing council. A society of self-governing associations leaves people free to choose the extent of their involvement. It does not compel endless hours of voluntary service above the demands of home and work.

But how to create a society of associations? How to tackle the current big corporations? How can one seek the greatest measure of equality possible when top tycoons are paid up to £1 million a year? Clearly, big business would regard the conversion of firms into self-governing associations with horror and would resist it root and branch. But if the public could be persuaded of the virtues of democratically accountable business, top managers would find themselves in the predicament that they are relatively few in number and that even executives in their subsidiary firms might welcome a reform. The most recent British Social Attitudes survey (1988) shows that the British public are anything but enamoured of the motives and performance of top management.

If a reforming government tried to convert existing firms into self-governing associations, what would that involve? Firstly, making management accountable to the relevant interests represented on a supervisory board of a company – let us assume that shareholders, employees and community interests have equal importance and that they should each elect one-third of the board. Secondly, creating a single membership status – *all* permanent employees to have the same rights and conditions of service, from the managing director to the lavatory attendant. Let us assume that inequalities in income will be flattened, to create a ratio of no more than 1:8. Thirdly, instituting a comprehensive system of co-determination, participation and consultation at all levels within the firm.

This is not so radical as it might appear. West German firms have comprehensive industrial democracy and co-determination measures, while many Japanese firms have single employee status, and in the period of most dramatic Japanese growth many companies had very low salary differentials. Nevertheless, it would be very unpopular with top management in Britain.

Measures likely to be unpopular with influential people need to be practical. How could these changes be applied to big conglomerate firms? While many aspects of industrial concentration may be economically unnecessary, there are many cases where large-scale organisations are essential. How can these organisations be effectively run by democratic methods? The simple answer to this is that if we believe *states* can be made democratically accountable to their citizens to some significant degree, then companies surely can. But let us accept that the structure and operations of a complex company may be difficult to understand and therefore difficult for representatives to govern. There are then two answers: unscrambling into their component parts those companies where size has little economic logic and creating different organisational structures for those companies where large-scale operations are necessary.

Firstly, large size can be attained by partnerships of semi-autonomous sub-units: firms that share work and contract one with another; firms that subscribe to marketing networks; firms that create collective bodies to represent their common interests or to provide common services such as training. These links can be by inter-firm co-operation alone or through linkage with and co-ordination by public bodies. In such cases firms enjoy all the advantages of scale, without the participating units becoming too large or complex to be democratically governable. These relationships are already common in the most successful regions of the Western industrial economies, and, far from being pie-in-the-sky, are widely identified as a key source of industrial efficiency, as many contributors argue in my edited collection (with Jonathan Zeitlin), *Reversing Industrial Decline?*[2].

Secondly, large firms can be stripped down to a 'core' of absolutely necessary activities that must be under direct control. Such a core might well be strategic management, research and development, and some crucial manufacturing operations. To get down to this core firms would follow a strategy of 'internal privatisation': sub-contracting non-core activities to co-operatives, promoting labour/capital partnerships and management-worker buy-outs of peripheral activities. For labour-intensive core activities the firm would contract with a labour co-operative on a fixed term deal. The result would be an economy of modestly sized units, capable of operating in combination on a very large scale. None of them would justify vast differentials of income, since firms would be smaller than the conglomerates of today and their internal hierarchies would be flatter. The over-paid top managers could be bought out as their positions were abolished by reorganisation.

How could one prevent such contracting out to labour co-operatives giving rise to iniquities as great as the conditions of gang labour in the Durham mines in the nineteenth century? Surely, management would exploit such changes to dump liabilities upon labour? But two ready answers present themselves: that the state requires compliance with a law regulating contracts with labour co-operatives and that trades unions remain to police and protect workers' interests.

Such a process of turning firms into associations and stripping them down by internal privatisation would create an economy based on manageably sized and internally accountable units. It would offer an end to the servile state, in which most people earn their living as employees without either a stake in or a measure of control over their workplace. It would also create a genuine 'enterprise society' in which there would be scope for individual initiative and responsibility. Mrs Thatcher's conception of an enterprise culture is one in which choice is offered to individual consumers through the market. But confronted with an economy dominated by big corporations, the individual's choice as employee or consumer is severely limited. This is exacerbated by the Conservatives' ruthless trimming of the countervailing power of the unions in defence of employees, and their indifference to the need to extend further the role of law and regulatory agencies to protect consumers' rights. As J. N. Figgis argued persuasively, it is difficult for individuals to pursue freedom except by freely associating with others. In an enterprise society based on self-governing associations, individuals have both opportunities for choice and the power to make those choices stick. Such a society permits a wide range of competing associations, and therefore choice based on genuine pluralism, and all the advantages of large scale where necessary, without unaccountable hierarchy. Through associations, such a society offers to its citizens unparalleled opportunities for individuation and freedom.

What About the Workers?

I have tried to indicate the ways in which an economy of self-governing associations would be possible and defensible against the hostility of management. But what about the unions? Surely, they have as much to fear from the growth of self-government at work? What would be the place of unions in such a scheme? The answer is: stronger certainly than in either state socialism or corporate capitalism, and more constructive than in either of them.

In an economy of self-governing associations the majority of workers would still receive the main part of their income in wages. Therefore, wage determination would remain important and would need to be institutionalised. Wage determination would take place at three levels:

1. national bargaining between the major interests – the state, associations and unions – leading to a fixed term accord for overall norms;
2. regional councils in which public bodies, associations and unions operate arbitration machinery to settle disputes about the application of norms to groups of workers in particular firms – at this level unions would also co-operate to ensure the provision of collective services such as training for firms and workers in the region;
3. unions would ensure the firm's compliance with laws governing labour contracts and ensure that wage norms were democratically arrived at.

There would be a positive right to strike, but the combination of internal self-government in firms and the unions' participation in comprehensive measures of collective wage determination would be designed to make strikes measures of last resort. The system of self-government in firms would be based on free votes of individual employees rather than through the union branches, thus maintaining the unions' independence and also preventing them from taking control of firms' internal decision-making procedures. Unions would therefore remain voluntary bodies to which individual workers could choose to subscribe. Like every other association they would be required to meet minimum legal standards of democratic self-governance. They would have the power to enforce fair contracts for employees; firms could not create 'labour rackets' under the cover of self-government.

In an associational welfare system the unions could greatly extend their role as providers of welfare and other services compared with their position today. Unions would be eligible to get funds under the 'write-in' provisions for 25% of the associational tax, to receive funds proportional to membership and to bid for projects from the reserves. Unions would potentially control very large funds to use for the benefit of their members. They would also contribute to training policy through co-determination machinery and control training funds and offer training themselves. The benefits of belonging to a union would be very real for members. Unions would provide benefits as associations in civil society and directly organise welfare. Socialists in combination with the unions would directly carry out policy instead of campaigning for it to be done by the state and they would be directly responsible to their own membership for the success of that policy. They would have to compete with non-socialist associations like churches in providing welfare.

Unions would not, however, directly organise or own production (such activities would be *ultra vires* under associational law). Thus associationalism would be quite unlike syndicalism. Workers would be free not to join unions and the self-government procedures of firms would be independent of the unions. Workers, therefore, would not be compelled to be part of a rigid corporatist structure, and unions would have to win and keep members to ensure influence. Workers would have the union to protect them if for some reason a firm became riven by factional strife or dominated by a management clique. They would also have unions to ensure that their job rates, skill classifications and training were protected. Unions would have an interest in and would help to maintain labour mobility and, therefore, the liberty of the worker.

Because it can be adapted to large-scale industry and permits a complex division of labour, associationalism is one of the few nineteenth-century social doctrines that remains fully relevant today. It combines liberty with effective management, and decentralisation and self-action with professionalism and efficiency. It offers a radically greater range of choice than most other social doctrines: greater consumer choice than state socialism and more real choice for the worker than corporate capitalism. Associationalism also allows diverse groups to choose their own form of social organisation: it offers possibilities of self-action to religious and other groups as well as to socialists. Because it avoids the authoritarianism of a socialist society fit only for dogmatic socialists, associationalism may appeal to enough groups in society for them to tolerate it and work along with it. It is the only socialist doctrine of which this can credibly be said, and therefore it is, in the long run, the only practical socialism.

THE SPIDER

Writing in a year of alternatives which would have seemed impossible such a short time ago – in Eastern Europe and Russia – and feeling more and more acutely the rigidity of the present regime in Britain (where the word 'alternative' is swept vigorously under the carpet) it seems fitting to remember the great philosophical religious poem of the twelfth century AD, from the Near East: *The Conference of the Birds* by Farid od-Din Attar. I quote from it below:

'Have you ever watched the spider and noted how fantastically she spends her time? With speed and fore-sight she spins her marvellous web, a house which she garnishes for her use. When the fly falls headlong into the web, she rushes up, sucks the little creature's blood and leaves the body to dry for use as food. Then, along comes the householder with a broom, and in an instant, web, fly and spider are gone – all three!'

Emma Tennant

Citizenship, Empowerment and Welfare

RAYMOND PLANT

The idea of citizenship has become prominent as a potentially unifying idea for a progressive, post-Thatcher agenda in the 1990s. However, the notion has to be made more precise than it currently is before it can function as a unifying concept and a broad guide to policy. Citizenship is a complex notion which avoids the simplicities of the free-market consumerism of the neo-liberal Right and the antiquated class analysis of the unreconstructed Marxists. However, if the 1990s turn out to be the decade of the citizen as Paddy Ashdown has urged, then we have to have some grasp of the complexities of citizenship in its political, civic, economic and welfare forms if we are to rally people to a citizen's agenda. I will concentrate on citizenship in the welfare field, where I believe policy on the Left needs more rethinking than its policy in relation to politics and civil society. In the context of the latter, the idea of a greater protection of civil and political rights, greater democratisation, and the need to strengthen an autonomous civil society of sub-political groups and initiatives are the basis of an agenda discussed elsewhere in this book, and the basis also of a growing consensus on the Left.

However, before going on to state the case for social citizenship in a new and revised form I will first say a little about why the ideal of citizenship is a very salient one for the Left. It challenges two approaches to the politics of the Left which have failed. The first is a class-based approach to politics; the second an interest group approach.

The Marxist, class-based analysis sees the citizenship approach to policy as fatally flawed for reasons which Marx set out with crystal clarity in his great essay on the Jewish Question. Marx claimed that civil and political aspects of citizenship and emancipation could not be put into practice against the background of social and economic inequality which in turn was a necessary feature of the private owner-ship of the means of production. It was not possible, Marx said, to create the conditions of effective political citizenship without social and economic citizenship, but this was impossible within an economy with private ownership of the means of production. Social democrats were quite mistaken, he argued in the Critique of the Gotha programme, in thinking that it was possible to produce a fairer distribution of social resources for citizenship in a privately owned economy. The social democratic project is flawed because it assumes that within a capitalist society it is possible to formulate a programme for greater effective citizenship. However, this assumes that there are common values in a capitalist society, a common good in the context of which the idea of citizenship could be formulated. In Marx's view such an assumption involved ideological distortion. In a class-based society class interests are antithetical, and while in periods of prosperity it may be possible for there to be a veneer of agreement between classes, this always embodies false consciousness: the reality of class division and domination is still there and will reappear in periods of recession when the apparent gains in terms of citizenship and social and economic rights will be eroded and cut back.

Social Citizenship

It is obviously impossible in the confines of a short chapter to provide a full critical discussion. However, two things are worth noting in relation to this class-based analysis of political culture. The first is that, with the collapse of Marxist regimes in Eastern Europe, even Marxists – particularly those associated with *Marxism Today* – are moving towards a more citizenship-oriented approach. And secondly, the class-based approach is becoming more and more a recipe for purist impotence on the Left. The working-class base is narrowing all the time and in any case workers do not currently share one class interest (unless one appeals to the notion of false consciousness to demonstrate that there is indeed only one class interest and that those who do not accept it are misled in various ways). Unless there is some way for the Left to reach out to other groups in society it will not gain power. It will only reach out to such groups by appealing to common values which cut across class: the idea of citizenship is central to this.

The concept of citizenship also contrasts with the other view of the future of the Left in Britain, namely that it should become a coalition of interest groups. However, there are deep difficulties associated with interest-group politics of this sort. Unless a political party has a set of core values against which to test and evaluate interest-group claims it will merely fall prey to the most powerful and articulate groups. Policy-making will then be little more than reaching the lowest common denominator between them. There must be some filter for interest-group claims at the policy-making level and one obvious way of achieving this would be to establish an integrated set of citizenship values. None of this is to deny that interest groups are important – far from it – but it may be that the claims which they make would be enhanced by being put into a broader framework which would seek to determine what are the rights and obligations of citizens in a more democratic and equal society.

The common basis for citizenship is to be found in an account of the set of rights and obligations in a democratic and progressive society, and in the remainder of this chapter I shall look at the rights and obligations in the field of social citizenship and, in particular, in the context of welfare.

Over the past ten years the social aspects of citizenship have become gradually eroded. This is not to be wondered at, given the neo-liberal domination in government policy and thinking. For the neo-liberal the only common goods are basically law and order, which define the necessary boundaries of a free society, and the only public goods are those which the market for technical reasons cannot produce. The duty of a citizen is to sustain this framework of law and to pay the taxes to produce the resources to maintain a more limited government. In the view of the neo-liberal, citizenship does not really enter into the social and economic sphere. Citizens do not have genuine social and economic rights in virtue of citizenship and the wider ideal of social citizenship is deeply antithetical to the maintenance of a free market economy in the version preferred by the neo-liberals, a point which should be clear enough given the government's reaction to the European Social Charter.

According to the government, conditions of work should be the result of a piecemeal process of making contracts between workers and employers, and welfare should as far as possible be a matter of producing a minimum floor – not of securing the conditions of life which are necessary for all members of society to be integrated into that society and participate in the activities which are characteristic of it. This point was made clear in the 1970s by Lord Joseph (one of the leading figures in the neo-liberal counter-revolution within the Conservative Party) when he argued in his essay 'Stranded on the Middle Ground' (1976) in relation to poverty:

> An absolute standard of means is defined by reference to the actual needs of the poor and not by reference to the expenditure of those who are not poor. A family is poor if it cannot afford to eat . . . A person who enjoys a standard of living equal to that of a medieval baron cannot be described as poor for the sole reason that he has

chanced to be born into a society where the great majority can live like medieval kings. By any absolute standard there is very little poverty in Britain today.

These ideas were repeated by John Moore in his speech on the nature of poverty in May 1989 when he rejected the idea of relative poverty in favour of something like Lord Joseph's ill-defined 'minimum standard' relating to a view of the absolute needs of the poor. Poverty according to this view is destitution, that is, not a just share in social resources which would allow all citizens to participate in those activities which are regarded as standard or normal in our sort of society. In the view of the neo-liberals there is no need for a politically guaranteed set of citizenship rights in the welfare field outside the market beyond preventing destitution. Indeed, from the neo-liberal view, to concede this would be to concede a strongly anti-capitalist point: that an able-bodied person has a right to certain sorts of resources independently of performance in the market. The status of a citizen is primarily a civil and political status, not an economic or social one.

In the view of the neo-liberals, economic status is best conferred by the market and the worst-off members of society will be best served not by securing the welfare rights of citizens but by the trickle-down effect of the private market economy, whereby what the rich consume today will be available more widely to all sections of society as time goes on. The neo-liberal will claim that while the market economy has indeed led to an increase in inequality: nevertheless the poorest groups in society in work have in fact increased their take-home pay in their own terms more quickly than they did during more regulated regimes in the 1970s. What matters for the neo-liberal is not the gap between the rich and the poor, but whether the poor are increasing their income on a year-by-year basis. They argue that statistics show this is happening.

Power

The neo-liberal will say that if we are interested in empowering citizens as individuals, the most effective way of doing this is through the trickle-down effect of the market and not by political means of securing a politically allocated welfare status outside the market. Thus, the real need is to get those not in work into employment. In the view of many neo-liberals influenced by American welfare theorists such as Lawrence Mead and Charles Murray, we need to concentrate on the dispositions, the motivations and indeed the moral values of the poor. They have become apathetic and dependent as the result of welfare and the operation of welfare professionals and welfare bureaucracies. The answer, therefore, is to break through this apathy.

A good example of the government's attitude here is the welcome which Mrs Thatcher gave to the Chief Rabbi's response to 'Faith in the City' (the Anglican report on urban deprivation which argued for a more collective response to these problems than the government is prepared to countenance). Lord Jacobovits argued that the Jewish community had managed to escape from the ghetto and begun to climb the economic ladder as the result of the self-help which the ghettoised communities were able to engender without state help and without the intervention of community workers, other welfare professionals and welfare bureaucracies.

This idea is linked too with a critique of the role of professionals and bureaucrats in the welfare field largely derived from the work of public-choice theorists such as Buchanan and Niskanen. This view of the role of bureaucracy and the professions challenges the public-servant view of such groups which has been dominant in British public service and goes back to the nineteenth century (and has its theoretical roots in Plato and in the early nineteenth century in Hegel). The challenge here is to argue that the motivation of people in bureaucracies and professions is the same as it is in economic markets, namely the maximisation of utility.

However, because in welfare bureaucracies this pursuit is in a non-market context, in this case maximising behaviour means not the production of commodities for which there is a consumers' market, but rather the attempt of people in these circumstances to pursue their utilities through enhancing their prestige or acquiring greater job opportunities, more power, larger budgets to control, and so on. If we compare such behaviour with those in the market we can see that governmental agencies do not have to reveal the cost of a unit of output at different levels of production and this means in effect that bureaucracies have a monopoly of information about the costs and benefits of what they are doing. This monopoly of information is protected by esoteric and professionalised language, together with the reputation of sanctity of professional and clinical judgement which keeps accountability at arm's length. The attempt to secure the social rights of citizens through the provision and delivery of services has led to increasing bureaucratisation and dependency in the view of neo-liberal critics, a development which they feel could be avoided by rejecting the role of rights altogether and, instead, relying on the trickle-down effect within the framework of civil and political rights to empower people in more effective ways.

In addition it is argued that to talk about the social rights of citizens is in fact a mistake. There can be no genuine social rights because such rights are asserted to scarce resources and there can be no rights to such resources. Civil and political rights, on the other hand, can always be realised because they require other individuals or governments to abstain from acting: that is, interfering, coercing, assaulting, and so forth. We cannot run out of people not harming one another and not killing one another. However, social rights such as rights to health, education and welfare are of necessity rights to scarce resources and there is no way that there could be individually enforceable rights to such resources. This idea also finds some favour on the Left. Because of the difficulties about social rights, and because of the importance of civil and political rights which could be put into a Bill of Rights, it is argued that we should not muddy the waters of the claim to civil and political rights which are clear, categorical and justiciable by importing alongside them a set of rights which clearly are not so easily enforced.

Although the Left talks of rights such as rights to education and health care, it has not challenged a status quo where general principles are laid down by law but where individual rights are impossible to enforce. For example, in health the Secretary of State has a generalised duty according to the 1977 Health Service Act to provide a comprehensive health service. However, this does not yield individually enforceable rights to treatment, as the Barber Baby case in Birmingham two years ago demonstrated. The aim has been not to go down the road of developing enforceable rights but, by arguing for strengthening the pressures on government, to make sure that its duties in this field are properly fulfilled. This can be done by parliamentary scrutiny of ministers or through select committees, together with inspectorates such as the HMI in education or the Labour Party's proposed Health Inspectorate. The response is a traditional administrative one, not one which seeks to put power into the hands of the individual in relation to the services provided under the Secretary of State's general duty. Indeed, the Left has talked the language of social rights for forty years now, but has not gone beyond thinking that these rights are satisfied if government undertakes a generalised duty to provide a service, rather than providing individually enforceable rights.

So is there space for a more radical egalitarian vision of social citizenship which can meet these criticisms: one which sees that empowerment cannot be produced by the trickle-down effect, which will avoid some of the problems of bureaucracy in the field of welfare and one which can put real power into the hands of individuals? Indeed, these features of citizenship are interrelated. If there are social rights of citizenship this seems to imply some basic commitment to greater equality, and individually enforceable rights which would in turn control some of the power of bureaucracies in the welfare field.

The New Right's argument that we do not need elaborate rights of social citizenship, because the trickle-down effect will empower the poor more effectively than politically conferred rights, fails because it does not attend sufficiently closely to the nature of power. The free market may be able to make consumer goods trickle down through the population and to spread around the results of economic success. However, at the moment it is doing this at the cost of a very significant increase in inequality. In the view of the New Right this does not matter; they believe what concerns the poor is not the gap between themselves and others so much as the fact that their income is increasing on a year-by-year basis and that this brings extra power into their lives. However, this assumes that power is like a consumer good: that there is an indefinitely large amount of it which can be subject to the trickle-down mechanism.

Many critics suggest that power is not in fact like this, that it is rather a 'positional good', the value of which decreases the more widely it is distributed. A paradigm case of a positional good (as Fred Hirsch, who first wrote about the idea, argued in *The Social Limits to Growth*) would be standing on tiptoe to see a procession better. While I am the only person standing on tiptoe I gain an advantage over everyone else, but as the habit spreads among the people in my group then the advantage is gradually lost, and when everyone stands on tiptoe then the advantage is lost altogether. It can be said that power is like this: if it trickles down to all equally it is gradually lost. The possession of power depends upon inequality, and that is why empowerment cannot come to all through the market against a background of growing inequality. To empower one group must mean diminishing the power of another group if power is a positional good. This cannot be achieved by the market and does depend upon the collective conferring of rights on less powerful groups, rights which will challenge the power of other groups.

Empowerment cannot just come through the market, it has to come also through political mechanisms. However, the New Right are correct in their view that the forms of empowerment which have been tried in the welfare field have very often spawned large bureaucratic forms of service delivery which have sought to provide services to meet pro-fessionally ascribed needs to individuals and have left little scope for individual choice and initiative. The challenge to the Left, therefore, is to try to devise forms of individual empowerment through rights which will give people more control over their own lives in the welfare field. This has to be a gradual process, but we do have to get away from the idea that having welfare rights just means a service provider having a general duty to provide a service without that conferring any rights on the recipient of the service and which can be delivered in a highly discretionary manner. The Conservatives have already understood the salience of this idea and they are already trying to tie service delivery much more to people's entitlements. So, for example, in the field of health the new doctors' contract – whatever its other defects – does in fact yield for the first time individual entitlements to treatment in specific areas. In the case of education there will be a duty on all schools to produce a report on performance under the national curriculum. The Left cannot ignore this movement in favour of more bureaucratic mechanisms such as strengthening the HMI or creating a Health Inspectorate to ensure reasonable service delivery. It has to be prepared to put power in the hands of individuals.

In the case of civil and political rights it has been assumed that the enforceability of rights has to be in the full sense of justiciability through the courts and this has deterred people from thinking of social rights in the same way. However, there are a range of other alternatives. We do at the moment define some social security benefits in terms of legal rights and entitlements and it would be worth trying to extend this pattern. In general a rights-based approach would move more in the direction of cash payment rather than service delivery, so that instead of the state providing the service, it might rather regulate, to ensure basic national standards, a range of different private service deliverers with cash or a cash surrogate such as a voucher to be cashed within one of these services which would compete for the voucher. Other additional measures could include changing the contracts of service providers such as teachers, doctors or social workers so that it became part of their contractual duty to provide a service of a specific sort at a specific level which would then yield entitlements under the contract. This is already beginning to happen in education and medicine (though to be fully effective it would have to be tied to clear sanctions in case of non-fulfilment of the contract).

Other alternatives would be to insist on a public stake in the formulation of codes of ethics in the professions such that these conferred some rights on the clients of the professions. It has been assumed that professions are guided by a public service ethic, rather than a personal utility maximising one, but if this is doubted, there is a case for making sure that the self-regulating professions do have a responsibility to take fully into account the rights of the clients of such professions, together with clear and adequate forms of redress when those rights are infringed or not adequately protected.

A rights-based approach to citizenship could open up a number of privileged areas of British life (the professions and producer groups in the health, education and welfare fields) and to move to confer statutory rights in the public sector would mean lifting Crown immunity in the areas in which the rights were conferred. The combination of a Charter or Bill of Rights in the sphere of civil and political liberties, together with a pluralist and eclectic set of ways of conferring and protecting rights in the public sector, would constitute a radical post-Thatcher programme, looking for alternative ways of empowering the individual alongside the market mechanism on which Thatcherism has typically relied.

Rights

However, to be plausible we have to consider ways in which such rights might be developed, and clearly the toughest case here is in health, because of the unpredictable nature of the needs involved and the relative scarcity of resources. What is clear is that health resources will always be limited because of the relationship between medical need and technology. Because technological developments breed new needs, demand is never likely to be satiated and a level plateau of funding reached. A right to health care would have to recognise such limits: there clearly cannot be an enforceable right to unlimited resources to keep a person alive whatever the circumstances. However, these limits already exist, although they are set not in a public and transparent way but according to the professional discretion of doctors and administrators. Decisions about resource allocation are not clinical judgements (which are the proper preserve of professional authority) but are essentially moral or political judgements about the best use of scarce resources.

A rights-based approach would therefore first have to recognise these limits in a more obvious way than is the case at the moment and then go on to try to define entitlements within these limits. There are various ways in which this might be done. One would be to try to seek some kind of consensus on basic medical needs. It might be argued that this is impossible given what is often regarded as the incommensurable nature of medical needs. However, some progress has been made in this respect in the USA where in the Health Maintenance Act of 1973 a set of basic health services are defined. This idea is used by Enthoven in his idea of a Consumer Choice Health Plan in which an insurance plan would have to cover these basic health services. In Enthoven's plan, private insurance would yield rights to health care under the terms of the contract of the insurance, and these rights would be to these basic health services. However, there is no reason of principle why the same policy could not be adopted in the NHS if we were able to develop some kind of consensus about medical needs. Is there any reason why we should not, if the debate were to be fully opened up? We do manage to reach a rough-and-ready consensus at the moment about what is needed to protect a right to security or privacy. We do not think that this consensus is vitiated by the fact that there is no such thing as absolute privacy or security, so why in health should we not recognise limits and seek a consensus within those limits?

[41]

There are two other alternatives. One is to define a right to a certain level of service in monetary terms. This could be done by averaging the cost of the health service over the population and defining entitlement at the individual level in those terms. The problem with this view is that health care is skewed in Britain in a middle-class direction and a more egalitarian policy would be to try to average out the cost of middle-class usage of health facilities and define entitlement in those terms. This approach would be the equivalent of a health service voucher. The difficulty again is that a voucher gives a very clear limit on entitlement. However, as limits are endemic in the system in any case, the question is whether these are set in some public way so that people know in advance what their entitlements are and might then make their own provision beyond their strict entitlement as happens in other spheres. The police protect my property but beyond that I buy various security devices; the same would happen in health and indeed happens already.

The third alternative is to go down the road of performance indicators. This would mean trying to establish performance indicators for the standard health services available, based obviously on what already happens, and then defining entitlement in terms of a right to expect the achievement of those indicators within one's local health authority or being able to exit to another authority or the private sector at the local authority's expense. Again this already happens implicitly and the rights approach would make these avenues of exit a genuine entitlement.

If we are to take the idea of rights seriously, we have to be serious about how they relate to enforcement at the level of the individual. As I have argued, there is no painless way of empowering individuals and social rights, if taken seriously, would clearly involve a considerable reduction in the power of professionals, bureaucracies and producer interest groups in the public sector. However, if we do not believe that we can go down this road, it would be best to abandon talk about social rights altogether because, as the Labour policy review argues, 'Rights without the means of enforcement are a fraud.' The history of social rights in this country since 1945 shows that such rights have yielded very little in terms of individual entitlement. We are now at something of a watershed in this debate. Either we see citizenship as involving fully developed individual social rights without which civil and political rights will not be very powerful, and we seek imaginative ways in which those rights can be conferred. Or alternatively, we abandon the search for individual rights in this area and argue that all that citizens can expect is a general duty on the state to provide services to be scrutinised by inspectorates and by Parliament, but not yielding individual entitlements. It is difficult to see how a radical agenda for citizenship can fail at least to explore the first of these routes.

The Best for the Most

ROY SHAW

Before the 1987 general election, all but one of the parties produced detailed policies for the arts; and the one which did not was the Conservative Party.

This might lead cynics to say that not only are there 'no votes in the arts', but that it is a positive disadvantage for a party to have an arts policy. Certainly it is true that while many people are interested in the arts themselves, far fewer are interested in arts policies, not realising that such policies can seriously affect the health of the arts they enjoy, for better or worse. But that is changing, and we can accelerate the change.

If the Tories did not bother to submit to the electorate a considered policy before the election, the Arts Minister, Richard Luce, lost little time in announcing one *after* it. He did not, however, announce it to the voting public, but to the arts community at a conference (8 July 1987) of the Regional Arts Associations. Moreover, he did not invite discussion, but admonished his audience to accept the government's policy whether they liked it or not. The speech was effective and the arts community has been ominously quiet ever since, apart from one prominent member of it, Sir Peter Hall, who spoke out vigorously before and after resigning his post as head of the National Theatre.

Before considering the alternative – and the point of the Luce speech was to echo his mistress's line that there *was* no alternative – it is important to consider the main drift of the speech and the climate in the arts world which it powerfully helped to create. First, he admonished the arts community not to be Jeremiahs, which meant they should stop criticising the level of government subsidy. Second, they must abandon 'the welfare state mentality', which he defined as a belief that the taxpayer owes them a living. Third, he did not see public subsidy as crucial to the wellbeing of the arts and warned that the majority of taxpayers were highly sceptical about it. It therefore followed that the arts community must accept the present economic and political climate. In that climate it was clear to him that traditional arts

[43]

funding led to a 'dependency culture' which must be replaced by an 'enterprise culture', in which arts organisations would get more of their funds from the private sector, mainly from business sponsorship, while the level of government funding would be maintained – a euphemism for 'frozen'.

All this was not new. It was a logical development of the warning that Mrs Thatcher's first Arts Minister (now Lord St John of Fawsley) had issued in 1979; that the arts world 'must come to terms' with the fact that government policy in general had decisively tilted away from the expansion of the public sector. One of his successors, Lord Gowrie, put it more sharply: 'The party's over.' Richard Luce has been even more stern and the arts community seems to have 'learned its lesson' and keeps quiet, in public at least, though many of them have said to me privately, 'We're very glad you're criticising the present situation, but you realise that it is difficult for *us* to speak out.' (They fear they might harm their own prospects of Arts Council grants.)

In 1988, Richard Luce repeated his warning to the arts community to 'abandon preconceived ideas about arts funding', by which he meant what he saw as discredited sixties collectivism. It really meant abandoning bi-partisan arts policies forged in the heat of World War Two and put on a permanent peacetime basis in 1946 with the founding of the Arts Council. Even as late as 1977, Norman St John Stevas, the Tory shadow minister for the arts, was affirming that the arts were as important as health or housing as an aspect of public welfare. The Thatcher Government may have abandoned that belief, but Luce was quite wrong to affirm that the public had as well. The independent Policy Studies Institute found in 1989 that 51% believed in keeping public subsidy at the same level (currently £175 million), 35% wanted it increased, only 4% wanted it reduced and a meagre 2% wanted it stopped. So it is clear that when all the opposition parties at the last election promised to increase spending on the arts, they were reflecting public opinion more accurately than the government.

One of the plausible but false claims made from time to time is that the needs of the arts are boundless and no government could hope to meet them. Each year the Arts Council assesses the needs and submits them to the minister and the sums they ask for are not astronomical, but about 50% more than they actually get. So about £90 million a year extra would meet the needs of the arts community and remove the constant anxiety under which they all currently live. Meanwhile it is not a whingeing arts Jeremiah, but a political commentator (Peter Jenkins) who has written that while M Mitterand's monument will be the splendid Musée d'Orsay, Mrs Thatcher's will be a bucket catching raindrops from the leaking roof of the Tate Gallery.

It is clear then that the necessary increase in arts funding would be a very tiny sum in the national budget. Moreover, it has repeatedly been demonstrated in the last few years that grants to the arts are not a welfare dole, but an investment which brings back to government more money than the amount spent. Of course, the value of the arts cannot be estimated in cash terms alone, though it is important to realise that even in those terms, the arts pay their way.

Certainly, the Thatcherite belief that public subsidy is not crucial to the wellbeing of the arts and that it encourages dependency are belied by my own ten years' experience of the assessment and funding of all forms of arts, though the Thatcher Government's two choices of Arts Council chairmen, Lord Rees-Mogg and Peter Palumbo, seem to think so. Mr Palumbo has even said that public subsidy also encourages bureaucracy, a strange misjudgement for one who now leads a team of arts administrators whom only their enemies describe as bureaucrats. Moreover, the Arts Council is advised by peer groups drawn from the arts world itself who are better judges than either politicians or businessmen. Despite that, it has been Thatcherite policy to give an increasing role to business sponsorship of the arts.

I do not oppose sponsorship as such, but I do deplore a policy which keeps government funding too low and looks to business sponsors to bridge the gap. In late 1989, sponsors themselves complained strongly that the government was passing the buck to them, and they might pull out. This led to the largest increases for a decade in the government's funding, though it was still far from enough to meet real needs. In a post-Thatcher arts policy, there will be a place for business sponsorship, but then the arts community will look to it only for icing on the cake and not, as it increasingly has to do now, for its bread and butter. The minister quite wrongly believes that in the USA, where he goes shopping for policies, business is the prime source of arts money. Moreover, sponsorship is regularly described (not least by grateful arts bodies) as a form of philanthropy; but a leaflet sent by the arts minister's office to prospective sponsors is more candid: sponsorship, it said, is 'a commercial deal . . . not a philanthropic gift'. It is a form of advertising and the Association for Business Sponsorship of the Arts advises business firms that if their sponsorship is to qualify for tax relief 'it is important that advertising is seen as the sole objective of payment'. After Thatcher, politicians and the arts community may wish to consider whether it is desirable for the arts increasingly to be a by-product of the advertising industry.

There are many drawbacks to sponsorship which cannot be detailed here. They are talked about in the arts community, but few have dared to put their heads above the parapet. One was Lord Rayne, who said, on retiring from the chairmanship of the National Theatre, 'It is a hazardous business relying on sponsorship.' Another was Sir Peter Hall, who revealed after his retirement that one of the questions theatre directors now have to ask themselves in choosing a play is not just 'Is it good?' or 'Will the public like it?', but 'Will the sponsors like it?' Terry Hands, having announced his intention to resign as director of the Royal Shakespeare Company, spoke of sponsors telling him 'You'll have to kow-tow to us.' That, said Hands, was the future, and he wanted out. Clearly, an alternative arts policy will remove the pressure on arts bodies to accept business sponsorship at any price.

It is perfectly possible for government to ensure that the arts are adequately funded. They have been starved of funds, not because the money was not available and certainly not because taxpayers did not approve of their money being spent on the arts, but because it was against the Thatcherite free-market ideology to make it available and the government also curbed the power of local authorities to do so.

We do not need a brand new arts policy as some on the far Left and the far Right believe. We need 'to fight to recover what has been lost', and the conditions for doing that are now less unpropitious than they seemed through most of the eighties. Some fine tuning will of course be needed, but the main need is to rediscover lost ideals, including the one which was formulated in 1940, when government first began to fund the arts. It is: 'The best for the most.'

After the Right

ANDREW GAMBLE

Is there an alternative to Thatcherism? That depends on what is meant by the term. Thatcherism can mean simply the government headed by Margaret Thatcher, and the policies and political style associated with her. But it can also mean the long-term strategy for transforming British society on which the Conservatives embarked when Margaret Thatcher became their leader.

The two meanings of Thatcherism are often confused. Thatcher established such an ascendancy over her party and over the opposition that at times there really has seemed to be no alternative either for her party or for the country. She has so far overcome all opposition to her leadership within her own party and for much of her ten years of office the opposition has been weak and divided.

But no political leader is indestructible. Thatcher has suffered troughs as well as peaks in her fortunes, and at times has been lucky to survive. She has already lasted longer than any other Conservative leader or Prime Minister this century, but the challenges to her position have increased since 1987. There are now several alternative leaders within her own party, one of whom (Heseltine? Hurd? Baker?) may be the actual leader before the next election. She has recently also had to face a more united and effective opposition. Labour was finally rehabilitated by the media at the end of the 1980s as an electable alternative government. It achieved this feat partly through the disarray of the centre parties and partly by dropping the policies which had made it a stark and not very popular alternative to the Conservatives. With Conservative policies themselves unpopular, in early 1990 the Thatcher Government was at its lowest electoral ebb.

The re-emergence of two-party politics, the speculation over the Conservative leadership, and the prospect of a much closer contest between the two main parties at the next general election, now give clear signs of the emergence of an electoral alternative to Thatcherism.

What is less clear though is that there is a political and ideological alternative to Thatcherism, one which offers not simply a different leader but also a different set of ideas and sense of direction. Thatcherism was conceived as a particular political project aimed at creating the political conditions for breaking from the failed policies of the past and reshaping the balance of power within British politics and society.

The nature of this project and the degree of its success, even in its own terms, is disputed. But there is little doubt that it has been a major factor in forcing the Left to rethink its own position. The Left today has become uncertain of the truth – and even the desirability – of some of its most basic beliefs, and its confusion has been seized on by the New Right. A chorus of voices proclaims that ideology and even history itself are over because capitalism and liberal democracy have been proved to be the final forms of human society.

None of this is particularly new. In the 1950s Daniel Bell announced the end of ideology. But at that time the final form of the good society was seen as the Keynesian mixed economy and the welfare state. Harold Macmillan said after the 1959 election: 'The class war is over and we have won it.' The same claim is being made today, only with redoubled force, following the sudden collapse of the communist regimes of Eastern Europe in 1989.

The question, then, is not whether there exists an electoral alternative to continued domination by a Thatcherite Conservative Party. The rather low level of electoral support which the Conservatives under Mrs Thatcher have achieved at general elections means that the Conservative position, although strong, is not impregnable. The present electoral system much exaggerates the degree of support the Conservatives enjoy.

The real issue is the purpose of such an electoral alternative. Is it to install a different group of leaders, who it is hoped will be more competent and accountable, and will manage affairs more sucessfully? Such a modest objective, although seldom achieved, has often been scorned by the Left. Managing capitalism, many have argued, should be left to the capitalists: what socialists wanted was an alternative to capitalism. A socialist government would not be content to manage the capitalist economy but would actively seek to transform it.

The precise nature of this transformation, however, has seldom been clear. Belief in the possibility of an alternative society has always been central to socialist politics but there has been little clarity as to how such a society would be organised, or by what political means it might be brought about. Rhetoric about an alternative society has often been combined with pragmatic accommodation to the existing society. The result has frequently been disillusionment and disorientation among the supporters of radical change.

Those who hope to offer more than simply an electoral alternative to Thatcherism have to learn some lessons from how Thatcherism developed. Any viable political alternative would have to be based on a different vision of the good society, capable of being articulated at different levels for different political contexts. It would also need to be embodied in a political strategy which identified the policies which could simultaneously win popular support and advance towards longer-term objectives.

Trade-Offs

It is because Thatcherism marked out a political alternative to the policy consensus of the past three decades that it has been so much discussed. The 1980s will be remembered under different names in the Soviet Union, France and Iran. But in Britain it will always be the decade of Thatcher and Thatcherism.

Thatcherism first had to prove itself electorally. It had to prove that it could win votes. This is the first test for any political alternative. Thatcherism passed it with ease. Having lost four of the five general elections before 1979, the Conservatives have won all the following three in a row and despite Labour's improvement in 1989 and 1990 may well win a fourth. They have managed three consecutive general election victories before, but not under one leader. A fourth consecutive victory really would be unprecedented.

The electoral triumph of the Conservatives in the 1980s is so marked that it obscures the real nature of Thatcherism by focusing attention on the personality of the leader. Yet a little leader worship is understandable. Margaret Thatcher has not just presided over Conservative success. She has personified it. Any leader who had survived for as long as she has done would have attracted attention. But Thatcher has not just survived: she has dominated the political landscape in Britain in a way few of her predecessors managed.

Many explanations have been offered for Thatcher's dominance of British politics in the 1980s: the electoral system, the disarray of the opposition, and the political skill and opportunism of the Conservatives are all important factors. But the ideological ascendancy which Thatcherism gave the Right was important as well. After 1975 the New Right increasingly set the terms of the political and ideological debate. Its central doctrines could be applied to theoretical issues, to policy issues, and to issues of ordinary life, and its arguments appeared plausible and coherent.

It was able to do this both because of the failures and disarray of the Labour Government and because of the greater readiness of the Conservatives to respond positively to new issues and new opportunities created by rapidly changing patterns of work and leisure, and an increasingly open and interdependent world economy. The initial spur behind the development of Thatcherism was the strong reaction in the Conservative Party against the record and the policies of the Heath years. But its momentum was maintained by the flow of ideas and policy discussion which came from the New Right and by fast-moving world events.

The impulse behind Thatcherism was the need to restore the state's authority and reverse the decline of the economy. Although the New Right is made up of many groups which have tended to become more rather than less diverse, they were united in the early years of Thatcherism by the need to free the economy from the controls and burdens of collectivism, while at the same time strengthening the authority of government by limiting its size and its scope.

The Thatcherite project was driven by the belief that the postwar accommodation between the interests of labour and capital could no longer be sustained, and that this was leading to accelerating inflation, rising unemployment, and a growing burden of public expenditure. The market economy was being buried under an avalanche of controls and regulations, and the state paralysed by strong pressure groups.

The New Right favoured a return to the principles of classical liberalism – free markets and limited government. Limited government does not mean weak government. The state has to be strong to police the market order and provide those goods such as security, competition, law enforcement, and stable prices which the market cannot provide for itself. If the state takes on responsibilities beyond these it risks losing its authority and its effectiveness. It has to be above the fray of competing interests in civil society, which means that the state should not become involved in administering major spending programmes, such as education and health, or economic enterprises, such as coal, electricity, and telecommunications. Its role is to encourage families and individuals to be self-reliant and independent of the state, relying on the market rather than on public services for the satisfaction of their needs.

This image of the good society, based on a free economy, a strong state and a stable family has been central to Thatcherism. It has been the inspiration for many of the policies and strategies of the Thatcher Government. It is the ground to which Margaret Thatcher returns again and again. From it have sprung a number of separate if related discourses – commonsense homilies about the economy as well as sophisticated disquisitions on macro-economic management and public choice.

Thatcherism is sometimes presented as though there existed a set of policy blueprints in 1979, ready for immediate implementation. No actual policy process could ever work in that way. What distinguished the Thatcher Government from its predecessors was not detailed policy plans but its strategic sense of its long-term objectives, and its pragmatism concerning the means to achieve them.

Many of the policies for which the Thatcher Government is noted were not in fact planned in detail in advance but were improvised according to the particular circumstances and opportunities the government encountered. They include the legislation on trades unions, the abolition of exchange controls, and the privatisation programme. Subsequently some of these programmes, most notably privatisation, were dignified with more coherence than they had at the time.

The lack of policy planning does not mean that this government governed in the old Tory fashion, according to circumstances rather than principles. It had very firm principles which it was not prepared to compromise, but it had enough political grasp to realise that short-term tactical retreats and compromises were often necessary. The government – like all governments – had many different objectives, not all of which were compatible. In order, for example, to ensure that the privatisation of nationalised industries proceeded smoothly it had to enlist the support of their existing managements. But this meant giving guarantees about the future shape of each industry which were very damaging to another of the government's main aims – encouraging competition.

It had constantly to find the trade-offs that worked politically. More than most governments it proved successful in doing this, while still presenting its policies as consistent and coherent.

The Thatcher Revolution did not extend to all areas of policy; defence and foreign policy were untouched. The major area of change has been economic policy. However, even many of these changes, such as the turn from Keynesian to monetarist policies in economic management, were already under way before 1979. The influence of events such as the ending of the great postwar economic expansion and the system of fixed exchange rates, as well as changes in the political and intellectual climate of the 1970s, would have ensured that the thrust of policy in the 1980s was away from state intervention. The political alternative which Thatcherism represented did not depend uniquely on the election of the Thatcher Government.

What the Thatcher Government did contribute was a fierce commitment to the ideal of a more limited government and freer markets, and a readiness to use the powers of the state to confront those groups which resisted. It achieved many successes against its enemies, most notably its victory in the miners' strike in 1984–85. The ruthlessness and determination it showed in organising victory against opponents became a noted feature of its political style.

Long March

As the Thatcher era has lengthened, however, the contradictions and limits of the Thatcherite project have become more obvious. The fate which many predicted for Thatcherism – that its early radicalism would soon evaporate – has not occurred. Margaret Thatcher has repeatedly seen off those of her colleagues who have urged her to be more conciliatory, to adopt a softer approach, or to consolidate. There have been periods when the government has seemed to lose direction, but this has usually only been the prelude to a renewed burst of radical legislation.

Yet the government keeps driving up against a fundamental obstacle: the sharp conflict between its ideological and its populist objectives. The latter are crucial to maintaining the government's electoral fortunes, but tend to hinder the achievement of the longer-term transformation in attitudes and behaviour which the government is keen to promote.

The problem can be put another way. In seeking to dismantle the collectivist institutions that have grown up during the past hundred years, the government finds that whereas some of them, such as the nationalised industries and the trades unions, have little popular support, others, most notably the National Health Service, continue to enjoy a great deal. How are the voters to be persuaded that the changes which New Right doctrine prescribes will be to their advantage?

Conflicts such as these have tended to make the Thatcher Government extremely cautious in some areas. For example the move away from collectivist welfare programmes has hardly begun. Neither has the tax base been significantly broadened. The government has succeeded in reducing taxation substantially for the higher income groups, but it has not managed to reduce either the overall tax burden or the level of public expenditure.

Progress towards the ideal of the free economy and limited government has been slow. Its use of the powers of the state have made the Thatcher Government a highly centralist and interventionist government. Its supporters justify this by arguing that it is necessary first to centralise power in order to decentralise it. Only if the powers of government agencies, such as local authorities, are first repossessed by central government can they then wither away.

In order to unravel social democracy and the collectivist state, the Thatcher Government has been obliged to embark on a long march through the institutions of the extended state. In its reforms in the schools, in the hospitals, in the universities and in the media, the government has tried to alter the contexts in which individuals interact and make decisions, and to provide incentives so that those with a

[52]

vested interest in maintaining the status quo are compensated for relinquishing their opposition to change. In this way institutions can be restructured so as to promote the long-term objectives of reducing state expenditure and state involvement in people's lives and choices.

The problem with any such long march, however, is that it depends on the party in government continuing to be re-elected, so that further instalments of the reforms can be introduced. What the Thatcher Government has found is that many of its policy changes have become increasingly unpopular with voters. Selling council houses was a great success, but further opportunities for popular capitalism have been harder to find. Privatisations have had only limited success in expanding share ownership, and public opposition to privatisation of public utilities like water and electricity has been very strong. The government has insisted that its reform of the health service is not the first step towards privatisation, but the contrary is widely believed by many voters, and Conservative popularity has suffered as a result.

The community charge is another measure where the government, in pursuing its objective of forcing down local government spending and abolishing rates, has ended up imposing a new tax which makes many voters worse off. The New Right argue that no tax should be redistributive, but this principle conflicts with a widespread popular sentiment that taxation should be fair.

The opposition parties have taken to proclaiming that the government has gone too far. From a New Right perspective, though, it has not gone nearly far enough. On this view there have been important gains from the Thatcher years, but the danger of a reversion to extended government remains. By exploiting its powers under the British constitution with such determination, the Thatcher Government has shown successor governments how little they need to be bound by constitutional conventions. It wants a more limited state but refuses to contemplate constitutional changes, such as electoral reform and a Bill of Rights, which might make it permanent.

The Government claims to have made substantial progress towards its two major objectives, restoring state authority and reversing British decline. The first has been secured by forceful assertion of British interests abroad, whether in the South Pacific or in Brussels, and by challenging the power of organised interests, most notably the trades unions, at home. The second depended firstly on restoring stable prices through the application of a monetarist financial strategy and secondly on promoting supply-side policies which removed the barriers to the working of free markets. Under this heading was included tax reform, industrial relations reform and privatisation.

By 1987 the Conservatives were claiming a substantial success. The shakeout during the recession of 1980–81, it was argued, had helped to restore both corporate profitability and labour discipline, and the results were apparent in the steady growth of output and productivity between 1982 and 1988. The government boasted that it had achieved both popular capitalism and a new enterprise culture. Long-standing shortcomings of the British economy had been remedied.

Although the costs of the Thatcher years in terms of unemployment and poverty have been extremely high, the prosperity of particular regions and most sections of the working population has been real enough after 1982. In its 1987 manifesto the government was able to claim that it had banished forever the gloom of the 1970s. Abandonment of socialism and collectivism had created a prosperous, thriving economy.

Thatcherism certainly needs such an economy for its long-term survival. The evidence suggests it has not achieved it. The Lawson boom of 1986–88 triggered by private credit and fuelled by tax cuts assisted the government in winning re-election in 1987, but it proved unsustainable. By 1989 it became clear that while there had been some undoubted supply-side improvement, there had certainly been no miracle, and the productive base of the British economy was still too weak to meet the demands placed upon it. The result was the increase in inflation and a growing balance of payments deficit. The most alarming statistic to many observers was the deficit on trade in manufactures. A surplus of £4 billion in 1980 was transformed by the end of the Thatcher decade into a deficit of £14 billion. A structural gap of this magnitude posed grave problems of adjustment for the British economy in the 1990s.

Monetarists have been quick to blame the former Chancellor, Nigel Lawson, for the economic problems that were looming so large by the end of 1989. If he had stuck to monetarist principles and concerned himself only with the domestic money supply rather than trying to fix the exchange rate, they argued, all of this could have been avoided. But the idea that a return to monetarist principles offers a solution to Britain's economic problems has few political takers. The Thatcher Government discreetly abandoned monetarism after 1983 because its prescriptions were proving so unreliable. It reverted to political management of the economy, aimed at promoting economic conditions which would permit rising living standards, tax cuts, and the re-election of the Conservative Party. In 1987 the policy was triumphant. It looked threadbare two years later.

Bad Dream

The collapse of the Lawson boom will severely reduce faith in the Thatcher economic miracle, and will reveal the free market 'cure' to have had only limited success. One of its consequences is that Thatcherism is unlikely to dominate the 1990s as it dominated the 1980s.

Nevertheless the shape of post-Thatcher politics is far from clear. Any government that comes after the Thatcher Government will inherit what the Thatcher Government has achieved; the reduced role of trades unions, but also the reduced manufacturing base.

In its early days the Thatcher Government was fond of proclaiming that there was no alternative. In the electoral sense this is no longer true, although the size of the task facing the opposition should not be underestimated. Even with all its current difficulties the Conservative Party will be very difficult to dislodge from power. The importance of maximising the effectiveness of the anti-Conservative vote is still as great as before. Labour requires a much bigger advance in its vote than the Conservatives needed in 1979 to form a government.

Labour will need to identify a political alternative to the direction which the Thatcher Government has charted for British society and politics. There is still a tendency to think of the Thatcher Government as a bad dream that will pass. It is conceded that the Thatcher Government made breaches in the walls of collectivism and redefined what is politically possible. But, as is often pointed out, much of the old system is still intact, and surveys of opinion repeatedly show that Thatcherite values and policies are rejected by substantial majorities of the electorate.

Despite this, the initiative remains with the New Right, and the drift towards free market solutions continues. Collectivist institutions and the attitudes and values appropriate to a public realm will be further undermined, leading to a society characterised by large imbalances in power between classes, marked contrasts in wealth and poverty, both of income groups and of regions, and by a political process which is concerned with fewer and fewer issues and in which participation is low.

A political alternative to Thatcherism will need to start from an understanding of why Thatcherism was successful and what were the limits to its success. It will need to have a clear picture of the kind of society it seeks to create, and the stages of progress towards it. It will need to have worked out how structural reforms intended to have long-term effects can be combined with policies that maintain sufficient electoral support along the way.

The test of a revolution is the character of the successor regime and how much it seeks to undo the changes that have taken place. The Thatcher Revolution may be incomplete but it has altered the character of opposition politics, and has helped to shape the character of the alternative that can be proposed.

Among the more important changes that have taken place during the Thatcher years are, firstly, attitudes towards the national economy. National protectionism involving import and exchange controls is no longer a viable option for any party seeking government. The policy issue now is what kind of links should be developed with the world economy. Here the free market Atlanticist stance of Margaret Thatcher is countered by those who give priority to links with the European Community. The issue goes wider than economic sovereignty. It also concerns which model of institutional development Britain will follow in the 1990s – the free market of the United States or the developmental state of the German Federal Republic.

Secondly, the debate on nationalisation has been changed irrevocably. The question of ownership no longer has the importance socialists once attached to it. The nationalised corporation is not a form of state socialism anyone wishes to revive, even for water. The debate has passed on to how best to regulate the activities of corporations, whether they are in the public or the private sector, and how to alter the way in which different interests are represented within business enterprises. One of the spurs to this is the new awareness of environmental issues and the ecological damage being done by unregulated economic activity. The struggle to extend forms of democracy to the organisation of economic activity will seek to alter the balance of power within each enterprise, in order to alter both the context in which decisions are made and the substance of those decisions.

Thirdly, the old conception of the mixed economy has passed away along with the idea of nationalisation. The separation between production and distribution which so bedevilled the politics of the Left has not troubled the Thatcher Government. It has been noted instead for the unity between its economic and social policies – incomes and needs are determined through the market and welfare is a palliative which must not be allowed to encroach on the way the market works. Any viable alternative would need in its turn to establish a similar unity. It would have to find a way of removing the stigma which a market society places on poverty and idleness by providing everyone with a basic income.

Fourthly, Thatcherism has weakened Labourism – the old alliance between the Labour Party and the trades unions – significantly. The legal position of trades unions has been altered, and Labour will not seek to reverse it. Trades unions are not about to disappear, but the labour movement is no longer the key centre of radical politics that it could once claim to be. Ethnic politics, feminist politics, and green politics all challenge it. Labour's degree of dependence on the trades unions in the past made it difficult for Labour to project itself as a socialist party representing all citizens. Labour is now evolving quite rapidly into the kind of socialist party that is common in other parts of Europe.

Fifthly, the unrestrained way in which the Thatcher Government has used parliamentary sovereignty to force through many unpopular measures such as the poll tax, water privatisation, and NHS reorganisation, has focused attention on the importance of civil society and the institutions between the individual and the state, which include trades unions, local authorities, universities, schools, and voluntary associations of all kinds. These are often bulwarks against an overmighty state. Thatcherism has a conception of civil society as well, but it is defined almost exclusively in terms of markets, and is unconcerned about imbalances of power when these arise from the operation of markets. Through its actions the Thatcher Government has highlighted the lack of constitutional safeguards against arbitrary power in Britain. It supports a return to limited government, but its policies have often promoted the opposite.

This issue is likely to be at the heart of any radical alternative from the Left. A strong civil society is important not just as a counterweight to the state but as a counterweight to concentrations of private power in the market. The Left has to define anew the society it wishes to create. Earlier responses to the excesses of markets led socialists to favour the use of the centralised power of the state to protect individuals and communities. In recoiling from that solution many socialists now embrace free markets. Markets left to themselves, however, will not achieve the objectives which socialists seek. A market order is only tolerable if it is embedded in a strong civil society and a strong democracy which can counter poverty, oppression and injustice. Giving priority to the establishment of such a civil society and such a democracy is a basic condition for the emergence of a viable alternative to Thatcherism.

DISASTER

It's the time when Thatcher swoops down,
with her terrible 'caring' voice,
on the stricken village or town –
no, they won't get away
till she's had her full say,
they haven't any choice!

So beware of the wings and the beak,
of the shadow that blots the sun!
It's arranged, like a Cabinet leak;
troubles never come singly,
she will make you feel tingly,
a Horror to everyone!

Like a Stuka, a Dracula bat,
she hovers around the sky,
she's a hawk, you can't doubt that!
If you're accident-prones
you may hear those dread tones
and meet that baleful eye!

Gavin Ewart

From Nation State to World Society

MICHAEL YOUNG

'An interest-rate fluctuation in Tokyo kills a real-estate deal in Birkenhead. Bond swings in London spell the difference between the success or failure of a public offering in New York. The reckoning of Mr Gorbachev's support in the Politburo dizzies the price of wheat futures in Chicago. It's a small world, where financial and all other markets are connected like a hundred hair-springs in an Aladdin's watch; where a concert at Wembley can feed 100,000 children in Tigray; where events unfold faster; where the fluttering of a single butterfly's wings in the Amazon jungle can precipitate a storm over Pontypridd. Decisions are trickier. The future is more unpredictable. No one is better positioned in this global climate than, you've guessed it, our Neil. Vote Labour on Thursday and do your bit to bring the world under control. It's time for a change.'

It certainly is. But daring as Mr Mandelson is, come the next election I do not see him asking the party's advertising agents to seek out space for such a message. That would be the day. It will not happen, not yet, because Mr Kinnock has still not woken up from his long sleep in the same bed, on the same uptight little island, as Mrs Thatcher. Prince Charming is not even looming up over the Thames, and when he materialises it is not clear whom he will wake first.

Burden of the Past

Cut to the 1930s. Socialists were then almost automatically international in their outlook and not just because they shared the fascination of the Webbs with the Soviet Union. Take me, for example. Inconsistent I assuredly was, as much as anyone else in the party – on one day pacifist, on another prepared to rip up cobblestones in Cable Street to hurl at the Blackshirts; on one day for disarmament, on another shouting 'Arms for Spain!' as though my voice if raised enough would carry to the Ebro. Until I was cowed by the mounties who charged me and my mother and 10,000 others. We pressed ourselves against the walls of the House of Lords as though the very walls could protect us.

But on two other issues I and those like me were pretty consistent. We wanted the League of Nations to be given more power – perhaps it would be better to say just power. The vision was of a league in which high-minded and plain-living Britons like Philip Noel-Baker and Arthur Henderson and George Lansbury would represent Britain. I remember once being mesmerised by Noel-Baker, a Labour front-bencher, arguing the case for a world government which would hold in check the belligerent nation states as the state in its earlier stages had once held in check and then neutralised the feudal lords after the Wars of the Roses.

The other issue was the Empire. It was quite a lesson in political geography. Coloured red, it enveloped the world on the wall-maps in every school in the country. Every coin still bore the head of the Rex who was also the Imperator. The Bengal Lancers and the King's African Rifles were almost as much our regiments as the Seaforth Highlanders, the Irish Guards and the Devons. The Empire forced us into world-mindedness.

We had it both ways. We could enjoy the sense of power and also more than square it with our canons of morality by urging that we should give it all up: the subject peoples should be freed from the colonial yoke.

Annie Besant, the former member of the London School Board who had founded the Indian National Congress, was our intellectual forerunner. India was the centre of attention for millions of others besides the students like me who trailed over from LSE to do clerical work in the India League office in the Strand. Mr Krishnamenon, then a St Pancras Labour councillor and later independent India's first Foreign Minister, smiled at all of us. St Pancras had a constituency which stretched from the deserts of Sind, the Rift Valley of Central Africa and the Blue Mountains of Jamaica all the way to King's Cross. Mahatma Gandhi had our support too when he attended Round Table Conferences, partly because he did not lodge at Claridge's but at Kingsley Hall in the Darkest London of the East End.

After 1945 the focus gradually changed and the process of unwinding was never to be stayed. I remember writing to Harold Wilson in 1964 asking him if he would give an option to the people of islands like Mauritius, Fiji and Barbados to remain with Britain in the future if they wished and elect MPs to Westminster, in this like the French. But it was too late for that, even though we accepted for so long the overloading of the national resources created by the continuous support given to imperial preference, the sterling area, the maintenance of a military presence east of Suez and a higher level of military expenditure generally than any other country of Britain's size.

Hong Kong apart, the Empire was dismantled bit by bit and, as it all happened, we became more and more inward-looking. The broad, brilliant and vague sweep of socialist ideas which had prevailed in the 1930s and thrust forward the 1945 government gave way to the overweening details of Regional Board membership in the NHS and the demand for anthracite from South Wales collieries. We were building socialism in our one country, or we intended to. Once the Empire had gone and Stalinist Russia lost its appeal our socialist theory did not sail much beyond Dover.

In retrospect, it seems inevitable that the Labour Party should have withdrawn into intellectual isolationism. To have fostered or gone along with the liberation of colonial peoples was one of its achievements; but it was not one we could boast too much about when facing the electors. Whenever Labour was in government the leaders and their followers could in private hardly fail to lament the loss of power even while they blustered out in public a kind of denial that the loss had occurred at all, in this as much red- (or pink-) blooded nationalists as almost any Tory. Collectively we were transfixed by a political melancholia which prevented almost any new thinking on world issues. We were locked into our own variation of the 'Quebec psychosis' – frozen into a past we had lost. Our socialism has not been about equality so much as it has been about loss. We were behaving like a bereaved person who remains so much caught up in the past (without being able to admit it) as to be unable to let go – to let the past go – and start to rebuild a new life. As each new generation has been subtly infected by the one that went before it has been less a case of Perfidious Albion than of Bereaved Albion. The same thing has happened to many other nation states which have lost power, although less dramatically. They, too, have had to get over that sense of loss if they have faced up to it at all; and we could now after a long delay join them.

How else to explain the persistent standoffishness of all British parties to Europe? We would all (it seems) rather cling to a ghostly pre-eminence we no longer have than join in as just one of the partners in this new community. For some years in the war and after, the Labour Party behaved as though it really was a European Socialist Party. Denis Healey in his memoirs has described his zest as he moved from one socialist meeting to another when in 1945–50 he was the Party's International Department. He was a kind of Prince Charming for the socialist parties which had gone underground or into exile in the war. But we then turned our back on them and for many years were racked by the European issue. Time and time again it divided Labour as much as, in more recent times, it nearly destroyed Mrs Thatcher over the Westland affair (when she lost Heseltine) and over the European Monetary Union and what goes with it (when she lost Lawson).

Gatwicking

The withdrawal has been all the more perverse because the modern version of Little England (and Wales, Scotland and Ireland) has coincided with a steady growth in world interdependencies. The density of communication of every kind has increased steadily as measured by volumes of mail, phone calls, travel, students studying abroad, or almost anything else. If you misdial, the wrong number may be in Mexico City instead of Bournville. At the same time a common, shared technology has made for more homogenisation in lifestyle almost everywhere.

If people objected to what had happened there would by now have been a near-universal backlash against the world that technology has given us. Maypoles would have been set up outside every Sainsbury's and mead become a best-seller. But it has not happened yet and seems to me unlikely to happen for a good many years to come. Quite the opposite. The addiction to television is no less because it is shared by so many of the other inhabitants of the planet. They are happy to goggle at each other across national frontiers. They join in together to watch spectacles like the Olympic Games, the World Cup or pulling down the Berlin Wall.

There is also no sign as yet that travel is going to diminish because there is less and less to travel for. People are so much subject to the 'Gatwicking' of the world that the party member who lands in Athens or Miami can easily be in panic that the automatic pilot has flown the plane in a circle and landed it at Gatwick again, for all the difference he can distinguish. But the airlines will not go bankrupt because all their destinations are lookalikes. People do not travel in order to arrive but in order to travel. They travel because they worship movement, as witness the earnest, down-to-business, dedicated look that people have when they leave behind the lightheartedness they have at work and get behind the wheels of their mobile rooms or queue up to board another aeroplane even if they are so purposefully to go 'nowhere'. They are constantly on the move because they feel more significant when they are. However one interprets what is happening, their boundaries are no longer the frontiers of the nation state.

In this world of movement – not only of people but of ideas, goods, services, fashions, pictures, sounds – the power of nation states taken individually is bound to be diminished. We cannot any longer talk about the world outside; the world is inside. Labour's Chancellor of the Exchequer is not going to be any more capable than the Conservatives' of controlling inflation in Britain if it is raging in the world as a whole. The mortgage rate in Britain is going to be set not by our government but by Tokyo, New York and Frankfurt. Whether British exporters can succeed is more determined by other governments than our own. Government regulation of the City will matter less and less as there is a move towards a single financial market first in Europe and then in the world, and people anywhere can buy or sell stocks, or borrow or lend money, as easily and as instantly in Stuttgart or Singapore or Sydney as in Sheffield. The British Government is now like others in being unable to act alone. Its sovereignty – like the sovereignty of all the other states – is being ceded to forces which are not under the control of any of them.

Ghost of Noel-Baker

This being so, the opposition parties must surely rouse themselves and open their eyes to the new world which has been created (or has created itself) while they have been asleep. The Gorbachev phenomenon, and its repercussions in Eastern Europe, could be the catalyst. Instead of acting as a brake Britain could, with new leadership, become the accelerator to a more unified Europe and a parliament to match.

Before long that could become common ground to all parties. But the bigger challenge comes from beyond Europe and beyond 1992. The great question is whether the pragmatic co-operation which has distinguished the development of the Common Market could have a world-wide application. It is obvious that most of the problems are not European but world-wide. Europe is a rich continent. If there is to be any energetic move towards more equitable distribution between the rich and the poor on a world scale, Europe will need to push for it, and be prepared to lead it and sacrifice for it. If anything effective is to be done to conserve the environment it can only be done on a world scale. Strasbourg has no rain forests, no Antarctica; the beds of the world's oceans are not under its jurisdiction, or anyone else's; the fish do not spawn or swim to the orders of M Delors. A new Europe-wide and eventually world-wide tax and expenditure system is needed whereby the polluting countries compensate those whom they are polluting, and whereby the funds are generated for great conservation efforts whose beneficiaries will be every country rather than just one or several.

Multinational corporations cannot be stopped from becoming the organs of their own version of world government by any action taken in the public forums of Europe. Human rights cannot be protected except by means which extend to all humanity. Terrorism cannot be brought under some measure of control from Europe alone, for all its police forces, intelligence services and armed forces. Nor can the international drug trade, which could in the long run ruin Europe as it has ruined some districts in the United States. The grimmest scenario one can imagine is that international bandits – drug barons in alliance with political terrorists and the more shady multinationals – will equip themselves with more armaments (eventually with nuclear weapons) as ordinary states divest themselves of theirs.

It is heavy stuff compared to the hair curlers and the E numbers which have been food and drink for the EEC. This is not to say that a pragmatic approach could not pay off, each problem or set of problems being tackled, and anarchy held at bay, by co-operation between nation states and their civil servants. But it will not indefinitely be enough merely to have co-operation between states. Before long they could seem like boobies in a tarboosh. It will not be enough for the European Community any more than it was for the thirteen colonies of North America.

Something more comprehensive, more stable, more responsive to the people of the planet will be necessary. For if all the EEC did with its enlarged powers was to enable Europe to compete more effectively with North America and Japan (or Japan together with China if they ever form an entente more far-reaching than they have at present), the end result could be more friction on a mammoth scale, and more danger of war. If European countries are able to bury their hatchets, the example should be used in order to persuade others to bury theirs. Europe will only be at peace if the world is, and this may not happen without a world state.

So a world state is again forcing itself on to the political agenda, and with it the age-old questions of what a state is and what it is needed for. What kind of 'social contract' is appropriate? Certainly not the Rousseau kind in which there is a wholesale transfer of rights. The traditional idea of the sovereign state with a monopoly of coercive power is certainly not right either. To begin with, it may be better to think of the 'citizens' in this world state as being the nation-states themselves, but with individuals as citizens gradually establishing themselves on the stage. I doubt whether the old nineteenth-century idea of the 'night-watchman state' will be enough. Anything less than a state dedicated to more equitable distribution as a basis for social order may prove less than adequate to the new situation. Hume, Tawney and Rawls will all need to be drawn on in a new effort of practical imagination. The philosophers, the artists and the human scientists should lead at any rate the opening rounds of a debate which will continue to resound through the rest of this century and the early rounds of the next.

Perhaps Mr Gorbachev will prove to have been Prince Charming who was hidden all the time in the mists of the Thames above Westminster, even if he himself is eclipsed in the Soviet Union. If so, then in very different circumstances the spirit could be similar to what it has been before, with the aims being to enhance liberty on a global scale; to prevent the strong from exploiting the weak by establishing the rule of an even-handed law; to secure a more just distribution of the fruits of the earth; and to create a more orderly, less violent world society in which differences between people will be encouraged rather than extinguished. The ghost of Noel-Baker could ride again, on a caparisoned horse in the Gorbachev cavalcade.

POLICIES

Red and Green: Accounting for the Environment

PATRICIA HEWITT

One of the most exciting intellectual and political challenges of the 1990s is the need to integrate environmental with economic and industrial priorities.

Neil Kinnock, in his introduction to the Labour Party policy review, refers explicitly to the interdependence of economy and ecology and argues that: 'We cannot allow production to race ahead unchecked, paying no heed to the depletion of natural resources, the damage to the environment, the problems of waste and pollution . . . It is essential that environmental concerns are built into the production process.' Labour's environment policy similarly stresses the need to integrate environmental thinking into other aspects of policy.

Unfortunately, the policy review's chapter on economic and industrial policy contains little more than a nod in the direction of green concerns, with no suggestion about how economic and industrial policy might be adapted to environmental ends. So, how to proceed?

Firstly, what is required is a definition of environmentally sustainable growth. Secondly, Labour needs to develop the case for state intervention to provide an environmental framework for market operations, using charges and taxes as well as regulation. Thirdly, Labour should integrate environmental priorities with industrial, agricultural, energy, transport, fiscal and other aspects of economic policy.

A European perspective is essential. Many environmental issues such as air pollution can only be tackled effectively on a European (and some only on a global) scale. The environmental modernisation of industry is rapidly emerging as a central theme in the transformation of Central Europe. In Poland, for instance, where some villages are so polluted they are no longer habitable, environmental reconstruction will have to go together with industrial rebuilding. It is equally central to the programmes of EC and Scandinavian socialist parties. The British Left can learn much from its European socialist partners, whose thinking on these issues is often well ahead of its own. But we should also aim to make our own contribution to the development of European Community environmental policy – where the Conservative Government is, once again, increasingly isolated.

Slash-and-Burning

Much of the debate about environmental economics has centred on 'growth' versus 'no-growth'. The Green Party criticises both Labour and Conservative for being 'grey' – committed to industrial growth, whatever the environmental rhetoric. But it is a false antithesis. We continue to measure 'growth' through the Gross Domestic Product which draws no distinction between environmentally beneficial and environmentally harmful activity, and which omits many of the environmental costs which are being imposed on future generations.

Under current national accounting conventions, GDP is an incomplete measure of economic activity in Britain. Only marketed goods and services, or those funded from taxation (like the NHS), count towards national economic growth. An increase in car crashes, repairs and replacements, or an increase in double-glazing designed to compensate for a noisier environment all count as growth. Waste dumped in rivers or at sea, air polluted by carbon dioxide fumes or industrial emissions, water contaminated through excessive use of fertilisers, climates changed by the slash-and-burning of tropical forests, do not appear in the accounts of either companies or countries. The environmental resources which are damaged in these ways are, in economic terms, 'free goods'.

The environmental costs imposed by economic activity – the 'externalities' – may be experienced close to home, for instance by people living near a new waste dump. But the vast majority of costs are borne by other countries, or by other continents or by generations yet to come. Nor is it surprising that, when the costs are more remote in space or time, it is often difficult to reach agreement about who the polluter really is.

Bringing environmental costs home to the producer ('internalising the externalities') is an essential part of reducing environmentally damaging behaviour. It requires changes in the national accounts, as well as those of companies.

Attempts have been made in several countries, including France, Norway and Japan, to 'account' for the environment. The Japanese Government, for instance, publishes figures for 'Net National Welfare' which correct national income figures for environmental and other factors. Japan's growth rate is much lower according to these national welfare measurements than it is in conventional GDP figures.

GDP accounts will inevitably reflect political assumptions about what is to be counted. Putting a price on environmental resources will offend many people's instinctive understanding that some things are 'beyond price'. Definitions of benign and harmful activity may prove controversial. For instance, David Pearce and his colleagues who recently provided a report on sustainable development for the Department of the Environment[1], refer to 'business opportunities in leisure and tourism', but do not mention the environmental *costs* (such as pollution and energy resource depletion from air travel, the effect on traditional communities, and damage to fragile lands) which are also imposed by the international leisure industry.

From a different perspective, it should also be noted that 'non-marketed services' include the often invisible family and domestic responsibilities performed almost entirely by women. Nonetheless, identifying and valuing 'non-marketed' goods and services would greatly assist public debate about environmental, economic and social priorities. The technical problems of such an approach, although substantial, are not insurmountable. But there is a need for a *political* objective – to measure the 'quality of life' with sufficient precision to promote public and Parliamentary debate about improvements (or deteriorations) in the same way – and, indeed, at the same time – as the Budget itself.

But what about the question of 'growth'? Because 'growth' does not equal environmental and social welfare, 'no-growth' cannot be assumed to be environmentally desirable. High growth might be environmentally benign. Low growth might be environmentally damaging – and generally is in the developing countries. What matters environmentally is not the measurement of *growth*, but the measurements of environmental damage, restoration and protection.

In 1987, the Brundtland Commission, chaired by Norway's socialist Prime Minister, emphasised the concept of 'sustainable development' as the basis for reconciling environmental and economic needs[2]. In essence, environmentally sustainable development suggests that economic activity should leave to future generations an environmental stock similar to that inherited by the present generation; should not damage the ecological 'support system' (of which the ozone layer is a vital part); and should limit waste disposal to levels which can be safely absorbed by the environment.

The British Prime Minister and the government, in response to Brundtland in recent speeches, have stressed their commitment to 'sustainable development'. They have done little, however, to measure the changing value of the natural resource base – oil, coal, natural gas, forests and fisheries.

The treatment of North Sea oil is a good test of the government's commitment to environmentally sustainable development and, in particular, the principle that each generation should pass on to its children a sustainable environmental inheritance. The application of that principle to renewable resources is reasonably straightforward, requiring, for instance, trees to be replanted at the rate needed to preserve or increase the forestry stock. It can also be applied to animal and plant species, or, at a global level, the climate-regulating functions of the oceans and the ozone layer.

But *non*-renewable resources, such as coal, natural gas and North Sea oil, require a different approach. Obviously, if each generation were to pass on to the next the same stock of non-renewable resources it had inherited, those resources would remain unused. The environmental stock would be preserved, but at the expense of the greater economic and social welfare which could have been achieved through its use. An environmentally responsible approach would recognise that depletion rates should be carefully regulated and at least some of the benefits gained for one generation should be invested in a form that will create new sources of wealth and welfare in future. But the British Government's approach to North Sea oil, for example, is exactly the opposite: high depletion rates with the benefits to national revenue and the balance of payments used to finance short-term consumption. Although Pearce and his colleagues argue that sustainable development requires sufficient reinvestment of the proceeds of exhaustible resources to compensate for their depletion, they do not point out that this is precisely what the government has failed to do. The government's response to such a charge is usually to stress the substantial increase in *foreign* assets: but foreign investment by private individuals in projects whose environmental impact is itself unknown scarcely amounts to a 'sustainable' use of North Sea oil.

A Vision of 'Green Growth'

What are the prospects for environmentally benign growth in the European Community? Environmentally-led public and private investment would increase the output of 'clean' consumer goods, capital goods embodying low-pollution and low-waste technologies and environmental services such as waste treatment and disposal. Local, regional and national government would invest in energy conservation, the reconstruction of sewers and water treatment plants, public transport in and between cities, and the telecommunication networks needed for 'low transport' land use. The European Commission could serve as an investment bank, attracting resources to projects with environmental benefits such as reduced cross-boundary movements of pollutants.

Environmentally-led development of this kind requires a new kind of economic and industrial policy designed to integrate environmental values into the economic decision-making of individuals, companies and government. As the German SPD recognise in their new draft Basic Programme: 'The ecological reorientation and renewal of our national economy must extend from the product ideas and product planning via the production process all the way to consumption and the recycling of the used materials.'

In Britain, Labour's 'supply-side socialism' is directed to the long-standing weaknesses in Britain's real economy which manifest themselves dramatically in the deteriorating balance of trade. Raising the general education and skills level; investing in R&D and in science; modernising the railways and telecommunications; facilitating regional economic development; protecting companies against market short-termism and creating a framework for long-term investment are key elements in a strategy designed to achieve competitiveness by raising the value of labour rather than cutting costs of labour.

The environmental transformation of industry is not an *alternative* to this strategy: it is, or should be, a vital part of it. A shift from environmentally wasteful to more responsible forms of production is part of the fundamental change in the production process described by one leading German environmental economist as: 'a conceptual shift of emphasis from heavy industry to knowledge-intensive forms of production, from the ideology of tonnage to intelligent forms of production, from quantitative to qualitative growth, from industry to services, from standardised mass production to flexible production systems and from wasteful to ecologically more appropriate methods of production. Our environmental problems would be fewer if this reorientation were more than incipient . . . The central question – and not only for environmental policy – is how to make [this new paradigm] prevail.'[3]

Nor can Britain's balance of trade problem be separated from the process of environmental modernisation. As the demand for environmentally benign consumer goods and production processes grows, and as environmental regulation at national and European level becomes stricter, companies and countries with a substantial R&D base and the ability to make rapid changes in product design and production process will benefit from new export markets.

A striking example of this process is the recent surge of demand for disposable nappies produced without chlorine bleaching of paper pulp. The consumer campaign was triggered initially in Sweden by the Chemical Inspectorate's threat to seek a ban on chlorine bleaching. As the initially reluctant paper pulpers mended their ways, Swedish producers were able to beat British companies to a new product market.

If environmental and industrial modernisation are indeed part of the same strategy, the instruments of industrial policy should also serve environmental ends. Here, again, we can learn from other European experience. The Hungarian Environment Ministry, for instance, has proposed that loans for industrial projects should be subject to conditions on waste-free and non-polluting technologies; and that 'nature conservation pools' or 'eco-banks' should be established to invest in waste-processing and other environmental projects. I have already referred to the possibility of a European Commission 'eco-bank'. At least as important could be Labour's proposed creation of a network of *regional* industrial investment banks which could, simultaneously, act as 'eco-banks' promoting the environmental modernisation of industry.

Private Car

Environmentally sustainable economic development will mean growth in some activities and products, decline in others. A shift from short product life and high replacement rates for cars, refrigerators and other consumer goods, to longer product life, more repairs and lower replacement rates would imply less growth in traditional car and white goods production, higher growth in the output of spare parts, and a shift in jobs from production to repairs. A new demand for vehicles powered by alternative and renewable fuels (electricity, bio-alcohol or hydrogen) – which could be encouraged by tax incentives and regulations – could, on the other hand, promote R&D and, in the longer term, stimulate production and employment in the vehicle industries.

The Kreisky Commission on full employment in Europe[4] argues strongly for the employment potential of environmentally-led growth. Although some of the new jobs would be in capital and consumer goods, much of the increase in environmental employment would come in the service sector; some would require a high level of technical skills, others (such as driving small city buses) would be in areas where mechanisation is extremely inefficient.

The British Labour Party, like its EC counterparts, recognises both the necessity and the limits of the market. An environmental perspective strengthens that analysis of the need for a framework of regulation and intervention in the decisions of private companies and individual consumers. The great virtue of the market is that it allows for the decentralisation of millions of individual decisions about production and consumption. The sum total of those individual decisions may, however, be an outcome which nobody would choose. For example, more and more people choose to travel by private car: yet none of them *chooses* congested streets, polluted cities and damage to the ozone layer. Where substantial environmental externalities are concerned, the apparent self-interest of individuals acting in the market will produce results which are in no one's interest. Intervention is required, to set limits on various forms of pollution, to restrain certain kinds of decision-making and to integrate environmental costs into the prices of goods and services.

The environmental transformation of production and consumption – although a popular notion – will sometimes be painful in practice. A useful test case is the approach which a new government might take to the private car. Labour has long been associated both with the mass producers of cars and with aspirations to mass car ownership. It is not therefore surprising that proposals for curbs on private car use are often instinctively condemned on the Left.

But Labour will have to confront the problem of private car use, in local as well as national government. The benefits of private, door-to-door transport are obvious, particularly to those who use cars. The costs are less obvious – but just as real. Road traffic is a growing source of CO_2 and other emissions as well as a major user of non-renewable energy resources (accounting for nearly three-quarters of final oil consumption). Passenger mile for passenger mile, the private car uses more energy than any other form of transport, including a long-distance jet!

Despite Mrs Thatcher's new interest in global warming, her Department of Transport forecasts an increase in road traffic by 2025 of between 83% and 142%. The move to lead-free petrol, catalytic converters and cleaner engines cannot prevent, if the official forecasts are right, a substantial increase in vehicle emissions over the next fifteen years. If that were not bad enough, the land use implications of an unchecked growth in road transport are horrifying. The present government's transport policy falls far short of the Prime Minister's rhetoric about 'a full repairing lease' on the world of which we are custodians.

Direct restrictions on car ownership are politically impractical. Instead, the objective should be to make cars more environmentally acceptable and their use more discriminating. The withdrawal of Britain's present tax subsidies to company cars – a classic illustration of 'paying the polluter' – is essential. In severely congested cities like central London, as I have argued in a recent Institute for Public Policy Research paper[5], the most efficient, most environmentally effective and fairest form of traffic restraint available is road pricing; i.e. charging drivers in city centres during weekday peak hours. The use of road pricing as an environmental and congestion charge is designed to 'internalise' the external costs which drivers now impose on others. It would simultaneously free the roadspace needed to enable buses to become a fast and reliable form of public transport, and generate revenues which could be invested in computerised bus management and information systems and, in the longer term, in new forms of light electric railways.

Britain is unusual amongst Western European cities in combining relatively low car ownership with relatively high car use. Other cities, like Munich, have shown that lower car *use* (evenings and weekends rather than weekdays, leisure rather than work journeys, and so on) is compatible with higher car *ownership*. In this case, fears that environmental measures would hit manufacturing production and jobs seem to be unfounded. There will, however, be circumstances in which environmental priorities will require an end to some processes and some products: the response of Labour and the unions then should not be to defend the jobs whatever the environmental costs, but to manage the change into new, environmentally beneficial production and services.

Environmental Charges and Taxes

The example of road pricing raises the general question of how far economic instruments – charges, taxes and pricing policy – should be used by environmental socialists. In Britain, although the 'polluter pays' principle is widely accepted by both government and opposition parties, both have tended to see the use of market instruments for environmental protection as the property of the Right, with regulation or 'command and control' policies belonging to the Left. Thus, road pricing is often criticised as a 'right-wing' solution, as is the proposal for a 'carbon tax' made by Nicholas Ridley in a recent pamphlet[6].

Amongst other EC and Scandinavian socialists, however, the debate is not about *whether* to use environmental charges and taxes, but *how* to use them most effectively. The German SPD envisages a fundamental restructuring of the tax system for environmental purposes. The 'Progress 90' working group which is drawing up the SPD's next election manifesto says that: 'The SPD plans to use the dynamic and innovative forces of the market economy to preserve the environment. The basic idea is to give incentives for environmentally wholesome conduct through price signals to both the economy and the consumer.' At the heart of the new plan is a substantial shift in the burden of taxation from individual work – which, in itself, is environmentally benign – to the consumption of non-renewable energy. Energy taxes of DM30 billion (£10 billion) will be balanced against cuts in income tax and increased pensions and other social security benefits for non-taxpayers.

[78]

There are other examples to draw upon, including some from Eastern Europe. In the USSR, the government's price reform includes adding the costs of protecting and repairing the natural environment to product prices. In Hungary and Poland, putting a price on the environment through the use of economic instruments such as waste and pollution charges is seen as central to the creation of a new, socially responsible market system.

Considerable unease is sometimes expressed on the British Left about the 'polluter pays' principle itself. It is argued, for instance, that it simply gives the rich a 'licence to pollute' and that restricting or banning the polluting behaviour will be more effective as well as more just. In some cases, of course, regulation is essential: if a pollutant is lethal, it must be banned, not made more expensive.

Instinctive preference for regulation over pricing and tax mechanisms rests on the belief that, whereas regulation is designed to control and reduce environmental damage, environmental charges are designed to allow polluters to buy their way out. That is, in fact, precisely what has happened in non-market economies like the Soviet Union and China where charges or fines on polluters have been too low to act as a deterrent. In Western industrialised countries, too, environmental charges have sometimes been set so low that they become the equivalent of medieval 'indulgences' – a licence to go on sinning! This is not, however, an argument against economic instruments, particularly when it is remembered that ineffective regulation (under-staffed inspectorates, few prosecutions and low fines) has exactly the same effect.

Properly used, an environmental charge is an incentive to polluters to *change* their behaviour – particularly where pollution and other environmental damage is caused not by a few large companies but by thousands of small producers or millions of individual consumers. The charge must, of course, be high enough if it is to work, and is often most effective when combined with government standard-setting and other forms of more direct intervention. Under such circumstances, environmental charges are much more effective than direct regulation. Trying to inspect the use of chemicals by small drycleaning companies, or of fertilisers by every farmer, would require a large and expensive staff; imposing an environmental tax on the offending chemicals will prove more effective, provided always that the tax is high enough to persuade the users to use less.

The debate about environmental economics has moved beyond general reference to the 'polluter pays' principle to specific discussion of appropriate policies to deal with real problems. The objective is to find the most environmentally effective, economically efficient and politically acceptable policy. Since every policy may have an effect on the distribution of incomes, this must be examined. If the adverse effects are substantial, it may be necessary to find an alternative environmental policy. In other cases, it will be possible to offset an adverse impact on lower-income consumers (for instance, increased fuel charges could be offset by reduced licence fees for smaller cars).

Environmental taxes and charges – such as a tax on fuel or other energy consumption – must also be scrutinised for their possible effect on industrial competitiveness and the operation of the Single Market. The Labour Party, working with other European socialist parties, should take the initiative in developing a Community-wide policy on environmental charges – a subject to which the EC appears to have given little attention so far. One possibility worthy of further examination is the restructuring of VAT as a 'green' tax. Within such an approach, both the inflationary and the distributional consequences of environmental charges could be taken into account.

Hedgerows

One striking advantage of environmental charges and taxes over regulation is their revenue-raising potential. In the industrialised countries generally, the state has found its powers to raise and spend revenue increasingly constrained; demographic pressures and growing demands on the welfare state compound the problem. The costs of environmental repair and protection are simply too great to be met from national government revenues. Not surprisingly, therefore, many governments have used environmental charges more for the revenue they can raise than as an effective incentive to cut pollution. But environmental charges which are high enough to reduce pollution can also produce sufficient revenue to finance environmental modernisation. Formal 'hypothecation' of environmental revenue is generally undesirable, since the expenditure needed may not correspond to the revenue available. But a clear and public link between, for instance, road charges and public transport improvements will improve the effectiveness as well as the acceptability of the charges.

The attraction of using environmental charges and taxes to finance improvements in the quality of life is obvious for a Labour government whose ability to raise revenue from higher income taxes will be politically constrained. But environmental charges could also form part of a new system of local and regional taxation. Local councils could, for instance, trade off lower rates or local income taxes against charges on waste disposal or peak-hour city-centre traffic.

Environmental charges can also be used to redistribute income directly from polluters to victims. If, for instance, a waste-disposal company were required to pay for the noise and other pollution suffered by people living near its dump, the charges could finance compensation payments to the residents. (It is also possible, of course, that the environmental charges would make the waste dump too expensive to operate, thus creating an incentive to build more environmentally efficient waste-handling systems.) In Japan, charges on air and water pollution finance a system of compensation payments for the people whose health has been damaged.

A different approach is to use a charge on polluters to finance a grant or subsidy to non-polluters (a 'bonus-malus' system). Grants to farmers who restore hedgerows, for instance, or use other environmentally-sensitive farming methods could be financed by levies on pesticides or charges on farmers who destroy hedgerows.

It is clear that a wide range of economic instruments will be needed in the environmental restructuring of agriculture. The agricultural policies pursued in Western Europe since World War Two – of which the Common Agricultural Policy is a prime example – are designed to encourage national and regional self-sufficiency as well as to provide an acceptable standard of living for farmers. The results are well known: with the help of modern technology, farmers have responded enthusiastically to the unlimited incentives to produce more food. The result has been massive overproduction, which is only now being tackled, and a great increase in reliance on artificial fertilisers and pesticides which, together with the manure from intensive animal rearing, are now causing serious problems of water pollution in many parts of Europe. The Swedish Government has introduced a programme which includes a tax on pesticides as well as the inclusion of drinking water in food legislation, designed to reduce the use of pesticides by 50% in five years – without, they estimate, causing any significant reduction in yields.

The work of the SPD could also provide useful lessons for the British Left. A new government will inherit an electricity supply industry distorted and damaged by privatisation. It will need policies for energy production and consumption to stabilise and then reduce energy consumption, while at the same time increasing industrial production and tackling the problem of 'fuel poverty' – and to do so at the least possible cost. Detailed analysis of the environmental, economic and distributional consequences in Britain of a tax on non-renewable energy consumption is required. Subject to that analysis, an appropriate energy policy package might combine an environmental tax on fossil fuel consumption (which would, in itself, be an incentive to companies and households to invest in energy conservation) with insulation grants to pensioners and poorer families and, if necessary, an increase in both pensions and child benefit to compensate for increased fuel costs.

The present government has found in the environment a new

springboard for both its attack on the coal industry and its dedication to nuclear power. Coal-fired power stations are, of course, a major source of sulphurous emissions and, thus, of 'acid rain'. Flue gas desulphurisation can remove over 90% of those emissions. Its installation throughout all of Britain's coal-fired power stations is, however, threatened by the privatisation programme.

Environmental modernisation will not be assisted by dependence on nuclear power. Although it is true that – unlike coal – nuclear energy does not contribute to global warming, this problem is not the only environmental issue in energy policy. The problems of dealing with nuclear waste, the cost and difficulty of decommissioning old plants and the risk of a major accident are all part of the environmental case against nuclear energy. And nuclear power is also the highest-cost option. While a new government will face enormous demands on resources in an economy constrained by the balance of trade deficit, both economy and ecology argue for investment in energy conservation and renewable energy resources in place of dependence on nuclear power stations.

Third World

The most conspicuous environmental issues of the 1990s – climate change, carbon dioxide emissions, the destruction of forests, damage to the ozone layer, international movements of toxic waste – are irreducibly global. They cannot be resolved without co-operation between developed and developing countries. Nor can they be resolved by trying to prevent industrial development in the Third World, or by pauperising those countries and regions. In 1987, however, the developing countries paid $38 billion *more* to the developed countries in repayments of interest and principal than they received in public and private grants. That subsidy from the poorest to the richest countries represents an extraordinary reversal of the position only six years earlier (when net transfers in favour of the developing countries amounted to $35 billion). Sub-Saharan Africa, where the problem of desertification is particularly acute, experienced a *decline* in per capita GNP of 2.8% p.a. from 1980 to 1988 – a further reminder that no growth may not be environmentally beneficial.

As the Brundtland Report recommended, new flows of public and private investment are required to developing countries whose environmental problems are particularly great. Debt reduction schemes could be linked to international economic and environmental co-operation. The integration of environmental and economic policy at a domestic level must be mirrored by the integration of environmental needs into a new international economic and trading framework.

Green Europe

The vision of environmental development sketched here is consistent with many central themes of democratic socialism. Environmental protection demands a sense of individual responsibility to the community, to other countries and to future generations. It is wholly at odds with the 'I'm all right' short-termism which has characterised the Thatcher Governments. Individuals, regions, countries and continents are environmentally dependent on each other: there can be no opting out, no privatising of the environment. Thus, social justice has an ecological as well as an ethical foundation.

Environmental transformation – because it requires a willingness to use the tools of economic policy, at local, regional, national and European level, for environmental ends – implies a level of intervention with market operations which, again, is incompatible with the present government's economic philosophy. The integration of environmental and economic policy will help socialists to define a new relationship between market and state. In Eastern Europe, as people struggle to come to terms with the breakdown of centralised planned economies, environmental concerns caution against the import of an unqualified 'free market'. The creation of a free market is seen as a necessary but not a sufficient condition of environmental and industrial modernisation, and policy-makers speak instead of 'a combination of market and state control under close and powerful social supervision.'[7]

For Britain too, 'social supervision' is essential to our environmental goals. Community and consumer campaigns, particularly when they have the support of local and national media, can change producers' behaviour faster than any state agency could. An 'enabling state' can strengthen these democratic processes by requiring environmental freedom of information and opening up the decisions of companies as well as local, regional and national government to public scrutiny and debate.

The concept of 'Social Europe' – proposed by the EC social democratic parties in Bonn in 1973 – has always embraced 'Green Europe'. Environmentally led development in Europe in the 1990s requires a new role for the European Commission as well as substantially increased resource flows to the Third World and close economic relations with Eastern Europe. All imply close co-operation between democratic socialist and social democratic governments in Europe and Scandinavia.

THE ALTERNATIVE

The Labour Party is frequently accused of having become 'Thatcher-ite'. It is more likely that environmental concerns will force a post-Thatcher Conservative Party to embrace much of the interventionism of environmental socialism. The Conservative Party paid a high price in the 1989 European Parliamentary elections for Mrs Thatcher's resistance to European modernisation. In the next general election, a programme of environmental modernisation in Europe could be central to her defeat.

Rethinking Welfare: a Case for Quasi-Markets?

JULIAN LE GRAND

A striking feature of the first eight years of Mrs Thatcher's Government was how little impact it had on the welfare state. With the major exception of council house sales, the structure of the welfare state in 1987 was much the same as in 1979. Even the proportion of national resources going into welfare did not change greatly, remaining at around a quarter of the Gross National Product.

But all this was to change in 1988: a year that will come to be seen as critical in the history of British social policy. For it was then that the Conservative Government began its programme of radical change to the welfare state.

That year saw the passing of the Education Reform Act: perhaps the most significant Education Act since World War Two. It saw the setting up of a comprehensive review into the National Health Service, a review that finally reported in January 1989, with radical proposals for the reorganisation of the NHS[1]. It saw the publication of the Griffiths Report on personal social services[2], whose far-reaching recommendations were finally accepted by the government in a White Paper in November 1989[3]. Two major acts were passed in 1988 and 1989 concerning public housing.

All these reforms have a fundamental similarity: the introduction of what might be termed 'quasi-markets' into the delivery of welfare services. In each case, the state ceases to be both the funder *and* the provider of services. Instead it becomes primarily a funder, with services being provided by a variety of private, voluntary and public suppliers, all operating in competition with one another. The method of funding also changes. Instead of resources being allocated by bureaucrats to providers, a budget or 'voucher' is given directly to potential users (or to agents acting on their behalf), who can then allocate the budget as they choose between the competing providers.

These changes thus represent a major break with the past. They also present a problem for any critique of social policy from an alternative perspective. More specifically, what should be the attitude of an alternative government to these radical reforms? Should it simply accept them as a *fait accompli* and try to operate them as effectively as possible? Should it attempt to roll them back – to return to the pre-1988 welfare state? Or should it engage in a programme of radical reform of its own – one that presumably would involve neither 'old-style' welfare bureaucracies nor markets, 'quasi' or otherwise?

Quasi-Market Reforms

The 1988 Education Reform Act incorporates two quasi-market elements: open enrolment and the ability of schools to 'opt out' from local authority control. Under the open enrolment proposals, parents are permitted to enrol their child at any school of their choice; schools will then receive a funding allocation based on the numbers of pupils enrolled. The opting-out provisions permit schools to opt out of direct local authority finance and control and instead to receive a grant directly from central government. The two sets of provisions together can be viewed as the introduction of a form of education voucher funded by central government, with the setting up of essentially 'independent' schools and with the allocation of state resources to schools being determined by the pattern of parental choices, instead of through a state planning process.

The current proposals for the National Health Service and for social care also include quasi-market reforms. Hospitals will be allowed to opt out from health authority control; these and other independent hospitals and health clinics will be able to tender for contracts with health authorities; and general practitioners with practices over a certain size will have budgets for each of their patients that they will be able to spend on hospital and other treatments of their choice. The proposed budgets for health authorities and GPs to be spent on patient treatment provided by competing independent institutions is again a proposal for a form of voucher, with the difference that the choice is exercised not by the actual consumers, patients, but by the GP or the health authority acting as their agent.

Under the proposals for social care (the care of elderly, mentally ill, mentally handicapped or disabled people), a 'case-manager' would be appointed for each client to construct a package of care for the client concerned, based on a predetermined budget. In making up the package of care, the case-manager would consider bids from competing provider-organisations, including public, voluntary and private-sector agencies.

The proposed system can be viewed as essentially a voucher system with case-managers allocating vouchers on behalf of their clients between competing institutions. Again the allocation of resources is determined by client choice (as delegated to case-managers), instead of by central allocation procedures.

Under the 1988 Housing Act, the state will continue to subsidise local authority tenants (primarily through housing benefit); but they will be able to choose their landlords from competing suppliers. The mechanism of choice is slightly different (voting by tenants), but the principle is the same: the choices of consumers, or agents acting on their behalf, not those of the state bureaucrat, determine the allocation of state funds to providers.

All these developments thus involve the introduction of quasi-markets into the welfare state. They are 'markets' because they replace monolithic state providers with competitive independent ones. They are 'quasi' because they differ from conventional markets in a number of key ways. The differences are on both the supply and demand sides. On the supply side, as with conventional markets, there is competition between service suppliers. Thus, in all the schemes described, there are independent institutions (residential homes, housing associations, private landlords, schools, hospitals) competing for customers. However, in contrast to conventional markets, these organisations are not necessarily out to maximise their profits; nor are they necessarily privately owned. On the demand side, consumer purchasing power is not expressed in the form of cash; instead it takes the form of a budget or 'voucher' confined to the purchase of a specific service. Also on the demand side, in some of the areas concerned such as social services and health, the immediate consumer is not the one who exercises the choices concerning purchasing decisions; instead those choices are delegated to a third party (a case-manager, a GP, or a health authority).

These welfare quasi-markets differ from conventional markets in one or more of three ways: not-for-profit organisations competing for public contracts, sometimes in competition with for-profit organisations; consumer purchasing power in the form of vouchers rather than cash; and in some cases, the consumers represented in the market by agents instead of operating by themselves.

Vouchers

So what should the alternative's reaction be to these reforms? There are three possible courses of action: to reject them entirely, either by rolling them back and returning to the pre-1988 welfare state or by replacing them by other, quite different institutional structures; to accept them *in toto*; or to adapt (and even extend) them so as to serve alternative ends and values.

The first alternative – rolling them back or replacing them with other radical alternatives – would be immensely costly, both in terms of administrative resources and, perhaps more significantly, in terms of morale among the providers of the services concerned. Another large-scale change, especially, as in the case of the pure roll-back, one that lacked the motivation of novelty, might irretrievably traumatise services which by then will have suffered more than enough organisational upheaval.

Moreover, there may be a sense in which it is not possible completely to overturn the quasi-market phenomenon. As Paul Hoggett has pointed out, shifts of this kind are not confined solely to the public sector. 'Post-Fordist' changes of a very similar kind are occurring in the private sector, with companies that were hitherto vertically integrated and tightly controlled from the centre now increasingly contracting out their operations and engaging in other forms of decentralisation[4]. More widely, there is a general move away from large-scale bureaucracies: most obviously in Eastern Europe, but in most Western countries as well.

The reasons for this trend are not entirely clear. The advent of new technology permitting decentralised budgeting and other forms of information processing is undoubtedly a factor, as is a world-wide disenchantment with the perceived inefficiency and dehumanising character of large organisations, public or private. Whatever the reason, the very universality of the phenomenon suggests that there are fundamental forces at work here which it may be difficult, if not impossible, to buck.

So, totally dismantling the quasi-market reforms does not seem to be a practical option. Moreover, even if it were, it would not necessarily be desirable. Part of the pressure for the quasi-market reforms in the welfare area arose because there were perceived to be real problems with the previous system – problems that the introduction of quasi-markets could help resolve. From the Right came the accusation that the welfare bureaucracies were wasting resources on excessive administration; that they protected their employees' interests at the expense of those of their users; and, more generally, that they were unresponsive to their clients' needs and wants.

One aspect of this last point was echoed by other critics more sympathetic to the basic values that underlie the welfare state. They argued that the welfare system was particularly unresponsive to the needs and wants of the very people it was set up primarily to help: the poor and disadvantaged. Resources and facilities were often diverted to those best able to manipulate the system: the educated and articulate middle classes. Thus there is evidence that the middle classes make more use of some parts of the National Health Service and the education system than the less well off; they benefit more from local services, such as school transport, libraries, museums and parks; and, because of mortgage tax relief and other tax loopholes, they receive more by way of housing subsidies[5].

The introduction of quasi-markets may help resolve some of these problems – at least in theory. The introduction of competition is supposed to encourage a more economical use of resources, thus improving service efficiency. More importantly, the introduction of competing suppliers means that welfare users, or their agents, have an alternative. Confronted with the unco-operative teacher, with the insensitive consultant, or with the recalcitrant housing clerk, they can take their business elsewhere. This not only extends the choice of users, it gives them real power; in the battle for resources, the unco-operative, the insensitive and the recalcitrant will lose out, while the helpful, the considerate and the flexible will flourish. It may even help the poor, for they will have a measure of real economic power; if suppliers do not respond to their wishes, they can take their business elsewhere.

Thus quasi-markets may have some advantages over their predecessors. But this does not imply that the second of our possible reactions – uncritical acceptance – is correct. The arguments usually adduced in their favour gloss over a number of serious problems, in particular the existence or otherwise of choice, and the promotion of social inequality and injustice.

A major justification for the introduction of quasi-markets is that it would increase the range of choices for welfare users. But this could be challenged. Will there necessarily be more choice in quasi-markets than under bureaucratic systems? How much choice do parents have if there is only one school in an area? How much choice will patients have if there is only one local GP, or if changing GPs is difficult? How much choice is there for either patients or GPs if there is only one local hospital? Will enough potential landlords offer themselves to the tenants of problem estates to allow a real choice? Under the Griffiths proposals, how much choice will the clients of case-managers actually have? Will they, for instance, be able to choose their case-manager? (Indeed in this case the proposals could be viewed as restricting choice, in comparison with the previous situation. The elderly in need of residential care already had a kind of voucher: a social security payment for that care, for which entitlement was simply a test of means. Under Griffiths, the entitlement will now only be established by professional assessment.)

Sink Schools

The second major problem for quasi-markets relates to inequality and injustice – an issue of little concern to the current government, but one that should be a high priority for any alternative. A common criticism of conventional markets (and a frequent justification for their replacement by bureaucracies) is that they foster and maintain inequalities and therefore social injustice. Quasi-markets may well have similar effects. In education, selective schools may arise that cream off the most able pupils, leaving 'sink' schools for the remainder. Health care providers, such as GPs with practice budgets, or self-governing hospitals, will compete for the custom of the young and comparatively healthy, while ignoring the elderly or chronically sick. In social care, residential homes will compete for healthy elderly people, ignoring those who are senile and incontinent. Since there is likely to be a greater concentration of the 'bad risks' among the poor and deprived, the latter may end up receiving fewer services relative to those received by the better off, thus widening inequality.

Although there are many potential problems with quasi-markets, the old-style welfare state was itself far from perfect. Is it possible to adapt the quasi-market ideas so as to reap some of their undoubted advantages over the old system, while resolving some of their difficulties?

To begin with the issue of choice. We identified two factors that might in practice restrict users' choices: the absence of competitors in the local area and the fact that, in some cases, it is not the users themselves who make the relevant decisions but agents acting on their behalf.

So far as the absence of local competition is concerned, one answer could be transport vouchers. These could be given to parents to accompany education vouchers, for instance, enabling them to select schools outside their local area. Travel vouchers could also be given to prospective patients who have to travel to a distant hospital – and to their families for visiting them.

One answer to the restrictions on choice that may arise from the use of agents is to ensure that potential users can choose the agent who is to work on their behalf. Michael Young[6] has devised such a system for GPs, to replace the present system of capitation fees. As at present, doctors would receive a payment for each patient they had on their list.

Unlike the present system, however, every year patients would have to choose their doctor, or confirm the choice they had already made. In Young's view, 'this would bring it home to patients that it is they, as taxpayers, who are paying the doctors; and likewise to the doctors who would be less likely, when faced by patients who have their doctors' salaries in their pockets, to consider they are being paid by "the state"'. Accountability as well as choice would be enhanced.

This idea could be extended to social care. People in need of such care could be allocated a voucher and allowed to choose their case-managers who would help them decide how the voucher would be spent. Their need or entitlement could be established by a relatively simple procedure, based on age, degree of disability, or, in the case of those with learning difficulties, on a test of mental aptitude. Whatever the system, the principle could be established that assessment for entitlement for the voucher should be separated from the decision as to how the voucher should be spent.

Finally, the question of inequality. A possible solution to this is the positively discriminatory voucher or PDV. Here poorer individuals and/ or those with greater needs are given larger vouchers or budget allocations. This gives providers of services a greater incentive to take on such people; indeed if the discrimination is large enough they may specialise in the provision of services to them. PDVs in education could be used to give schools an incentive to take on children from poorer backgrounds; similar schemes in health and social care would encourage suppliers of such care to look after those who need it most.

A difficulty with PDVs is that, if income were used as the basis for discrimination, so that in general poorer families received larger vouchers, there might have to be some elaborate means test, with the attendant problems of stigma, administrative complexity and low takeup. An attractive alternative here is to use place of residence as the basis for discrimination, with the larger vouchers being given to families who lived in poorer areas. The wealth of an area could be assessed by a sample survey of the gross capital value of houses in the area. This would have the advantage of impeding the relatively wealthy from moving into the area to benefit from the larger voucher; for if they did so, the demand for housing in the area would increase, house prices would rise and the value of the voucher would fall.

Coin-Shaped

Not only could the quasi-market ideas be adapted to serve progressive ends, they could be extended. Patricia Hewitt has suggested applying the voucher idea to child care for the under-fives[7]. The voucher would be given to each parent at the end of the period of parental leave. Parents could then 'spend' the voucher on a range of approved child-care provision. The value of the voucher could be higher for single parents and for children with special needs; it could also be a PDV, with a higher value for those who live in poorer areas. It would have the advantage over cash that the amount to be spent would be determined by the value of the voucher; and that the voucher could only be spent on approved facilities. Both of these features would ensure that quality would be kept up.

A number of private companies, including Luncheon Vouchers Ltd, have just introduced vouchers for child care. However, these are rather different from Hewitt's idea for local authority funded vouchers. The private schemes involve employers including child-care vouchers as part of employees' pay packets. The vouchers have the advantage over a straightforward cash supplement to wages that they are exempt from National Insurance contributions and that income tax on them can be deferred for one year.

These schemes are essentially tax-avoidance schemes and, as Hewitt points out, all such schemes end up discriminating in favour of the better-off (who pay higher rates of tax and thus benefit more from anything that reduces taxable income). Instead of providing indirect subsidies through the tax system, it is far better for governments to finance vouchers directly. This avoids an open-ended subsidy to the well-off and allows for discrimination in favour of other, more deserving groups through a PDV mechanism.

The voucher idea can be applied at the other end of the education ladder. The present cumbersome system of university and polytechnic finance, whereby institutions receive a direct subsidy from the government to cover their teaching costs and students receive a means-tested (and inadequate) grant to cover their subsistence requirements, is about to be made even more cumbersome by the introduction of a top-up loans scheme for students. A simpler, quasi-market alternative would be to allow institutions of higher education to charge full-cost fees, and to offer all students a non-means-tested grant (or voucher) that would cover those fees, with a generous allowance for maintenance.

There is an equity issue here, in that many students (indeed most) come from well-off backgrounds; moreover, many will go on to well-paid jobs as a consequence of the education they have received at the public expense. But this could be overcome by the introduction of a

[92]

graduate tax, such as that currently being implemented in Australia. This would be a tax set as a proportion of income levied on higher education graduates and collected through the income tax, or, as recommended by Nicholas Barr, through the National Insurance system[8]. The advantages of the graduate tax would be that, unlike the repayment of conventional loans, people on low incomes would pay less than those on high incomes: hence any deterrent effect on graduates from taking up low-paid activities would be reduced.

Another area where the voucher idea could be applied is transport, where vouchers could be extended so as to cover all concessionary fare schemes. The problems with the latter are numerous. They are usually confined to one form of transport (such as buses or trains) thus disadvantaging those who, for one reason or another, cannot use that particular form (such as those in wheelchairs, for instance). They are also usually specific to one area, so that they provide no help for cross-boundary travel or for travel outside the area. And for the authority operating them they represent an open-ended commitment, with little idea of exactly how much they will be called upon to contribute.

It is not widely known that there is a system of transport vouchers already in operation. A consortium of the larger public transport organisations, together with British Rail, has set up a non-profit-making company, National Transport Tokens Ltd, that provides transport vouchers to local authorities or any other authority operating a concessionary fares scheme. The issuing authority buys a quantity of vouchers (in the form of coin-shaped tokens) from the company and then issues the tokens to eligible concessionary travel users. They use the tokens as full payment for their travel to any participating operator (buses, trains or taxis). Finally, the operator returns the tokens to the company, which redeems them at their face value, plus a handling charge. Any surplus from the scheme is shared with the operating authorities.

To the users the scheme offers far greater flexibility than concessionary fare schemes. And to the issuing authority it offers budgetary certainty: they know exactly when, where and how much they are paying for the service.

Experiments

There is much yet to be discovered about quasi-markets. Some of the consequences of introducing them may be good; some may be bad. What is important is that any 'alternative' government should not take an *a priori* stand against all the ideas. In some ways the present government has made a gift to any incoming government: by the time the latter takes office, a set of quasi-market experiments will be up and running. Properly monitored, these should be able to provide us with evidence as to whether, suitably adapted and extended, quasi-markets constitute the way forward – or whether some other alternative has to be found.

Arts: An Endangered Species

MELVYN BRAGG

The alternative is to employ imagination. To start again in a clean part of the field.

All societies can turn ugly. A decent society spends much of its energy resisting that potential disorder. The Lord of the Flies will rule unless he is ruled. Even over the meagre span of ten years we have seen the ugly emerge more strongly in our own society, clearly delineated like the bottom of a river in a drought. Child beggars I see every day on Waterloo Bridge; adults living underneath it in cardboard boxes; rubbish on the streets, in tabloids, in dogmatic arguments; petty authoritarianism and mendacity from some of the police; universities undervalued, research underfunded, schoolteachers hectored; 'public service' becomes an unmarketable phrase. Hedging it all about is the Gradgrind world of greed now considered respectable. The only alternative is to invent or rediscover better ways.

To stick to my own corner: the arts. It is interesting that we have won every argument and every debate on subsidy over the last decade but persistently lost the vote. It is now truculently agreed that the arts provide employment, revivify inner-city centres, plump out tourism, help ethnic groups, cohere communities – but still the tap is inexorably being turned off. Time to say – forget the materialistic arguments!

In any world league table Britain is a rich country. Its sense of its own richness and society's duty to make sure that the richness is shared ought to be enough. We know that once the basics are achieved, many people feel more fully alive through the arts, through seeing plays, listening to music, dancing and seeing dancing, going to galleries, and we know it needs time and patience to give more and more people a real opportunity to try and taste and perhaps come to love these things.

We ought to have at least a dozen more opera houses in a country as wealthy and as various as ours, a dozen theatres for dancers and realistic working subsidies for another dozen large repertory companies, photographic galleries and craft centres in all cities, art galleries

[95]

whose directors are not worried about the roof falling in, art classes in schools and colleges which have confidence in a future and touring companies which can persist and persist until the walls of every hitherto ignored remote Jericho begin to crumble.

We need to take the best to the most in chariots of delight so that the real glories of the past and the present – the thought, the art, above all the imagination – can truly ignite the lives of people in this country too long shut out by the unspeakably arrogant walls of indifference.

Think how we would sing then! Think how the cities would revive, the towns regain a sense of particular place, the whole country hum because quality and excellence were at last being offered without meanness, without condescension, without the strings which become bonds.

And the same could go for the best of radio and television – sneered at by snobs who as often as not turn out to be hollow, piping the tunes of the nanny past for fear of the rough brotherhood of the present – the quality of these too should be shored up and cultivated, increased and broadcast so that variety, dissent, beauty, opposition and curious matter would be on the agenda and available to all. And there would be positive discrimination in the first ten years for those areas which we as a society have allowed to fall so cruelly far behind in all that could grace a life in our times.

None of this would cost much money. When the then Chancellor Mr Lawson last coughed we lost more than the budget for five years of the above. All it needs is the will and imagination. What I propose is neither idealistic nor utopian nor any of the words so easily turned to cynicism. We are a small post-imperial island awkwardly cut off from Europe, with nothing to gain but by our brains and imagination. If we do not nourish the one and try to inspire the other we will continue on our Hobbesian course of turning this country's life and people into something nasty, brutish and short on everything that really matters.

The Democratic Deficit

RICHARD HOLME

What is wrong with the way in which we govern ourselves in Britain that wouldn't be put right by a change of government?

Mr Roy Hattersley, and traditionalists like him, would probably say 'very little'. But I want to suggest that the process of British government is at least as much of a problem as its products, and indeed that a distorted, secretive and in some ways undemocratic process contributes materially to unacceptable policies. It is difficult to imagine, for instance, that the poll tax could have emerged from a political system which was more open and responsive and had better checks and balances.

If democratic self-government is the ideal – and, at the moment when Eastern and Central Europe re-discover the values of liberalism, why should it not be? – it can scarcely be denied that a widening gap exists in Britain between this ideal and the very different reality of the top-down impermeable institutions of authority and direction which characterise our system of government. That this democratic deficit can and should be eliminated by thoroughgoing constitutional reform is now a matter of commonplace agreement among many – or even most – thinking people.

Constitutional reform raises detailed legal and mechanical questions, but perhaps the most fundamental question is what should be the values which infuse the new constitution, the spirit or *geist* which animates the dry bones?

Partisan Trap

Before discussing the values of a reformed British constitution, though, it is worth identifying the trap into which advocates of constitutional reform fall easily and often; that of partisanship.

Many of us are partisan in our politics, but to go on as a result to evaluate each and every proposal for reform exclusively in the light of the effect it might have on our particular party can only impoverish the argument.

Such an approach subordinates shared civic life, and the institutions and processes which make it possible, to the claims of party. This subordination may derive from an apocalyptic view of society as a battlefield, on which, *pace* Mrs Thatcher, socialism will be 'destroyed', or on which the proletariat will first triumph and then dictate. That is why ideological fundamentalism, seeking a victory for its own all-encompassing creed, so easily becomes the enemy of liberal democracy which by contrast seeks to de-limit, define and disperse the power of government so that it can be multiplied in the hands of people and their communities rather than held tightly at the centre.

Yet even those who, like the vast majority of British people, are not fundamentalists are inclined to ask of any proposed reform, 'Would it be in the interest of my party?' The fact that this question is often asked first – and last – betrays the one-dimensional nature of British political culture and the thinness of received ideas about what makes a liberal society.

The very notion that there is, or could be, a common ground of shared values, assumptions and institutions which delineates the way we govern ourselves and which precedes, and provides the ground for, the struggle over policies and priorities between people and parties is relatively alien to the British political class.

The sense of a 'public interest', which might sometimes cut across party lines but would constantly infuse the institutions of government and give them life, is very faint. If there is an animating spirit in the British constitution it is by contrast a sort of historical nostalgia which encrusts everything it touches with the ceremonious conservatism of tradition and thus forms a façade behind which raw power can be exercised without check or balance.

For a party to get its hands on the levers of power of the British state may seem to be a great prize. But those who, for reasons either of ideological conviction or power-seeking cynicism, believe that the only worthwhile project in politics is to win the prize of power without limit for their party are unlikely to be rational guardians of the public interest.

Yet they should not be entirely blamed, for this very partisanship authentically represents the predominant value system of British politics. The onus which this places on the advocates of comprehensive constitutional reform is to articulate a better political value system as a basis for a change of political system. A better system would be more solid because it articulated core civic values, rather than mere short-term calculation of party advantage.

What that civic value system is, and how it might be expressed and reflected in particular proposals for reform, is mainly what I want to explore here.

Key Civic Values

Each of the qualities or values which I believe should characterise reform of our institutions and constitutional practices can be viewed in reverse in the darkened mirror of the way we govern ourselves now.

Thus the counterpart of *pluralism*, the first of my suggested core values, is the concentration of power and orthodoxy and the intolerance of diversity and dissent which has gathered pace in the last decade. A similar tendency is the drift to ideological monopoly, not only in the narrow political sense of the relegation of local government to the margins of a highly centralised process, or in the constriction of the wish of the people of Scotland to govern themselves in the iron mould of a unitary state but also in the denigration of such institutions as the BBC and the Church of England. The freedom of competition stops short apparently at the borders of politics and ideas.

The same double standard is true of the second and related core value, *liberty*. Rather as in the classroom of a bad school, liberty in Britain is increasingly restricted to the freedom to compete, for scarce resources, books or examination grades – but just try questioning teacher's judgement. Freedom of expression, freedom of thought, freedom of information and freedom from oppression by authority are all constrained seriously enough in contemporary Britain to make a mockery of the rhetoric of our national adherence to conventions guaranteeing human rights and fundamental freedoms.

As in the bad classroom where students are pitted against each other, the third core value, *community*, or partnership, is also at a premium. The House of Commons sets the current pattern: confrontation. There is almost no process of public co-operation: between parties; between central and local government; between government and industry; between public and private investment; between professions and regulators; above all between government – central or local – and the citizen. The epitaph of Britain's failing elective dictatorship is 'divide and rule' and as a result all community of interest seems to have become suspect. Even the most basic community of all, the village, small town, ward or district, receives no encouragement to be J. S. Mill's 'seedbed of democracy', making its own decisions and learning in the process how to contribute to the wider world.

That which people might have a chance to learn from genuinely decision-making democratic local self-government is *citizenship*, my final and in some senses overarching core value. Certain Tories, such as Douglas Hurd, have made attempts to appropriate the notion of citizenship. Dismayed by the raw greed which Thatcherism has unleashed in society, they now seek to enjoin the affluent 'to do their bit' for society by charitable good works. But citizenship is a much more radical and powerful idea than philanthropy, for it is about the dreaded 'E word', equality.

A civic society would guarantee each person equality in society in certain fundamental respects. I would argue that these should extend to equal entitlements, to education and to social services and to a basic citizenship income for example. However, in the context of constitutional reform citizenship means not only equality before the law but an equal status and value in the public sphere. Instead we have a voting system which distorts the value of each vote according to where and for whom it is cast and a political system which disadvantages ordinary people against the big battalions. To take but one instance: the way in which business and unions pay for parties and therefore enjoy privileged access to power discriminates against the citizen.

The task, therefore, is to evaluate each of the main proposals for constitutional reform, in the light of the core values I have suggested: *pluralism*, *liberty*, *community* and *citizenship*.

So what should the principal planks of the reform platform be? Some would concentrate on the whole platform and urge a written constitution, as Charter 88 – and Lord Scarman earlier – have done. However, desirable as this may ultimately be, it can only come at the end of a process of reform rather than at its beginning; for our existing constitutional arrangements codified, as Vernon Bogdanor and other constitutional scholars have pointed out, would consist of one brutal sentence: 'What the Crown in Parliament decides is law.' Moreover it may well be that a process of step-by-step reform is necessary to create a political culture in which enduring support could be secured for a rational and democratic constitution as a whole.

Others would concentrate their reforming zeal on particular institutions and practices: seeking to reform political financing; the procedures of the House of Commons; the composition of the Second Chamber; the training and selection of the judiciary; or the role and structure of local government. Yet others would concentrate on the democratic deficit in the European Community, as economic and monetary integration proceeds apace. My selection of electoral reform – the Bill of Rights, freedom of information, open government, and Scottish devolution – is certainly not to deny the urgency or validity of any of the other proposals for reform.

Grundgesetz

I have selected these four reforms partly on their merits and partly on political grounds because of their popularity as demonstrated by repeated opinion polls and their significance in acting as levers on the whole system. The British constitutional monster, with its wide-reaching tentacles, is rather like William Cobbett's 'Thing'. It is necessary to select the parts of its anatomy where reform will wound it most deeply and thus assist its early decease.

Proportional representation has exactly this sort of leverage; it is an indispensable reform which would trigger a change in the political culture and make other reforms possible. The catch-22 of constitutional reform is that those who have to enact it have the least interest in its enactment. Single-party majority governments which have conjured their majorities from a minority of the electorate invariably find that the status quo has a great deal to commend it.

It is significant that one of the strongest calls of the reformers in Eastern and Central Europe, as they shake off the monopoly of communist power, has been for a multi-party system. Their banners have certainly not been inscribed with moving appeals for a two-party system. Perhaps they realise intuitively what the Westminster system has shown, that duopoly is not a sufficient step forward from monopoly.

Pluralism should start with the parties, and therefore with the electoral system. Opinions will differ as to whether Britain now has a multi-party system, a three-party system or a two-and-a-half party system, but the consistent inability of the two major parties over twenty years in polls and elections alike to get much more than three-quarters of the vote, just like the inability of either of these parties to achieve an overall majority of those voting, seems to indicate that duopoly is not good enough for the British either. The winner-takes-all electoral system has acted as a sort of market-sharing cartel but, despite the disincentives it provides to voting for third or fourth parties, a large part of the British electorate has sought other alternatives, even if their votes cost a great deal more in the electoral black market to which they are relegated.

As a matter of *realpolitik*, it is certainly true that the prospect of any process of constitutional reform now depends on inter-party negotiation, thus increasing the premium on electoral reform as the first goal of reformers in a hung parliament, in order to institutionalise negotiation politics. Yet some would argue that electoral systems are not fundamentally constitutional issues but second-order questions of detail; the electoral system does not, for instance, form part of the post-war West German constitutional settlement, the *Grundgesetz*.

However, I would suggest that, mired in the stagnant swamp of the British constitution as we are, electoral reform is the compass which could lead us to the high ground of liberty and constitutionalism. There must be an electoral system which protects liberty, in the shape of genuine freedom of choice between parties and candidates, and which also protects equality, in the sense of attaching an equal weight to every vote and ensuring that the character of the legislature bears the imprint of every voter instead of the minority of them who vote for winning candidates. If reforms are not made, our representative institutions will continue to be seriously deficient in legitimacy and the gap between the citizen and his or her parliament will continue to widen, and both will lose by it.

But if representative institutions and equal votes are important, not least for their enabling effect, they are by no means the whole story. With proportional representation Britain might legitimately claim to have a genuinely majoritarian democracy but, as Ronald Dworkin has pointed out, majoritarian democracies are by no means necessarily also communitarian democracies. The will of the majority would make a nice change in Britain but only if it is exercised in a way which respects the rights of minorities and which is centred on the inalienable civic equality of every man and woman. This leads inexorably in the direction of a Bill of Rights, a measure which has grown noticeably in popularity during the heavy-handed Thatcher years, but nevertheless runs into resistance in those parts of the Labour Party where citizenship is still subordinate to class.

Setting on one side apprehensions about the attitudes of British judges to human rights (attitudes which are likely to persist as long as the selection and training of judges remains closed and incomprehensible) the main objections to a Bill of Rights are either that it would impinge on the sovereignty of Parliament or, a related complaint, that it would not look after 'our people'.

Proposals to incorporate the European Convention on Human Rights into UK law, turning a treaty commitment into an indigenous Bill of Rights, would be more practicable, if less perfectionist, than setting out (like Canada, for instance) to draft a bill from scratch. However, it would also neatly sidestep the question of parliamentary sovereignty. Such a bill could be repealed by a subsequent Parliament and therefore not diminish parliamentary sovereignty in any respect, although its protagonists would hope that it would speedily become politically so difficult to repeal that it would become morally entrenched.

Lawyers, who always look to the worst case, naturally hope that with a Bill of Rights case law would develop. But it is also worthwhile considering its normative effect of ensuring that legislators drafted new law with the requirements of the bill in mind, and that administrators were aware of its constraints as they set about those of their activities which impinge on the citizen.

However, it might be as a symbolic change in our constitutional culture that a Bill of Rights would come to be seen as most important. For those who put class first above the citizen, for those who see the state in terms of power rather than enablement, and for those who think that in politics you cannot make ideological omelettes without breaking human eggs, the bill would be an historic defeat. Their defeat would at the same time be a victory for a bottom-up citizen-centred system of government enshrining the modern democratic revolution that Britain never really enjoyed, despite – or perhaps because of – the Civil War and the Glorious Revolution.

Individual rights rest most securely on a basis of shared knowledge and commonly held information. One objectionable feature of what is in many ways an admirable British Civil Service is how closed and secretive it is. For example, the perceived point of vulnerability to the dangerous world outside, the humble parliamentary question, is prepared for with a paranoid vigilance which might be regarded as excessive in the run-up to an arms treaty. Yet this secrecy is intrinsic to the nature of British government, in direct lineal descent from the unaccountability of the medieval crown to its subjects and of 'the mysterie' which necessarily surrounded the 'divine right' of the monarch.

The notion that the state, and its governors, are in some crucial ways above and outside the law and not accountable in every respect to the people is deeply ingrained. Our culture is still one of subjecthood, at its best paternal and at its worst authoritarian, rather than one of citizenship; a tradition of top-down direction rather than bottom-up participation.

The significance of freedom of information, which – like the other reforms suggested here – would be taken for granted in other democracies, is not that it would transform overnight the British political system, but rather that it would enable a process of change to get under way and symbolise that a new value system was in operation.

That each citizen should know, as of right, what is done in his or her name, particularly where it affects the person closely, is to view the benefits of freedom of information from the perspective of the individual and the community. Yet the benefits should also be felt in the process of government itself, making it more difficult for the enemies of the open society to conceal their mistakes and thus impede the learning process of that society.

The purpose of exposing maladministration is often misunderstood. It is not primarily to discipline administrators who have got it wrong but to learn from their mistakes and thus improve future policies and action. A strong case can now be made that one of the reasons for the relative failure of the British official class and its political masters to chart a successful course for this country since World War Two has been its reluctance to learn from repeated past mistakes; for instance the persistent inability to opt wholeheartedly for a European future and make the necessary adjustments in social and economic policy.

Perhaps official secrecy is not only the product of the history of the British state, but is in particular the result of the adversarial process, and its characteristic defensiveness, which makes governments intensely reluctant to share information with the legislature, let alone the citizen. Thus, as is so often the case in the British system, what appear to be random pieces of the jigsaw actually fit together snugly.

The British state is not only top-down and secretive, it is also unitary and monolithic. All power and decision-making rest in London, which, since it is also the commercial and cultural capital, makes it the centre of the United Kingdom in every sense, in a way which does not characterise the capital cities of other democracies.

The abolition of the GLC and metropolitan authorities, whatever its merits or disadvantages, was lively confirmation that local government's very existence, let alone its powers, is at the whim of Westminster and Whitehall. The hostility of the Thatcher Government to other centres of power within the United Kingdom has been so extreme as to lead it into a dangerous extension of centralisation in a way which many Conservatives themselves regret.

Most constitutional democracies are characterised, as Britain is not, by a balance not only between the branches of government and between the state and the citizen, but also between the centre and the localities. It represents a constitutional protection of the pluralism which is necessary for a vital and diverse democracy. The British Government, by contrast, will not even sign the European Charter of Local Self-Government for fear that its accession will seem to represent a commitment to a permanent place for elected local authorities.

In the long term, reform of local government and the establishment of elected regional authorities are probably the way forward, but in the near future the question of breaking the iron grip of the centre will come to a sharp focus on the issue of a Scottish Parliament.

Of course Scotland is a nation within the United Kingdom – as many would claim Wales is too – and should therefore not be discussed under the rubric of 'local government' or even that of 'regional authority'. But what the Scottish question does illuminate, and in the most dramatic form, is whether the central British state, and its tame legislature, is capable of co-existing with another point of autonomous decision within the same borders.

The Claim of Right and the Constitutional Convention in Scotland draw on a different tradition of government and citizenship than the top-down institutions of the United Kingdom, a tradition which is just as ancient but more truly democratic since it is rooted in popular sovereignty. One of the most heartening products of Labour's re-think since the seventies is the fact that it is now, as all the other opposition parties have long been, wholeheartedly committed to self-government for Scotland.

Self-government for Scotland within Britain will raise squarely the question of shared sovereignty. Britain's future in Europe depends – as it could be argued does the future of a democratic Europe itself – on the same question of creating a framework for sharing sovereignty. What were once the preoccupations of constitutional experts are rapidly becoming the bread-and-butter issues of politics in the new age.

The crucial test for any alternative government which purports to succeed an administration which has been proficient in the use and abuse of power but deficient in the practice of democracy, is whether it is prepared to open up a closed system. It is time that Britain's government was put up for popular ownership, with protection for every owner. There are risks in a constitutional revolution but the potential benefits, in social, political and even economic terms, now vastly outweigh them.

Economics to the Left of the Right

CHRISTOPHER HUHNE

The economic agenda of the next government will be dominated by one overwhelming problem – the correction of the exceptionally large British balance of payments deficit. That deficit is the result of living beyond our means, of buying more than we produce. It entails a prolonged period not merely of living within our means but of consuming less than we produce in order to reduce the deficit. The sea swell of the Lawson boom has ebbed away, not to return for many years. The first instalment of the work-out was due in 1990. The rest of the correction may be postponed in the run-up to the 1992 election, but it will have to be resumed shortly thereafter by whichever government is elected. Against this sombre economic background, it will be particularly difficult for any left-of-centre administration to shake off an aura of Crippsian austerity and to show that its values of fairness and social justice can be combined with the pleasures of the consumer society. The remodelling of a left-of-centre programme could hope for easier times.

The peak deficit in 1989, estimated by the Treasury in its autumn statement that year at 4% of national income, represented a record excess of British purchases of overseas goods and services over foreigners' purchase of ours. The largest previous deficit, compared with the size of our national income, was in the wake of the first oil crisis and before the advent of North Sea oil. At that time, unlike today, we could plead that many other countries were in the same boat. The deficits which are the legacy of the Lawson boom are altogether different in that no other country has managed to land itself in such a predicament. Since it is *relative* success which matters in the marketplace for currencies, the legacy is altogether more worrying.

Foreigners are building up claims on the British economy in the form of IOUs at an unprecedented rate. The key problem is what happens to sterling when foreigners decide they are holding enough of it at the present price. Even though the deficit is coming down, the stock of sterling assets held by foreigners must continue to mount so long as there is any deficit. It was, after all, not until 1976, after the peak deficit in 1974, that the sterling crisis really began in earnest. Not surprisingly, holders of sterling were already becoming concerned in 1989. Both of the final two percentage point rises in interest rates during that year were in response to massive selling pressure on the pound. Despite the rate rises and heavy buying of pounds by the Bank of England in order to support its exchange rate against other currencies, the pound sagged sharply through 1989, falling by more than 11% on its trade-weighted index against other currencies. This was, as we shall see, a necessary part of the measures needed to correct the deficit. At the same time, however, it entailed an inflationary boost to the economy which came at a difficult time. About a third of all the goods and services bought in the UK are foreign, which means that a 10% fall in the pound eventually leads to a 10% rise in import prices, and a 3% or so rise in the overall price level. With inflation already edging up, it was not a prospect which the government could consider with equanimity.

Indeed, none of the prospective policies needed to reduce the deficit to sustainable levels – which probably means a rough balance and certainly no more than about 1% of national income – is politically painless. Devaluation certainly encourages the supply of British goods to export markets, and hence reduces the likelihood of output growth stalling and of an outright recession. But it also pushes up inflation. The only other measures which could help curb the deficit – and which most economists argue need to be put in place alongside any fall in the pound – are tax increases and spending cuts. Such fiscal tightening would curb domestic spending and hence the demand for imports, but it would also curb the demand for home-produced goods and services which could not conceivably be exported: haircuts, cinema seats, restaurant meals, bus services and so on. It is essential to cut the gap between spending and producing – or between demand and supply. But the problem is that any cut in demand also tends to dampen supply as well. The deficit will cast a long shadow for many years.

New Optimism

In fairness to the Conservatives, however, there are three respects in which it is easier to solve the balance of payments problem than might have been the case in, say, 1974 when the last Labour Government assumed office. First, the world environment has improved consider-ably. The Organisation for Economic Co-operation and Development in Paris underestimated world growth for three successive years from

1986 to 1989. Moreover, the new optimism is particularly great in Europe, which is the key export market for the UK, taking well over half of our exports. The former talk of Euro-sclerosis has given way instead to a bullish assessment of the prospects for growth and investment as a result both of the creation of the European single market in 1992 and of the increased demand and supply potential opened up by the democratisation and liberalisation in Eastern Europe. The European economy appears to be on the edge of a new golden age every bit as successful as the postwar reconstruction of the fifties and sixties.

Secondly, there is a good deal of evidence within Britain that the economy has become better able to produce goods and services efficiently. The rate of growth of output per person – productivity – is not the be-all and end-all of economics, since it does not much profit a country to produce more per person if the overall amount produced is cut back. But labour productivity growth has tended over time to be the well-spring of rising living standards and an augury of a generally improved performance. It implies greater international competitiveness and a higher potential to produce with the resources available. There can be no doubt that labour productivity growth has improved sharply during the eighties. It was much better than in the seventies, and much better than that of most of our economic rivals. The only dampener is the fact that it is running at about the same rate as during the sixties, when we were far from happy with our performance. Nevertheless, the relative improvement is marked and should enable a better inflation and trade performance than would otherwise have occurred.

Thirdly, there is a political opportunity for whichever government holds power in the nineties to repeat the trick which Mrs Thatcher and the Conservatives managed to pull off during the eighties. Although North Seal oil is running out (and its contribution to the balance of payments is going into reverse, thereby necessitating a rising contribution from other tradeable sectors merely to leave the accounts where they are), there is another factor which could potentially yield similar benefits – namely defence cuts. The collapse of the Soviet empire in Eastern Europe, combined with the likely preoccupation of Soviet leaders in holding together their own union of fissiparous nationalities, means that there is no longer any justification for a British level of defence spending running sharply higher than the NATO average. A cut to Danish levels of some 2% of GDP would, for example, yield tax cuts (or increases in other items of spending) worth at least five pence in the pound. Moreover, there would be trade gains too from any foreign currency savings made in cutting the British forces in Germany.

Four Objectives

But these benefits are only relatively minor offsets to the besetting problem of moving back into broad payments balance. All governments have to attempt to meet four broad objectives of policy, the achievement of one of which often conflicts with another. First, external balance is important simply because of the retribution which the markets can exact if it is not achieved. In other words, net exports – exports minus imports – have to grow broadly in line with the overall growth of the economy if inflation or recession are to be avoided. It is this constraint above all which the Conservative Government ignored. Secondly, the domestic sources of inflation must be kept under control. Spending power in the markets for products must not be so buoyant that companies are able to raise prices instead of increasing output. Nor can the demand for labour grow so rapidly that wages and salaries are bid up higher than the rise in output per person plus the old inflation rate. If it is, then wage inflation will accelerate, leading to increasing costs and prices. For example, 7.5% earnings growth is consistent with 5% inflation if output per person grows by 2.5%. If earnings growth rises to 8.5% the inflation rate will tend to rise to 6% and so on.

Both the external constraint and the domestic capacity constraint imply a concern for inflation which some have argued is misplaced. Why bother with rising prices? Low inflation is a necessary economic objective in part simply because high inflation is so unpopular politically. If inflation continues to accelerate, most governments find that unpopularity forces them into choosing recession as a means of curbing demand and prices. But there are sound economic reasons for curbing inflation too. The reason which appeals to common sense (though, ironically, there is little hard economic evidence for it) is that high inflation requires people to spend time in avoiding its consequences. High inflation also tends to tip over into accelerating inflation, particularly if its source is a wage-price spiral.

The third economic objective for any government is a steady growth of living standards at the highest possible rate. Growth is likely to remain a sensible objective, even if the purchases which comprise growth shift their pattern and become more environment-friendly. After all, growth simply measures the increase in gross domestic product, which is a benchmark of economic activity. Many 'green' technologies will themselves open up new avenues of opportunity for industrial growth. Moreover, many of the products for which there has been highest growth in demand over the last decade are already lean in their use of materials and relatively pollution free. For example, the word processor on which this essay was written uses less copper than an old electric typewriter because printed circuit boards have economised on its use. It is obviously crucial that government should have an active role in banning or limiting the use of products which are toxic and noxious. But there is no reason to believe that it needs to stop growth altogether in order to do so. It can define, as it always has done, legitimate areas for private activity and assume that private contracts and exchange to the mutual advantage of both parties are innocent until proven guilty.

The fourth economic objective is low unemployment, about which there is relatively little disagreement save on the means of achieving it, which are ferociously controversial. An expansion of demand (through tax cuts, public spending increases or a devaluation) may cut unemployment in a recession. However, it was fairly clear at the end of the eighties, when companies were working at full capacity and pushing up the prices of their products and when demand for labour was pushing up wage rates, that a boost to demand was more likely to increase prices than output and jobs. In other words, the rate of unemployment at which earnings would not accelerate (assuming that there was no increase in inflation from other sources) was about 6% of the labour force. To all intents and purposes, this appeared to be the non-accelerating inflation rate of unemployment (NAIRU) or 'natural rate'. An attempt to push inflation much below this level could lead not merely to rising wages and prices but to accelerating wages and prices.

Redistribution

These four classic objectives of economic policy should be supplemented, in the case of left-of-centre governments, by a fifth. It is not merely important that living standards rise, but that living standards should be fairly distributed. At the very least, there must be an effective attack on poverty consistent with maintaining incentives to work. Egalitarians would wish to go beyond the alleviation of hardship and add the objective of equality in its own right. The traditional economic case for redistribution of the spoils of the marketplace is as applicable in the nineties as at any previous time. An extra pound is substantially more valuable to an inhabitant of London's cardboard cities than it is to the Belgravia multi-millionaire. The government thus increases the overall welfare of its citizens if it redistributes money from the millionaire to the pauper. There is another leg of the case, based on the philosopher John Rawls's veil of uncertainty. If we were each able to disregard our future place in society, by arranging that we stood behind a curtain in ignorance of what occupation and status we would eventually assume, what would we regard as a fair distribution of income and wealth? It seems unlikely that we would justify the abject poverty of the single homeless, or the failure of more than one in ten of the population who are unemployed or are pensioners relying on the state minimum to participate in the real rise in living standards of the last decade. Inequalities would be justified only to the extent that they serve the general interest in rising prosperity, including rising prosperity for the least well-off.

We thus have five broad objectives: growth, equity, full employment, low inflation and external balance. At the end of 1987, before the then Chancellor, Nigel Lawson, added his budget tax cuts of March 1988 to the fuel of rapidly expanding mortgage credit, it was possible to imagine a policy which could build on the Thatcherite legacy without making hard choices. The mix of growth, inflation and unemployment would be politically tolerable, while a left-of-centre government would define itself by cutting taxes less and spending more on public services and on transfers to the needy (and, of course, to its own constituencies). This would have suited the Labour Party very well, because it would have put on to the backburner many of the thorniest issues in its own relationship with the trades unions. The debate about the means of running the economy could be delegated to the technocrats, while the politicians concentrated on values. It is much easier, as Anthony Crosland argued, to take a slice of an expanding income than a slice of a stagnating one.

However, it is no longer clear that this relatively easy option is open. The problems left behind by the Lawson boom have substantially aggravated the arithmetic of any economic policy. Even if the 1990 correction is relatively successful in reducing the payments deficit, it is unlikely to fall to less than 2–2½% of national income – still a large deficit by historic standards. Growth will be the more difficult to attain because of the need to dampen demand and hence imports in order to correct the external imbalance. The same problem will sustain the pressure on the pound and therefore inflation, while the slower growth will also imperil the objective of reducing unemployment. All these problems in turn aggravate the difficulty of finding resources for priority spending programmes – for the public goods such as transport and the arts and the health service on which the Left is agreed – and for the attack on poverty. In order to keep all the balls in the air, tougher and harder choices will have to be made than looked necessary before the Lawson boom.

The policies needed to tackle this combination of late-eighties problems come in any number of permutations: it is perfectly legitimate to be in favour of credit controls and against fixing the exchange rate, or vice versa, or indeed to be against or in favour of both. But for ease of exposition it makes sense to stylise three competing alternative programmes which are broadly those within the non-Tory arena at the beginning of the nineties. It also helps to concentrate the mind on what is and is not practical politics and, equally importantly (since self-delusion is a beguiling weakness of politicians), practical economics. A final advantage is to give some historical perspective on the particular problems which were faced by the Labour Government of 1974–79, the last non-Tory government. I have specifically avoided saying that policy three is John Smith's and David Owen's policy, or policy two is Bryan Gould's, or policy one is Roy Hattersley's, simply because this would traduce the sophistication of all and any of the said gentlemen. Their views do not package so easily: my categories are caricatures. In a final section, I attempt an essentially liberal synthesis which tries to answer the question of what, in economic terms, is to be found to the left of the Right these days.

The Keynesian Social Democratic Programme

This is essentially the sort of policy mix favoured by the 1974–79 Labour Government, and by the Heath Government in later years. The management of demand is secured by the use of fiscal policy (tax and public spending decisions) plus interest rates (which may or may not be aimed in part at some monetary target which is meant to reveal the growth of total spending) plus possibly direct controls on credit or indirect inducements to the banking sector to limit the extension of credit. External balance is addressed in part by managing demand so as to avoid excessive imports, and in part by using the pound to encourage net exports if necessary. This does not rule out membership of the European Monetary System, but it does mean that the policy pursued within it is likely to be the maintenance of price competitiveness through devaluation.

This, however, may lead to greater inflationary pressures. Inflation in turn has to be dealt with through income restraint: some sort of incomes policy. Equity is secured through the tax and spending system and possibly through other measures such as statutory minimum wages and particular formulae for pay increases allowed under the incomes policy (such as Jack Jones's famous flat-rate pay rise). The long term ability of the economy to grow is meant to be helped by an active industrial policy of succouring high technology industries and research and development, and ensuring adequate education and training.

The Achilles heel of this policy is simply the failure of the trades union movement to deliver its members in support of incomes restraint, without which the only weapon the government can use against domestically generated inflation is a tougher demand management policy: i.e. deflation. It can raise the pound, and squeeze import prices, but at the cost of imperilling external balance and the health of the tradeable sectors like manufacturing. It can raise taxes and cut spending, but at the cost of its popularity, its social objectives and its commitment to lower unemployment. It can raise interest rates, and hit private sector demand and jobs. Without incomes policy, all the orthodox options look unpleasant.

However, there is little real hope that the trades unions could make incomes restraint work. Their membership is in decline, and in many key new areas they are simply unrepresented. Their whole institutional function and their leaderships would be compromised by wage restraint, which is like asking a lion to become a herbivore. Moreover, there are other serious problems in running any incomes policy. Unless there is some credible means of enforcing restraint, why should I believe that you will play ball? Why should I not bust the policy?

That was precisely what happened at the end of the seventies with the Ford workers, which is why the then Chancellor, Denis Healey, toyed with the idea of applying some form of sanctions to norm-busting companies. His proposed withdrawal of public sector contracts was an excessively blunt weapon. It could not hit companies which did not supply to the public sector. The best means of plugging this gap in the armoury, and breathing some form of life into this orthodox policy mix, is a tax-based incomes policy. Firms which paid over the norm would be subject to a higher tax on their pay bill, the proceeds of which would be recycled back to all employers in the form of lower National Insurance contributions. The nub of the scheme would be to raise the prospective penalties which firms faced for conceding inflationary pay bargains to ensure that the social as well as the private consequences were taken into account. This tax-based policy was advocated as a reserve power by the SDP-Liberal Alliance in both the 1983 and 1987 elections, though it was understandably not popular with either management or workforce. (Unpopularity in economics is not necessarily a bad thing: after all, such an anti-inflationary weapon would primarily serve the interests of those who are actually or prospectively unemployed, inevitably a minority. The majority may believe themselves better off with no restraint.)

The prospect of any effective incomes policy seems remote, though, while the trades unions have such an important constitutional role within the Labour Party, and while it is inevitable that the Labour Party is the senior or only party in a non-Tory government. Both Sweden and Austria are small countries with concentrated union movements which have long traditions of corporatist activity. Their examples do not easily transfer. Ironically, the union links of the Labour Party preclude an easy corporatist option in Britain. In summary, it is not impossible that hard circumstances may require the sort of incomes policy advocated by the traditional Keynesians but it is politically still a far from popular commodity.

The Left Keynesian Programme

The left Keynesian programme – known during the seventies as the Alternative Economic Strategy, though this sometimes entailed more Marxist elements – differs from the social democratic strategy merely in its willingness to do more violence to postwar institutions (such as free trade and free markets). Not believing in the possibility of incomes policy, some of its adherents hoped that if real incomes could rise by a given target each year then wage bargainers would moderate their demands and inflation could be kept in check. The main reason why the economy could not deliver that sort of high and sustained wage growth, they argued, was because of its tendency to slip into payments deficit. Devaluation could not work, because it raised import prices and hence curbed real wages. So the best option was to impose controls on imports which would directly check the payments imbalance without raising import prices or turning the terms of trade against us. Any additional revenues from import tariffs could be used to reduce indirect taxes like VAT and excises.

Quite apart from the problems which this strategy would cause for British membership of the European Community and the General Agreement on Tariffs and Trade, there were real question marks over whether it would allow real high wage growth, and whether this would moderate pay demands. Its most prominent academic supporters, the New Cambridge group, have now disbanded. Professor Wynne Godley, its leader, has conceded that Britain's European attachments probably rule out the essential control on imports.

Domestically, alternative strategists argued for a much more interventionist industrial policy, with some advocates proposing the nationalisation of key parts of the economy. 'Planning agreements' would be concluded between businesses, unions and the government, which would help to accelerate growth by specifying increased investment and product development, if necessary supported by public funds and protection. A taste of these proposals survives in the Labour Party's policy review document under the classification of 'supply-side social-ism' though it sits uneasily with the apparently new enthusiasm for the market allocation of resources. In reality, any form of highly interventionist planning is doomed before it begins. It has not been successful in any economy as advanced as Britain's, and has failed in a number of economies which were substantially less developed (including those of Eastern Europe).

The experience of Japan's Ministry of International Trade and Industry cannot easily be used to support the case for intervention, since its activities are becoming steadily less influential as Japan reaches the frontier of economic progress. State planning is relatively easy when the processes are simple and when there is an enormous amount of catching up to do with a trading partner which has a defined system of production. It is next to impossible in conditions of uncertainty. Two examples of Japan's vibrantly competitive internal markets suffice. The first is the failure of Sony to establish the Betamax as the industry standard video recorder. JVC's VHS system won instead, causing considerable losses both for its rival and for consumers who had invested in the alternative. Nor is there much sign of MITI planning even in quite traditional product markets like cars, where the market shares of the main Japanese car producers have changed dramatically over the last ten years. This hardly suggests that there has been MITI-inspired planning and collusion. Even the French system of indicative planning, which was much admired on the left in Britain during the sixties, has not stood the test of time, as a recent OECD country report on France showed[1]. In Britain, an additional problem is that the civil servants in the Department of Trade and Industry who would in the first instance be reponsible for such planning agreements have little or no experience outside the civil service.

However, there is a more fundamental and philosophical objection to the whole notion of direct government intervention in relatively detailed decisions, which is that government cannot be trusted to act in the social interest. It is just as likely to act in its own interests, which may be to maximise votes in marginal constituencies or to buy off powerful vested interests because they are powerful rather than because they are deserving. The whole thrust of the Left's strategy appears to assume that markets can fail, but that governments cannot. In fact, there is almost as much evidence for government failure as there is for market failure. Look at the cancelled TSR2 project, or Blue Streak, or the disastrous decision to proceed with the Advanced Gas Cooled nuclear reactor, or the backing for prestige projects like Concorde. Indeed, there is now a burgeoning economics literature devoted to nothing else but government failure and the way in which politicians act in the market for votes: the 'public choice' literature. This research will never allow a naive belief in the altruism of government again.

One of its implications is that the scope of government action should, whenever possible, be confined to policies which have a relatively general application and do not require arbitrary and discretionary decisions on the part of ministers. For example, ministers may be quite good at designing policies to improve the education and training of people who may work in a number of different industries, but rather bad at deciding that a particular company should receive public funds to support its investment in, say, motorcycles or micro-chips. They are less able to serve their own private interest, as opposed to the public interest, with policies of wide and general application. Picking winners too often means playing lollipop politics with your friends.

Similar objections apply to the notion that public ownership of the means of production would solve problems. Clearly, the Eastern European example shows that public ownership en masse tends to degenerate into bureaucratic control. Nor is the argument in equity a strong one. Despite the government's wider share-ownership programme through privatisations, the proportion of shares in UK-quoted companies owned by institutions like pension funds and life assurance companies for the support of retired and distressed working people has not ceased to rise and is now more than three-quarters. In reality, the British economy is already socialised, if ownership were really what mattered. In truth, the precise ownership matters less than competition in product, labour and capital markets. Bad producers lose market share, and are disciplined by consumer choice (if the consumer has a choice, which he or she does not in the case of monopolies like water). They may also be subject to takeover if they inefficiently use their assets. Managers have the incentive to provide the owners with the returns they expect from competing investments. For all these reasons, the interventionist left Keynesian programme would be a blind alley which is best avoided.

The Left Liberal Programme

The left liberal (or social liberal or social market) programme strongly avows the advantages of markets as a means of providing people with the goods and services they want. There is a presumption that the market should be allowed to get on with its job, and that any intervention should be very carefully justified before it occurs. Demand is managed so as to curb inflation, and any resulting unemployment must be dealt with through measures such as increased training and tougher benefit testing for those out of work for long periods of time. Private ownership or devolved collective ownership (such as co-operatives or employee share ownership plans) are regarded as superior to public ownership because of the interest of the owners in the greater efficiency of capital, but the government has to attempt to introduce competition wherever it can. It is competition which ensures that the consumer is properly served.

Is this merely Thatcherism? Not necessarily, since there are both technical and moral differences between the two. The left liberal may well be ready to fix the exchange rate in the European Monetary System as part of the discipline to be exerted on inflation (by ensuring import prices do not rise) rather than by allowing the pound to float freely as Mrs Thatcher prefers. Indeed, the left liberal is more likely to recognise the interdependence of the world's economies and seek internationalist remedies. On another technical matter, the left liberal also tends to be suspicious of the claims made for a particular type of monetary target. He or she may even be prepared to introduce a type of indirect credit control so as not to use interest rates excessively to bear down on borrowing.

The left liberal, compared with the Thatcherite, sees a much larger role for the government in addressing market failures which conspicuously affect whole sectors or the whole economy – such as the shortfall in education and training predicted by economic theory. The emphasis is on changing the climate within which business operates, rather than attempting, as the left Keynesian does, to direct rainfall to the top of a particular hill. The most crucial difference between Thatcherism or the right-wing liberal position and the left liberal is over inequality and poverty. The left liberal is prepared to make substantial transfer payments to reduce inequality. Some argue for a basic income guarantee which would give everyone an income entitlement. Others argue that such a universal benefit would become marginal to the attack on poverty precisely because any increase is so expensive since it is going to everyone rather than merely those who need it. The use of the tax system to claw back benefits from those who do not need them, even at the cost of relatively high effective tax rates of benefit withdrawal, would allow a politically feasible attack on poverty. In both cases, though, the concern for redistribution is marked.

The left liberal position has enormous political advantages. It removes the government from the tarnish of the trades union movement and from the need for incomes policy, which in turn reduces the risk of the government's credibility being undermined by a policy failure. It naturally runs with the grain of much of contemporary thinking about the belief in individual responsibility rather than collective intitiative. It is suspicious of the state and its motives: indeed, it has been called 'socialism without the state'. However, it also implies that a left government must lower its sights and those of its supporters on many substantial issues of reform. Most importantly, it implies that a government has to be prepared to see unemployment rise if inflationary pressures begin to mount. It has no cogent alternative to deflation and unemployment as a weapon against inflation. Moreover, the levels of unemployment which may be required will be all the higher if the government is forced by internal pressure to concede changes in trades union law which strengthen the unions' ability to insist on pay rises.

Which of these three broad 'schools' offers the greatest potential for the Left? The clever money has to bet that whatever non-Tory government is eventually elected will increasingly adopt something akin to the left liberal position, if only because of political expediency. The writers of *Marxism Today* and the *New Times* point to the breakdown of 'Fordist' types of mass production and the working-class political alienation which went with it. The modern economy is more complex than the old. Just in time manufacturing methods have broken down the 'any colour so long as it is black' mentality and introduced variety into production processes. The decentralisation of the British economy into smaller units, the gradual marginalisation of the traditional unionised cloth-cap industries, the fact that white-collar workers now outnumber blue-collar workers, the majority of owner-occupiers and the traditionally liberal suspicion of the state in Britain all point to the likely success of individualist rather than collectivist mores. The successful left coalition will have to pull together people who share a common belief in the importance of democracy, individuality, fairness and the beneficent activity of the state in limited areas of so-called 'public goods' like education, health and social insurance or security.

Some of this programme is going to sound very right-wing to old-style social democrats. If low unemployment is to be reconciled with low inflation, and incomes policy is rejected, it is essential to ensure that the power of 'insiders' in the labour market is curbed. This means responding to sharp rises in pay for groups in short supply by an exceptionally active programme of training, if necessary supported by government subsidy to ensure an adequate quality of recruit. It also means pursuing a Swedish-style employment policy rather than a Beveridge-style benefit policy: instead of someone who becomes unemployed assuming an automatic right to draw benefit with no strings attached, they should instead go into an active programme of counselling designed to propel them quickly back into the labour market. It also means continuing to curb the power of trades union 'insiders' to limit entry to their occupation and hence restrict supply and bid up wage rates. The first hint that the Labour Party front bench was beginning to accept this agenda came with its abandonment of the closed shop – the insistence on union membership – as inconsistent with the EC social charter. The greater the limitation on privileged groups – print workers or journalists, colliers or power workers – to hold their employers to ransom, the easier it will be to make high union membership compatible with low unemployment.

This need not, though, sound like a programme for shifting labour market power from employee to employer. Mrs Thatcher has implemented part of a liberal agenda by limiting the power of the trades unions. She has not conceived of ways in which employees could equally insist on individual rights. In product markets, it is often regarded as an anti-competitive practice to insist that a customer can only buy a particular product if they also buy various others. It is a way of using the leverage of something in scarce supply to strengthen the sellers' market position. Yet there is little restriction on employers who bundle up a series of decisions within the act of employment. Why, for example, should employees be forced to subscribe to a company's pension scheme in order to receive the company's pension contribution? The government has made some progress towards fully portable and transferable pensions, but it is still often worthwhile for an older employee to continue in a job which they may dislike and otherwise prefer to leave because of the subsequent pension advantages. If labour market flexibility requires that it is easier for employers to fire their staff, then it is only fair that it should also be easier for employees to leave jobs they dislike. There might be similar rights to split jobs so that young mothers could find it easier to leave the labour force, and married women could find it easier to come back into it. Men would find it easier to take more leisure and less money if they so wanted. In short, the government could encourage a major unbundling of options which currently have to be accepted as a package.

Another element of the social liberal agenda ought to be to encourage further moves towards profit-sharing. The trades unions have traditionally opposed profit-sharing because it has been seen as a way of shifting risk from employers to employees. This surely made sense when earnings were low and a fall would entail serious hardship. As earnings rise in real terms, this is surely a much less pertinent objection. It must make social sense for the total remuneration of all employees to vary a little rather than to have a shedding of the most vulnerable employees during any downturn in the business cycle. Given the long-term consequences of unemployment for motivation and skills, there is a substantial public interest in avoiding any incidence of it. In addition, the experience of companies like the John Lewis Partnership and the National Freight Corporation suggests that nothing legitimises employee criticism and employee involvement more than an element of employee ownership or profit-sharing. Since the greatest repository of knowledge about any company is its own employees, this is the best way of unlocking a gold mine of ideas for improvement.

In product markets, the government has to hunt out any improvement which will reduce the power of producers to fleece consumers. Bureaucratic regulation is always less effective than competition wherever it can be introduced. Competition not only broadens choice, but it sharpens the edge of the producers already in the market. The launch of the *Independent*, for example, improved the quality of *The Times, The Daily Telegraph* and the *Guardian* merely because the competition hotted up. The anti-trust and anti-monopoly policy should be ruthless, not merely confining itself to examining proposed mergers but also looking at the prospective break-up of large companies (like AT&T in the United States recently) with dominant positions in particular markets. Existing restrictive practices, such as the way in which car-producers limit the import from the Continent of cheaper cars in order to stop their exorbitant prices from being undercut, should be cut back actively by the Office of Fair Trading and the Monopolies and Mergers Commission.

There is a final and crucial caveat about the social liberal policy compared with the old social democratic consensus. The social liberal is concerned about the provision of high-quality 'public goods' and about ensuring that people receive their proper entitlements to services like home helps and education. However, there is no need for these services to be provided within the public sector by public sector bodies if private sector firms can do it better. There is a crucial distinction to be drawn between entitlements to services and the formal provision of them. Public procurement should be opened up to greater competition. The links which often exist between local government and local trades unions whose members provide local services should be cut in order to minimise the potential for corruption. The social liberal recognises the essential flaw in traditional socialism: the blithe assumption that the government and the state will act in the social interest rather than in their own interests.

The most potent appeal of Thatcherism to traditional constituencies of the Left is its anti-establishment radicalism. The only way of undermining that appeal is to trump it in the areas where it is weakest. In part, this means highlighting the failures of social provision – health, education and public transport – which are becoming such an obvious feature of Britain in the nineties. But it also means stressing the incomplete and even sham nature of Mrs Thatcher's liberalism. It is sham most of all because it is combined with illiberal political instincts and actions. The Prime Minister is a liberal in her economics, but an authoritarian in her attitude towards the individual in any other context. Her economics, too, involve increased private choice only to the extent that there is no inconvenience to those with existing property or ownership rights. The social liberal agenda can and should go wider than she has dreamed in the extension of property ownership, employee rights of choice, and opportunity. The extraordinary failure of the Left during the eighties is that it ever allowed Mrs Thatcher to borrow the slogan 'Trust the people'. It is high time it got it back.

London Transport

PETER NICHOLS

If you asked the Man on the Clapham Omnibus what he thought of the private car, he'd probably say he'd like one. That's if you could find him. Once he was the voice of the people. Nowadays on most buses, he'd be a black or Asian woman or child, a pensioner or an adventurous tourist. What they would all have in plenty would be time to answer, as their bus made its slow, serpentine way between the ranks of parked cars and through jams caused by other cars, mostly occupied by one person each.

London's traffic may seem a quirky topic for such an anthology but so many issues beloved of political journalism or conjecture have a remote, almost metaphysical look – as of angels on heads of pins, fascinating but far from urgent. Even health, education and unemployment rear their heads only at intervals in our lives; but no one can avoid facing the problem of traffic every day, wherever they live, and in central London that means an unholy mess that worsens by the week and that no democratic government dare take on. All parties admit the need for some sort of transport policy and at intervals parties even publish these works of fiction, which are variously well reviewed, soon remaindered and pulped within the year. Obviously the only solution is banning private cars and replacing them with a working public system, which is abhorrent to the Right and impossible for the Left, with another election coming up in four years time.

If cabinet ministers had to use the tube, it would all be reformed within the year, but that's not going to happen because *they* wouldn't want it. Yet I remember sitting opposite Aneurin Bevan on the Circle Line when he was Minister of Health. That was before the car-owning democracy really got going and turned every city street into a parking lot. The road I live in has 250 vehicles parked along its kerbs at the moment. At a low average estimate of £5,000 per vehicle (from Land Rovers to Minis) the cost to their owners was £1,250,000. Multiply by all the streets in London and it's clear where the money could come from for an efficient, free public service – and that's not counting the cost of repairs, parking fines and permits, fuel, insurance, road tax and theft. Nor the cost to us all of road maintenance, traffic control, treatment of dead and injured and damage to the ozone egg-shell by all the poisons farted out in those daily traffic jams. Nor can the streets be cleaned any more: those gutter-brush and spraying vehicles appeared briefly and were scrapped long ago as local authorities gave up the struggle. Even to clear domestic rubbish is to work in warlike conditions, with furious rat-running motorists blowing horns at the slightest delay by a double-parked scruncher.

Sooner or later doubt will be cast on the idea that cars are male genitals or flying carpets and some Saatchi will be paid to put the word around that buses are sexier, classier and greener. The solutions, because they are and must be radical, involve all the left/right, gradualist/sharp shock, market forces/public ownership battles so precious to all parties. Tinkering won't solve it. Finally it will all seize up, but before that how can a democratically elected government face such an initially unpopular measure? Well, unpopular measures are imposed now and then, even in democracies — for instance against hanging and for homosexual tolerance. Some towns *have* got good transport — travel on Newcastle's spanking Metro. One city has no cars at all and, though Venice may not have much else to do with any other place on earth, it does have a multi-storey block at its entrance where the cars are left. The number of public and private vehicles on the canals is strictly controlled as a few too many would wash the place away — and much more of this muddle may do something similar to London. Private cars are wonderful in the countryside or on motorways; in cities they're as anti-social as private sewerage.

The huge capital investment people make in their cars could give us an immaculate, free mixture of punctual buses and trains (the only appealing aspect of Fascism) with far more and far cheaper taxis. We'd be able to see and clean the streets again. All the vehicles would be moving, not parked for eight hours while their owners work or sleep. The pedestrian would cease to be a bullied victim or (as the AA once described him) 'the greatest menace on the road today'. Apart from the car-makers, everyone would be better off.

But would the electorate ever vote for it, and if not, how can it be done? And if it cannot, we have to wonder whether democratic socialism is more than a forlorn dream.

Social Policy: New Models for the 1990s

NICHOLAS DEAKIN

Peering into their clouded crystal balls, the pundits have detected persuasive evidence that the nineties are to be the 'caring decade'. If that is indeed to be the case, there is one conspicuous gap in the range of public policies that will have to be filled as a matter of priority. This is the space once occupied by social policy. The 'orphan child' (as Rudolf Klein termed it) of the eighties must find parents prepared not just to demonstrate their concern for caring values but to commit both their brains and pockets to the task of producing a comprehensive reconstruction of policy.

The real scale of the task only becomes evident when the full record of the eighties is laid out. For a large part of that decade, a government has devoted considerable energy to denying not merely the desirability but the very existence of an autonomous and coherent set of objectives that could be labelled 'social policies'. Challenged on this precise point, Norman Fowler – ministerial architect of the government's social security 'reforms' – told the House of Commons that Conservative policy objectives were: 'to control public spending and to bring down inflation . . . Our social policy objectives are the same as our overall policy – to achieve a stronger economy and tackle unemployment,' (*Hansard*, 22 April 1985).

Such extreme reluctance to contemplate the possibility that there might be legitimate social policy concerns which could pose questions of choice or even conflict has been based on a series of negative perceptions – three, in particular. First, there has been a pervasive concern, dating back to the mid-seventies and extending well outside the ranks of the Conservative Party, about the 'burden' of welfare expenditure and its potential for slowing down or compromising economic growth. Second, there is the anxiety (originally associated with Hayek but taken up subsequently by Conservative politicians) about possible distortion of the public policy process through the activities of pressure groups pursuing special interests (usually in the area of social policy) under the cloak of an assumed common interest – or, worst of all, 'social justice'. The activities of the so-called 'poverty lobby' are a case in point. Finally, there is the concern repeatedly expressed by the Prime Minister about the corruption of character and sapping of the national will for enterprise by creeping dependency brought about by an over-comprehensive welfare system. Since her agenda has always been fundamentally about hearts and minds, not economics, this underlying concern has been a constant factor in the shaping of policy.

In addition, the government has sometimes been surprisingly defensive about the presentation of some of its social policies. Thus, Conservatives frequently observe that evidence of negative outcomes stemming directly from the application of narrowly defined economic priorities has been exaggerated by the media. Television – especially the BBC – is often singled out as a particular culprit: the treatment of issues like homelessness and the social consequences of mass unemployment are cases in point. Furthermore, analyses of developments in social policy (even as the government has chosen to define it) within the academic world are frequently dismissed as grossly biased. Witness, for example, John Moore's attack on the academic members of the 'poverty lobby' shortly before his departure from office as Secretary of State for Social Security, dismissing their research as a misguided attempt to come to the rescue of socialism when it 'was in danger of being dismissed as a serious political ideology'.

Equivalent views have been expressed in the United States. But in discussion of poverty and welfare American New Right theorists do at least have the advantage of a substantial corpus of social scientific work to support their perspective – an advantage not enjoyed by the New Right on this side of the Atlantic, who have only a slender output of equally slender pamphlets from the think tanks to underpin their large generalisations.

Despite this paucity of hard evidence, members of the government – and their outriders as well – have chosen to continue presenting social policy as 'welfare', and welfare as inevitably promoting dependency. They argue that, politically and socially undesirable as it is, the state should sustain this activity at the minimum feasible level compatible with the overarching economic objective of facilitating wealth creation through growth. Defined in this way, social policy – 'shaped to fit', in The Times's phrase (7 May 1983) – can serve an acceptable subsidiary function. So, when management 'does the right thing' (in City analysts' definition) by shedding labour, the welfare safety net ensures that this can be done without intolerable – that is, visibly unacceptable – consequences.

But apart from minimum cash support to individuals, specific services should be provided, on a stringent test of need, only to those who cannot otherwise secure access to alternatives through their own initiative, either in the marketplace or through self-help. Care of the indigent elderly without living close relatives would be one example of a group that can legitimately be helped in this way. But such formal services of last resort should be provided wherever possible not by state agencies but by voluntary bodies (preferably supported by self-generated funding). Informal care is even better, supplied ideally through the family; or, failing that (and family failure is a continual cause of concern to the New Right) through what is represented as 'the community', a congerie of volunteers and 'active citizens'. Providing care in this way is not merely more efficient and less costly, it is also (at least according to Douglas Hurd) ethically superior (*Church Times*, 9 September 1988).

But even these are seen essentially as intermediate goals. In the long run, the main objective of any welfare system, however constituted, is to teach us to do without it; and this can only finally be achieved by fulfilling the Prime Minister's long-term objective of reinstating individual responsibility as the central value determining all behaviour in the social sphere. For the rest, sustained wealth creation on a sufficient scale will address all outstanding problems; first, by creating jobs – the only really efficient way of relieving poverty – and eventually resolving any outstanding issues of omission of individuals or localities from the general increase in prosperity. For, as Lord Joseph puts it, 'a rising tide lifts all boats' – and without artificial distortions introduced in pursuit of the chimerical objective of greater equality.

Why has this ramshackle collection of prejudices held the field throughout the eighties with such relative ease? There are a number of possible explanations. First, the government gathered momentum – and confidence – as it progressed from economic to social policies without encountering serious obstacles; the unthinkable rapidly becoming conceivable, and then achievable. The mirror image of this process was its opponents' disbelief as one sacred cow after another went to the slaughter, beginning with the deeply cherished belief that no government could survive the social and economic disruption that would be the inevitable consequence of sanctioning mass unemployment.

The inherent stability of British society masked for some while – even after the inner-city disturbances of the early eighties – the full impact of economic change (especially the accelerated erosion of the manufacturing base) on those least well able to cope with the consequences: the unskilled workers and their families. When these did become clear, they could be dismissed as the sentimentality of those who, in the Prime Minister's phrase 'drool and drivel that they care'. Or, more sternly, these became the unavoidable costs that had to be paid in order to achieve belated modernisation of the economy, through a 'supply-side miracle'.

Other more mundane factors helped to smooth the progress of the counter-revolution: individual ministers' ambitions to make their mark sustained spending in some social departments (following the example of Margaret Thatcher and Keith Joseph, the high-spenders in the forgotten Heath regime). Successive tenants of the Department of Health and Social Security were especially prone to try to make a virtue of what was often a necessity, since expenditure in some areas has been sustained by extraneous factors: demography (the growth in the early eighties in the number of school leavers) and the high rate of unemployment. 'Islands of Keynesianism' with high contra-cyclical public expenditure on infrastructure survived for reasons of political expediency along the Celtic fringe and most notably in Northern Ireland.

None of these factors, taken by themselves, would have been decisive without the remarkable accretion of power in the centre over the decade, and the absence of any constitutional constraints upon this process. The absence of any justiciable rights, either for the individuals whose lives were permanently marked by the impact of government policies (for example, through changes in the social security regime) or for the intermediate public institutions whose opposition to those policies marked them out for abolition, was a central element in determining the pace and direction of change. Since the vast majority of social policies depend for their effective delivery on local, not central agencies, the progressive restriction of the independent role of local government has been a particularly important change over the decade.

Apart from the increasingly significant role played by the European Court of Human Rights, where Britain has become known, ironically, as their 'best customer in Europe' (*Independent*, 20 April 1989), the power of the executive has been exercised virtually without impediment, and social policy has been one of the areas where it has been most vividly exhibited. 'Sentence first, verdict afterwards' has been the Queen of Hearts in Downing Street's style; dispensing with any attempt to establish a common basis either of opinion or even of fact, in diagnosis or prescription. The approach can be seen passing through successive stages of development, as the government has addressed, without benefit of royal commission or departmental committee, first the problems confronting the social security system (the Fowler review, with its limited number of public hearings), then public education (the Baker Education Reform Act, rammed through Parliament, despite an overwhelmingly unfavourable response to the government's published proposals) and finally the National Health Service review, drawing only on the confidential advice of the increasingly hyperactive New Right think tanks.

In such circumstances, it is hardly surprising that the quality of decision-taking has steadily deteriorated, despite the lavish camouflage provided by greatly increased expenditure on government publicity. Nor has this process been helped by the steady erosion of the standing of the social statistics collected and analysed by government agencies. Too often – most notoriously, in the case of unemployment statistics, where definitions of the unemployed have been altered more than twenty times, redefinition always (remarkably enough) producing a reduction in numbers – ministers have succumbed to the temptation to manipulate them, either as a substitute for action or to conceal the consequences of their collective activities.

In sum, the outcome of the past decade has been to marginalise social policy at a time when, as the divisions in society have steadily increased, effective intervention to modify or reverse the negative impact of those developments, especially on the most vulnerable, should have become increasingly important. But the form that these interventions take and the location of responsibility for taking them remains, at the end of the eighties, a highly contestable area.

Important though it is to reinstate social policy in its proper place, as an independent activity which has legitimate priority in policy-making, it is more important still not to overcompensate and assume that a new model social policy can be crafted in splendid isolation. Some sense of the overall direction that public policy should take, and the type of society that might emerge if it were adopted – however crudely sketched – are essential context if convincing alternatives are to be advanced.

The overall direction of such alternatives can be plotted, as the Thatcherite project has been, along the three axes of political, economic and value changes. As with that enterprise, the question of values takes priority. Put at its simplest, the objective for the nineties should be the reinstatement of the notion of a collective good; common interests binding individuals in a collectivity which we can still legitimately term 'society'. One of the most powerful instruments for defining and achieving that objective would be a reinvigorated social policy. General outcomes that will not be achieved through the sum of individual activities in the marketplace; specific setbacks which adversely affect the individual and his or her family and which they cannot hope to surmount through their own unaided efforts: both require systematic interventions defined (but not necessarily executed) by agencies acting to uphold the public interest. Environmental policies (as both Patricia Hewitt and John Rentoul argue here) are an important illustration of an area of activity where the state must necessarily take a leading role if the sum of individual activity is not to produce outcomes which can be severely damaging both at the personal and collective level.

But the intellectual decay of Thatcherism and its manifest unpopularity with the general public, explored elsewhere in this book, must not be taken as a licence to revert to the patterns of the past. Although empowering individuals as customers in a supermarket where choice is determined by ability to pay has grave weaknesses as an approach in the welfare sector, as the eighties have shown, the concept of an approach sensitive to choice has important merits – provided that market criteria are not the sole determinants of allocation. Dispersion of political power downwards to smaller units of government that will be both more accessible and more responsive to individual citizens needs to be married to increased choice. But such an approach raises difficult questions about the type of institutions that will be needed, their functions, responsibilities and accountability.

Defining the economic priorities poses a whole set of further issues about policy choices (for example, the priority to be given in industrial policy to training; and facilitating participation by women in well-paid and secure jobs). From the social policy perspective, it is the automatic assumption that economic policy goals must have priority and be addressed first; next come the linkages between economic and social policies (breaking away from the 'safety net' approach to welfare) and the setting of goals which are mutually reinforcing. The Swedish Budget statement (1988/89) sets out national policy objectives in a style which is refreshingly novel to a British reader: 'The primary goals of economic policy are jobs for everyone, a fairer distribution and good economic growth.' Reflex rejection of the Scandinavian experience as a model with any relevance for other advanced economies is part of the Standard Polemical Kit of the New Right apologists – one can well understand why they find any successes (as described here by James Curran) highly embarrassing when on a basis inexplicable in terms of their dogmatics.

The Shape of Things to Come

Within the context set out above, the task is to define a social policy for the nineties which:

- possesses intellectual coherence without imposing excessive uniformity;

- meets the full range of citizens' legitimate aspirations, not merely statistically determined basic needs;

- is consistent with policy objectives in other areas but not subservient to them;

- would be effective in execution.

The hinge on which a new social policy turns is the concept of citizenship and the rights deriving from it. One of the gross deficiencies of policy in the eighties has been the development of uneven entitlement; access for those empowered through the market at the expense of those who cannot – for whatever reason – take full advantages of the opportunities available there. This is not merely a matter of limitations externally imposed. There is also an issue of poverty of aspirations; an acceptance by a substantial part of the British population that they have no right to good quality services delivered in a way that does not demean those receiving them. Apparently interminable delay in operations to correct painful disabilities that may then be cancelled at short notice, and the squalid physical surroundings confronting users and staff alike in social security offices are two examples of circumstances that the middle classes do not expect to have to tolerate. Many women, a substantial chunk of the working class (especially the elderly, but including a disturbingly large number of the human casualties who have reached adulthood during the period of high unemployment produced by the blitz on manufacturing industry) and some – though not all – ethnic minorities: all these overlapping groups are at risk.

Choice is the key that will unlock the barriers that bar such groups from full exercise of their citizenship. One of the central tasks for the nineties will be to try to ensure that the choices that they can make are real ones. This certainly does not imply eliminating or restricting competition in the provision of services; the monolithic public bureaucracy as means of provision is dead – events in Eastern Europe at the end of the eighties delivered the deathblow. But the alternative is not provision through an unrestricted market in which public agencies either perform marginal functions, on sufferance, or else persist only on a 'sunset' basis, with built-in obsolescence. The nature and content of the social services, in particular, need a complete overhaul in which the users of those services play a central role.

Critics have argued that this approach is too complex and time consuming, and therefore inefficient, compared with the limited but clearly defined and planned range of options available through a state-run system, or the spontaneous responses generated by the signalling mechanisms in a market model. But recent experience suggests otherwise. Local authorities and health authorities that have experimented with the collection of user preferences through opinion research have found that the results provide sufficiently clear evidence about potential users' relative priorities to serve as an important element in drawing up strategies for service provision. Furthermore, such evidence can be used to assemble information about the amounts that users are able (and willing) to pay and the form in which payment can best be made. As for reactions to failures in provision, recent evidence suggests that the level of customer complaints, on which such weight is placed in a market-driven system, can be seriously misleading as an instrument of measuring satisfaction. Most dissatisfied users prefer to practice avoidance rather than go through the bother of making formal complaints or employing the clumsy and little-known ombudsman devices now being established in a number of private service sectors (i.e. banking and insurance). Here, the public sector, with well-established channels for communicating discontent – the local councillor's surgery is the obvious example – may have a positive advantage.

This said, there are still major problems in making public provision more responsive to users. Even if adequate substitutes for market signals can be devised to identify user preferences and levels of satisfaction, there are likely to be problems of motivation among providers of services, of flexibility in provision and responsiveness. The revival of a sense of commitment to providing a high-quality service – and a restoration of public esteem for those who provide it – could eventually lead to the reinstatement of the 'public service ethic', as John Stewart and Michael Clarke have recently argued. But in this process the role and responsibilities of public sector unions are bound to remain controversial. And market fanatics will continue to argue, whatever the objective evidence, that *a priori* 'the private sector is more efficient than the public sector. It is about style, about culture, about managerial freedom, about clarity, about accountability,' (Watts, *Independent*, 11 December 1988). The challenge for the public sector in the nineties is to disprove this proposition, in every respect.

In particular, the question of 'managerial freedom' needs to be addressed. One of the key issues to be resolved is that of how authority is exercised, and by whom. In a politically managed system the lines of accountability run, in theory, back to the electorate. This is the approach which the Conservative Government has attempted to override, by dismantling or hiving off directly accountable agencies and creating new ones which will function as far as possible solely in response to the disciplines of the market. Yet, its virtues notwithstanding, the market approach and managers trained to implement it have repeatedly shown themselves over the course of the eighties to be unable to respond effectively to basic consumer needs – for comfort, safety and reliability. London Regional Transport, which has failed in all these three respects under senior management installed with an explicit brief to bring market disciplines to bear, is every London resident's favourite awful example. But can agencies that function wholly or partly under democratic control show that they can meet these objectives at least as well?

This issue of where the ultimate responsibility is to lie and how accountability for decisions is achieved is fundamental. It must be convincingly resolved, and criticisms of the democratic alternative fully met, before the eighties model of welfare can be superseded by something better. Pessimistic arguments about the impact of mass democracy on the quality of decision-taking go back a century or more, to de Tocqueville and Bernard Shaw. They provide one of the cornerstones of the (American) New Right's arguments against public control of provision: the corruption (implicit or literal) of the process by the involvement of those likely to benefit personally. The alternative view is that altruism is still one of the guiding principles which the majority of the British people (of all classes and political opinions) wish to see adopted in framing social policies. After a brief period in the seventies, when concern about abuse of welfare produced a harsher climate of opinion, that proposition can be generally substantiated from the evidence contained in the successive British Attitude Surveys and other opinion polls. These have consistently shown that the majority of respondents want more, not less, to be spent on health and social services and most benefits; and are willing to face the financial consequences, in terms of higher taxation. From this evidence, it seems clear that a form of social contract survives, in which responsibility for the weak is still viewed as a collective duty – although the form in which that duty should be discharged remains a matter for debate. Keynes may be dead, but Beveridge is not, as Ivor Crewe commented after the 1983 general election; and subsequent evidence (notably, the level of public concern expressed about the funding and management of the National Health Service) strongly reinforces that conclusion.

Continued public support, after the experience of the eighties, for a series of basic services resourced from public funds but not necessarily provided in the public sector can therefore be taken as a point of departure for the nineties. But although opinion surveys can give general guidance, they are fragile – often fallible – instruments for devising more detailed policies, beyond the point of identifying a few favourite services and benefits. Even here, the ordering of priorities varies quite widely from time to time and poll to poll – witness the rise and fall of support for measures to mitigate the effects of high unemployment, where 'compassion fatigue' and the consequences of the massaging downwards of the unemployment statistics have both had their effects on public consciousness.

In a 'pure' democratic model, the election manifestos of political parties define priorities for public endorsement through the ballot box. But the inflexibility of this device (and the wide intervals at which the electorate have their once-for-all opportunity to respond) greatly reduces its value as a basis for policy-making. Some form of continuous accountability, beyond the formal constitutional safeguard of parliamentary debate (exposed in all its dignified ineffectiveness by the elective dictatorship of the eighties) is clearly necessary. Any new devices would need to take account of the impact of changing circumstances – often unpredictable at the time of the hustings – and the implications of interaction between different policy sectors, which have been so crucial, in the past, for social policy.

Effective policy analysis, based on reliable (and objective) information, can assist by helping to identify areas where variation in policy may be necessary. Promotion by ministers of open debate (as opposed to the characteristic closed policy-making style of the eighties) on priorities can also improve the quality of decision-taking. Parliamentary select committees and their newly televised hearings can provide an arena for such debate. Even the sclerotic internal machinery of political parties could be loosened up sufficiently to permit discussion and review of policy issues to take place. But all these are essentially top-down measures. The evolution of policy in a style that incorporates the preferences of service users requires a more radical departure.

From Guardians to Enablers

To proclaim the virtues of a bottom-up approach, in contrast to the top-down perspective adopted by past governments of all political colours, is simple enough, but the execution is more complex. Put at its most basic, an egalitarian perspective, of the kind advocated here, is difficult to apply without a substantial element of central intervention. Setting a framework of fiscal policy is all very well; but how much discretion in raising and expending revenue can be allowed to devolved units of administration? Real devolution (as opposed to the botched seventies version) must confer such powers, at least on Scotland and Wales, and very possibly on English regions if the philosophy of 'home rule all round' is adopted. And opposition parties that have objected, with justice, to the stringent limitations on local discretion imposed by the Conservative Government (measures restricting local government's freedom of action, up to and including the poll tax) cannot consistently oppose attempts by local authorities to restore – even reinforce – such freedom of action, even if this involves systematic departures from national manifesto objectives.

Thus any restoration (let alone reinforcement) of local discretion necessarily brings with it wide variations in outcome. Unless strong compensatory measures are introduced, the success of the middle classes in diverting welfare resources in their own direction will be reflected territorially. Some special interests – those of women and ethnic minorities – may be neglected; others (producer groups?) will be able to assert themselves more freely. So while the locality is clearly the place to begin when contemplating reform – and one of the major deficiencies of past structures that must be corrected has been the scale on which they have operated – breaking up Leviathan into a pack of miniature beasts will not by itself necessarily give the desired result.

The classic answer, in socialist social policy, has been to send for the guardians: the high-minded incorruptibles who can be relied upon to put the common interest before their individual concerns. After a lifetime's search, the Webbs believed they had found them in the officials of the CPSU; that tattered illusion was another casualty of the events in Eastern Europe at the end of the eighties. The libertarian answer has always been the same as the spontaneous response of the Czech, East German and Hungarian people: throw the rascals out. But rethinking social policy comprehensively requires us to consider a wider range of options.

If local discretion based on choice is to be built into the new model as one of its fundamental characteristics, safeguards will need to be incorporated as well. Common standards and levels of provision will need to be set nationally, after open debate; their enforcement must be a matter for public agencies. Audit and inspection resume the central role that they once performed; but the supervision of the activities of the auditors should rest not with traditional government departments but with an expanded version of the new agencies – like the Audit Commission – created during the eighties, with their brief expanded to incorporate a concern with quality and accessibility of services, as well as efficiency and value for money. Subject to such safeguards, the approach should be to decentralise provision of services wherever possible to the lowest geographical scale, and distribute functions among agencies in accordance with capacity to provide. The issue of democratic control can be addressed by bringing local elected representatives together in different combinations to provide overall political direction in different policy areas. Problems of management discretion, overload on individuals and effective accountability will need to be addressed if this model (first advanced by the Webbs, as it happens) is to be successfully implemented.

If pluralism in provision under democratic control is to be achieved at local level, the implications for local government are far-reaching. It is not sufficient to talk in terms of the 'enabling' authority, as politicians of all persuasions have already fallen into the habit of doing. The means of defining what is to be enabled and how those made responsible for delivery can do so both effectively and responsively must be clearly defined. Inspection and audit at local level will be an essential element in the portfolio of tasks to be performed; but this is the bare minimum. Technical assistance to responsible agencies in defining and carrying out the jobs which they are contracted to perform; ensuring that the interests of service users are not lost sight of in the process of contracting; exchange of relevant experience with other areas facing similar problems; and co-ordination through establishment of networks involving both the providers and receivers of services are among the additional tasks that local government will have to consider taking on.

In this alternative scenario, voluntary and community-based bodies would have a greatly enhanced role to play, involving not only delivery of services but a place in the policy-making process. The introduction of the voluntary sector into the service delivery arena as a convenient means of cost cutting or offloading unpopular activities, or as at best a supplement to 'mainstream' public services, has been a feature of social planning in the eighties which must now be discarded. Another new feature of the eighties has been the rapidly expanding role of 'for profit' organisations, notably in the field of residential care of the elderly. Competition, locally and nationally, between different sectors should be encouraged provided that it benefits the users of services by increasing the choices available to them and the terms of the contest are clearly defined from the outset. But private sector monopolies or manipulation of the contract system to produce their equivalent in practice would fail this test as decisively as the public sector monopolies of the recent past.

In moving to a pluralist system of service delivery, however, it is important not to underestimate the role that the public sector can still play, and in particular to avoid the marginalising of its remaining clients. In this process, the attitudes and performance of those that provide the services are likely to be of crucial importance, if the risk of a two-tier system with a demoralised residue of public provision is to be avoided. Both in terms of material reward and morale, their interests need careful consideration. The encouragement of co-operatives, as a means of securing involvement and commitment of staff and hence helping to maintain quality of service, is one area in which local authorities have an opportunity to take new initiatives, given the requirements of recent legislation on contracting out of services. Encouraging employee 'buyouts' is one route that has already been explored. Other initiatives may be particularly appropriate in the case of services with substantial numbers of users from minority ethnic groups. Alternatively, if the scale of the operation is not sufficient to justify adopting this approach, the encouragement of self-help groups with logistic support and (where appropriate) funding from the local authority may provide an alternative answer. The essential point is that public sector involvement in delivery should not be dogmatically excluded, any more than it needs to be insisted upon; and that the experience of the past decade suggests a number of ways in which that role could be exercised which meet the criticism that past approaches have invariably had a disabling effect (Deakin & Wright, *Consuming Public Services*, 1990).

If delivery is to be locally based, varied in format according to local circumstances and discretion, and open to further variation in accordance with user preferences, what remains for determination at the centre? In a nutshell, a greatly simplified version of cash welfare. The struggle to achieve such a system has been long drawn out and many of the issues involved are highly complex and technical. Grossly oversimplifying, the major technical issue has been the problem of linking the tax and benefits systems in a systematic way; and a key policy question has been when and how recipients' benefits are to be phased out if the disincentive effect of abrupt loss of entitlement is to be avoided. The Right would want to stress the importance of not discouraging individuals from re-entering the labour market ('the employment trap'); the Left the consequences of loss of benefit for the poorer household ('the poverty trap'). Various devices have been put forward which might address all or some of these problems: a negative income tax, which would be operated through the Inland Revenue; a basic income guarantee rolling up a series of existing benefits; a national minimum wage. Now that the technology is available to address the practical difficulties, the time is ripe for a further review of the policy options – a more comprehensive and open one than its predecessor (the Fowler review).

Responsibility for the delivery of cash benefits is to be allocated, under the present government's proposals, to one of the agencies that are being hived off from the civil service to implement agreed policies (the so-called 'Next Steps' agencies). The implications for social policy of divorcing policy-making and the detail of administration are far reaching; but provided that clear policy direction and a proper degree of accountability are introduced, the principle is sound. Indeed, the concept of removing functions from the centre, both organisationally and geographically – the 'Next Steps' agencies are to be located outside London, a decision made for economic reasons which might be turned to political advantage if viable regional political structures can be created – is entirely consistent with the present argument.

In sum, the model for social policy will be pluralistic, and therefore quite widely varied in its different local forms and outcomes. It will be based upon citizen rights, and will lean heavily on audit and inspection to ensure that those rights can be exercised in practice. It will aim to incorporate, not exclude, market considerations by providing wider choice wherever possible for all users of services, where necessary through extending competition – not only in the non-statutory provision but across public and private sectors. (The 'quasi-markets' described by Julian Le Grand also have a potentially important role to play here.)

Securing and maintaining high quality in delivery over the whole range of welfare services would be a crucial objective.

Such a system would not be value-neutral or technocratic, resting as it would on responding to the concept of entitlement, deriving from common citizenship. The ultimate responsibility for meeting policy objectives would not rest with the bureaucracy, however well-instructed or public-spirited. Nor would it derive from the application of sophisticated management techniques developed in the private sector, though these have their place. It would be the outcome of effective democratic control. To achieve this would require a degree of political mobilisation, both centrally and (even more importantly) at local level, which has not previously been a characteristic of this society. However, the precise form of political involvement and the role of parties is not prescribed. Finally, the approach proposed does not fit traditional stereotypes, either of Right or Left. It may be all the better for that.

Down with Aunt Tabitha: a Modest Media Proposal

JEAN SEATON

Let us be ridiculously optimistic about the British media. Let us imagine that it is possible to do something by government action to make newspapers and broadcasting, not slicker and richer, but better.

Of course, such a notion is well known to be absurd. There are people (government ministers, for instance) who think that the worst excesses of the media, as of the trades unions, should be curbed. There are others (shadow ministers, for instance) who look for a means to correct political bias. There are very few other people, apart from the occasional idealistic journalist, who see a problem at all. On the one hand, action isn't considered necessary: Britain may have lost an empire, but it still has the best media in the world. On the other, any major interference would be a dangerous infringement of liberty.

But let us irreverently discard the conventional wisdom, and start with contrary assumptions. Let us assume that a rapidly changing industry needs to be guided. Let us assume that something which daily intrudes into our lives in ever more sophisticated ways needs to be, itself, the subject of continual public surveillance. Let us rashly state a new principle: the media interferes with us; therefore we have a right and a duty to interfere with the media.

Such assumptions are certainly extreme. But perhaps they may serve us better than the accepted ones, if only because the latter are humbug. People may be complacent about the British media – they have little experience of any other – but they don't trust it. Fifteen years ago (according to MORI), more than half the adult population claimed to believe what they read in the papers; in 1989 fewer than two-fifths did so; in the same period, the proportion of people placing their faith in television halved.

That this should be so is not just the fault of owners, editors and producers. It is also – most culpably – the fault of hypocritical governments, Labour and Conservative, which have valued their own

[139]

convenience above the liberal ideals which their own members publicly espouse. *Doublethink*, according to George Orwell, is 'the power of holding two contradictory beliefs in one's mind simultaneously, and accepting both of them'. Through successive regimes, *doublethink* has precisely defined the attitude of Downing Street towards the media.

Never, however, have the contradictions been so glaring as in the past decade. The politics of the eighties have been orchestrated in a language of freedom, choice, non-intervention, the withdrawal of the state; yet the same ten years have been pock-marked with government limitations on the public right to be informed. Where individuals have sought to challenge state manipulation of the news, the government has shown neither mercy nor moderation, in making an example of offenders. If the vital bond of trust between public and media has been eroded, the timidity of much current affairs broadcasting, which has been the direct result of government bullying, is one undoubted cause.

Britain may have 'the best media in the world'. But the effective range of discussion and investigation is certainly narrower today here than in most other modern democracies, including West Germany, France, Sweden and the USA. (It may not be long before the former Eastern bloc leaves us behind in the matter of media freedom. Who can imagine the Home Office giving a foreign camera crew carte blanche to film what they liked in the Maze Prison – in the way that the Soviet authorities recently provided open access to a Western team in one of the USSR's last remaining political gaols?) Meanwhile the media (and especially television) has been blatantly used for government propaganda – with a massive increase in public sector advertising, much of it for the furtherance of the Conservatives' privatisation ideology.

In addition, the government has encouraged the oligopolistic tendencies of the industry itself – in the name, of course, of freedom. If one contradiction of Thatcherism has been that free market rhetoric has been accompanied by interventionist practice, another is that talk about a media marketplace has been accompanied by its virtual eradication. Technological change – with its requirement of long-term investment and large-scale capitalisation – has produced a bureaucratic jungle of profit-taking conglomerates which own huge shares in all the media which the public consumes. The victims of media concentration are variety, creativity and quality; while the future proliferation of broadcasting channels in the hands of a shrinking band of operators is certain to make matters worse.

Mega-Star

The few corporate owners are not competitive in a sense that could conceivably be expected to produce an improved product: but their financial rivalry undoubtedly imposes pressure to produce a cheaper one. That means an almost inevitable lowering of standards: it is cheaper to buy in agency news than to send a reporter to the scene, it is cheaper to buy in internationalised soap operas than to make your own drama, and so on. In the last decade, commercial television revenue has doubled. Yet it has, significantly, been the small companies with the narrowest profit margins (frequently those dependent on Channel Four) which have produced the most innovative material. Big companies have tended to plump for foreign imports, and will be increasingly inclined to do so as the audience is sliced into smaller units by the extending range of channels.

Thus – whatever may be said of our assumptions – the need for a British media *perestroika* which disdains the old assumptions and abandons the pretence at laissez-faire, is overwhelming. The question is what direction it should take. Is there a need (as some suggest) for intervention, but only for the purpose of creating a freer market? Or is there a need for more regulation, in order to remove the commercial pressure and government interference that already exist?

One basic point is clear. You cannot reform by doing nothing. A government policy on the media which seeks to make changes is interventionist even when it claims not to be. For those who are not complacent about the present state of the media, the issue is not whether to intervene, but the purpose of intervention. Here, there can be differing answers. Let us, therefore, make a further assumption: that the objective in a democracy should be an accurate, multi-faceted, intelligent and responsible media, which believes in the people instead of wishing to pull one over them. If so, we may say that the aims of reform should be enabling, rather than prohibitive; they should encourage initiatives, and discourage caution; they should open doors, and not close them.

Reform, in short, must start with an unambiguous slogan which many – on the Left, as on the Right – will find frightening: down with the censor. Government policy towards the media for a generation or more has been the opposite. Behind the platform-talk of freedom and consumer sovereignty has lurked the real anxiety – that the media will make ministerial (and official) lives a misery by letting cats out of bags and teaching people things they ought not to know or understand. Such has been the psychology that has constrained British media institutions like a nervous, clammy hand:

Whatever you do
Whatever you say
Aunt Tabitha says
That's not the way!

So far from new technology loosening Aunt Tabitha's cloying grip, the development of video, satellite and cable, alongside the modernisation of print journalism, has been shadowed by an accumulation of supervisory quangos. In the new confusing environment Aunt Tabitha, like Dame Edna, has become a mega-star indeed. The mission for the 1990s – the true alternative – must be to send this powerful and debilitating matron packing.

Poodle

Now let us descend from romantic assumption into pragmatism. It is impossible to abolish the censor altogether. There will always be some secrets which governments will unshakeably insist remain secret. There will always be people who, quite understandably, will seek to protect their reputations against libel or slander. There will always be some kinds of behaviour or enactment – seditious, blasphemous, sexual, violent or whatever – which public taste and political necessity will dictate should be withheld or prohibited. We may dispute whether any visual or verbal messages are harmful, in themselves, to the recipients. (Has the crucifixion fetish of Christian art helped to create a more violent society? Has the theme of under-age sex in *Romeo and Juliet* created a less moral one?) We may think that the evils of suppression, and of sustaining the machinery needed to suppress, outweigh any possible offence to the public – which, in Britain, has been remarkably sensible, tolerant and adaptable over the last thirty years. However, for good or ill, the tide of opinion in this country (and probably internationally) is flowing in a different direction.

Yet to acknowledge that there are practical limits to extending freedom does not mean placing ourselves with those who would restrict it further. Indeed, for those who care about artistic expression and political liberty, the aim should always be to seek new opportunities for artists to reveal, disturb and shock, and to outrage establishment sensibilities. Experience shows it is the objectionable that lasts: the comfortable and easily appreciable is more likely to be forgotten. The object of reform, therefore, should not be to appease Aunt Tabitha but (if we cannot actually kick her down the stairs) to rouse her to a state of ineffectual fury: *the media we want must not be anybody's poodle.*

In any case, if there are practical limits to what may be permitted, there are also practical limits to what can be banned. Recently the Labour MP Clare Short led a feminist campaign against girlie magazines in W. H. Smith's – a left-wing echo of Mary Whitehousean prurience. Such a crusade, however, will soon be undermined by the satellite dish: an instrument of escape from any purely British attempt to blinker, which will eventually be almost universal.

What makes the scissors approach to the media so depressing, however, is not that it is ineffective (in politics as in sex, it fans interest in what it seeks to ban), or even, solely, that it dampens down experimentation. It is that it expends energy of a negative kind. The problem with the media is not, or only trivially, what it contains, but what it does not. What the eye cannot see, the heart does not grieve over: but it should. It is all those things – information, ideas, arguments, scandals, causes – that are *not* brought to the attention of the public that ought to be the focus of our concern, not the tedious violence or boring soft pornography or (from the government's point of view) the transitory embarrassment caused by a leaked story. A positive approach for the 1990s would be to look for ways to preserve and nurture what is good in the media, and waste little time on what is bad.

The really bad – the dull, bland and repetitive, rather than the outrageous – will always be there. The serious danger in the next decade is that, in the new technologically advanced environment, the good will find it impossible to thrive. Commercial television, hitherto, has produced great benefits. However, the underlying principle of all commercial broadcasting – that its primary concern is not the production of programmes but the production (or capture) of audiences of the right size, class, age and region to satisfy the advertisers who pay the bills – could have devastating effects in multi-channel conditions. There is certainly no reason to suppose that the abandonment of the public service ethic which has hitherto played a role in independent broadcasting, and its substitution by the laws of the economic jungle, will encourage a diversity of choice: what is far more likely is a competitive downward spiral towards the lowest common denominator. It is nonsensical to attack 'interference' as though it must amount to Stalinism. The need for interference to prevent a tragic degeneration of the media is as vital as, say, the need for interference in an urban road scheme: in neither case can a reliance on the rough-and-tumble of competing financial interests result in anything but chaotic failure.

Indeed, we are faced with the classic distinction – in Isaiah Berlin's terms – between 'freedom from' and 'freedom to'. The present government has (in theory) emphasised freedom from outside control while (in practice) seeking at every turn to restrict and control aspects of the media it does not like. The alternative approach is to perceive that the media *cannot* be free if they are left alone, except in the capitalist's sense of free to make money.

Changing of the Guard

What ought the media to be like? We have already sought partially to answer that question. Let us repeat and extend our description of the ideal. Few would care openly to dispute that the media should – at the least – provide wide-ranging and detailed information about recent events throughout the world, together with a variety of commentaries upon them; that it should give expression to the major concerns of the public; and that it should allow the public to see itself, as accurately as possible, as it really is. In the 1980s, the concept of 'society' (so we are told) went out of fashion. Yet the media has always been a peculiarly binding social force. In totalitarian regimes it is the key instrument of a unifying oppression; in democracies, it helps to provide a national and social identity. Media coverage of state rituals and major constitutional events – from royal marriages to general elections – helps people to define themselves. In addition, it is the media which helps to bring people together in fear, anger or grief at times of national trauma – the disasters, accidents, wars, crimes, epidemics in the history of any nation. Finally, the media provides the means by which a nation judges itself and its own members.

To inform, to discuss, to describe, to mirror, to bind, to campaign and to judge – these are the most important functions of the media in any free country. The purpose of reform should be to enable the media to perform them more effectively: that and no more and no less. It is a sufficiently ambitious aim, and it must take precedence over every other consideration – including anxieties about the supposed danger of intervention, and the political and moral fastidiousness of Aunt Tabitha.

If we are clear that the purpose of reform is so simple, then the solution becomes apparent. We should concentrate on positive incentive, not negative control. We should concern ourselves less with the highbrow (or, alternatively, the degraded) minorities with their specialised tastes, who can usually look after themselves, and more with the high proportion of the public who take what they are given. We should ensure that the newspapers with the largest circulations, the television and radio channels with the largest audiences, meet independently assessed standards in some of what they sell – while cheerfully permitting as wide a range of nonsense and banality as they may wish to disseminate in order to maintain their profit margins.

The well-educated – the *Guardian, Independent, Times* and *Telegraph* readers – set the agenda and will continue to do so. We need not worry unduly about them. But it is the purchasers of the *Sun*, *Mirror*, *Star* and *Sport* who provide the bulk of voters, the labour force, members of the armed forces, juries, strikers during industrial disputes and crowds at the Changing of the Guard. When we speak of democracy, it is their political and social role we have in mind, and it is to them that we need to turn our attention: their reading, listening and viewing habits and opportunities.

That it is *possible* to inject standards of excellence into a patronisingly dreadful means of communication like the British tabloid press is, to some extent, demonstrated by the tabloids themselves: the *Daily Mirror* has long had redeeming features, and so have the supposedly middle-market *Express*, *Mail* and *Today*. It is most convincingly proved by the most 'mass' medium of all, television, whose four earthbound channels manage to combine, in varying cocktails, but each to a still high level of refinement, the best elements of the *Observer* with the most condescending aspects of the *News of the World*. Television in the eighties has suffered but it is not yet supine: why the erosion of standards is so tragic is that, hitherto, television has uniquely retained its capacity to provide a quality-newspaper product – in drama and cultural critique as well as news and current affairs – to a huge, not entirely captive, tabloid audience. That millions of *Sun* and *Star* readers would recognise Muriel Grey or Peter Sissons in the street is a clue to what might be obtainable. It cannot be proved that the nation's health is improved because 2.5 million teenagers and pensioners do not automatically switch over from the *Media Show* or *Question Time* to *Dallas*. But it is hard to believe that it is not.

Let us therefore now unveil, not another principle, but a specific policy, tailor-made for the expansive, socially conscious, unstuffy, visionary 1990s. In the new age of newspaper and television proliferation, any channel, paper or magazine which reaches a very wide public – determined by independently audited readership or audience ratings – will have to accept, and be seen to operate, a reasonably strict code of political and cultural conduct: if it becomes even more popular, then the requirements made of it will become still more elevated, inspiring and onerous. Thus a high circulation or high audience enterprise will become both beneficiary and victim of its own success. As it passes a series of thresholds, the pressure will be on it not – as at present – to become worse, but to become better.

The traditional socialist approach to huge profits easily or exploitatively acquired was to seize them. Under the new dispensation of the post-traditionalist 1990s, owners, producers and editors will be invited, instead, to plough part of their profits back into their product, in order to make it more estimable. The intended consequence will be a media which (as is already the case in commercial television) links financial gain with quality and ensures that seriousness and populism live happily side by side; and which also discourages the apartheid between well-educated quality consumers and the mass market that is such a striking, and unhealthy, aspect of the newspaper press today.

Ideally, the media organisations will draw up such a code themselves: much as they have voluntarily adopted a code of practice over invasions of privacy. Whether this is possible or not, the content of such a document, which must be carefully and realistically drafted, is bound to be controversial. Certainly it should take care to avoid any political bias. It will need to specify quite closely the basic political ground to be covered, and the amount of space or air time to be devoted to it; it will have to insist on adequate opportunities for the expression of rival points of view, and by different sections of the community; and it will need to ensure provision for genuine reader, viewer and listener feedback. The rules must be firm, clear and legally enforceable by a small council or tribunal armed with sanctions. It is important to note, however, that punishments will be meted out for *failing to include* quality material. There will be no interference with the media merchants' legitimate business of making money by filling the majority of their pages, or hours, with whatever they wish. In short, there will be no censorship, direct or indirect.

Let us imagine (in the case of newspapers) a first ratchet at a million audited readers. A publication with 995,000 readers need do nothing but publish pictures and stories about sportsmen and pop stars to sustain its circulation, if it chooses. If, however, its tactics result in an increased circulation, then it faces a choice: either to ensure that its sales drop back below the threshold, or to balance its populism with material which may not offer the most obvious cash benefit, but which takes its obligations to the public more seriously.

In the very big league of multi-million circulation papers, only those prepared to take their informing, debating and teaching duties very seriously indeed will be allowed to compete. Yet throughout the range, there will be no attempt at all to tone down or cut (except as a proportion of the total) what makes a paper popular. The effect will be a social compact: high-selling papers will pay for their influence, actual or potential, over a widening section of the public with an appropriately widening recognition of their responsibilities. Much the same principle will apply to radio and to television where, at present, the system of franchising means that something like it is already in operation, but where deregulation and the consequences of the cable/satellite revolution will soon put the maintenance of standards in jeopardy.

Such a system, of course, has little in common with the 'Right of Reply' demands of the Left in the 1970s. The Right of Reply campaign was an understandable response to misrepresentations in the press; it was led by journalists and trades unionists who had been particularly angered by distorted accounts of industrial disputes. Yet the tit-for-tat theory on which the campaign was based – editors should pay for attacking a group of workers by having to publish the comments of the workers themselves – had little bearing on the real-world influence of papers on casual readers. Even when (as sometimes happened) editors *did* grudgingly publish a union response, they felt no incentive to do more than merely print it.

Zippy

The new, enabling media code will be both far more sweeping in its scope than anything envisaged by the Right of Reply campaigners, and also far more encouraging. Because a popular enterprise will recognise that it must offer quality for as long as it remains popular, there will be an incentive to make the 'duty' element a palatable part of the product. Editors may soon begin to take pride in their quality content, even to wear it (as commercial television does at present) as a badge of honour. It may not be fanciful to imagine a time when people buy the *Sun* because of its parliamentary coverage or books page, rather than in spite of them.

Like all revolutionary plans, this one is beset with difficulties. One is the problem of border zones: how do you treat a paper or channel that hovers on the brink of a threshold, bobbing sometimes above, and sinking sometimes below it? There is also the likelihood that some editors will simply go for the cheapest possible option consistent with the rules, making no effort, for example, to recruit suitable 'quality' staff. It will certainly be hard, and probably unwise, for a media council to act as judge of the quality of quality, except in very broad terms. There is the sticky problem of what sanctions to impose: should suspension or closure be the ultimate deterrent? Fines will have to be large to be seen as more than a form of profits tax.

None of these difficulties, however, should be insuperable – or need prevent the creation of a climate in which 'quality' becomes an integral part of all the popular media. None need obstruct the key aim, which is to be on the side of journalists and the public alike, to embolden and never to suppress. The introduction of the code should be accompanied by a lightening of wider legal and governmental restraints on publication. Meanwhile, there will be no persecution of small or medium-sized groups. Minorities below the lowest threshold – pigeon-fanciers, fashion fanatics, tit-and-bum enthusiasts or whatever – will be able to consume as unleavened a diet, within their own publication or channel, as their supplier chooses to offer them.

Will the code squeeze profits, and so end up as Aunt Tabitha in disguise, by pushing some publications out of the market? The risk seems small. When only unleaded petrol is permitted to be sold, no oil company will suffer. Similarly, once all popular newspapers start to carry regular quality features, there will be no reason why any of them should lose circulation, and the extra cost will be minimal. 'Quality', however, will be injected into the inter-tabloid market, and the *Sun* will have to ensure that its 'quality' features are as zippy as those of the *Star*. In the case of television, it has been 'quality' programmes that have sold best abroad. Thus, a measure that helps to nurture home-grown quality and to discourage cheap, low-grade imports, will do the industry a good turn and help the balance of payments.

There is much to be worked out. Defining 'quality', like defining 'public service', is a philosopher's nightmare. Everyone, however, knows the difference between quality and the opposite. And the purpose of the code, in seeking to inject quality into the popular media, will be to recognise and reinforce the centrality of the media in our national life: as the arena in which citizen addresses citizen, in which standards in art, literature and music are established, in which values are set, and in which the whole of our democratic life is enacted.

For Aunt Tabitha, the media is at best a circus, at worst an agitator. In the 1990s, we hopefully predict, Tabithism will be out of style. Let our alternative be to believe in, celebrate and develop the British media as the most free and ambitious – as well as the best – in the world.

'Ladies and Gentlemen'

MICHAEL ROSEN

'Ladies and gentlemen, Secretary of State, thank you for attending this conference: "Conservatives in Education: What Next?" I speak as an employer of many thousands of people and as an observer of change in our society over many years. Now, I know that one way to make myself popular in present company would be to tell you how the school-leavers coming into our industry now are less able to read, write or do mathematical calculation. I could also make myself popular by blaming teachers for this sorry state of affairs. To do all this, I fear, would be to miss the point. Let's be honest about it: schools never equipped our people for jobs. When we take on school-leavers we don't expect them to know the ropes from day one. Nor do we when we take on graduates. Industry has always had to train its new arrivals. When it comes to all this whingeing about reading and writing and maths, well I have to say I don't take it too seriously. We are never actually short of people who can read and write at the levels we require and anyway new technology has replaced many of the snag points of presentation and spelling and the like. I for one am quite prepared to put my hand on my heart and admit that I was never too hot on the writing front myself. I soon learnt that what I couldn't do myself could be done by someone else.

'So, am I saying that schools have been doing fine and really we have nothing to worry about? Nothing of the sort. It is just that I have another tale to tell. Think of it from my point of view. Every year, a number of my employees retire, a number of new employees arrive fresh from education. Every year a number of my managers retire and a number of new managers arrive mostly fresh from a work situation. Now, do these two kinds of newcomers fit the bill? The managers, mostly yes. We have a well-qualified personnel department in touch with the most modern American methods. Our managers need to be leaders, initiators, planners. The combination of school, higher education and experience seems to equip sufficient numbers of people able to do the job. The problems arise in the lower grades.

[149]

'Here we are not looking for people with management skills. We need people who are reliable, turn up to work on time, do what they're told, work hard, work extra hours when we're in a fix, see things the company way, are flexible about changes in work practice, are not too demanding on conditions at work and don't have unrealistic expectations in the way of remuneration.

'Now comes the basic educational question: have schools been giving us employees like this? I don't think so. I don't even think schools were addressing these basic requirements. I've seen schools spending hours and hours on "creativity", "discovery", "research", "questioning evidence", and the like. In heavens name, I ask, what use is this going to be to us as employers of these people? My employees don't need to be "creative", they're not there to "discover" things and they're most certainly not in the business of "questioning" what's going on.

'Now, I must say I'm very much in favour of the National Curriculum. Here at long last we have the possibility of an educational practice that mirrors work practice. Pupils will proceed in school right from the very start along the lines we operate with in industry: specific jobs required by management, done to order, within a time limit, followed by regular quality control and assessment. Abolished at a stroke is all that undirected business of teachers (or worse, children) inventing their own courses and topics. But even as I say these things I can hear very reasonable interjections from people: how will we train those people in our society who *do* need to be creative, make discoveries and question things? Well, it really is quite simple: these kinds of children won't go to the schools where the National Curriculum is compulsory. Independent, preparatory, private and public schools will expand just enough to take on all the children industry will need as adults to perform these more demanding functions of management and leadership.

'It should soon be quite clear to parents what different kinds of school are available for which kinds of end-product. You see, the major problem in the past was not "lowering of standards" and the like, as some of my Conservative colleagues have said. It has been that the process of education has been blurred. It is as if we had two production outputs but the two production lines kept getting muddled up. Pupils on production line "A" (for employees) kept getting treated as if they were heading for production output "B" (for managers). People coming into my industry as employees have not so much been *under*-educated as *wrongly* educated or often even *over*-educated. We can't have secretaries full of fancy ideas in their heads from reading intellectual literature. We can't have fitters full of ideas from GCSE sociology. Or the whole production system will go down the pan.

'In industry everyone has their place in a process: if someone on the line suddenly thinks he'd like to read a Shakespeare play or have a game of cards half an hour before his lunch break, he'd better forget it. At the same time we can't have children in schools spending hours of their time involved in what the educational establishment call "collaborative work". What sort of expectations do they think they inculcate with such methods? Obviously – collaborative ones. Well, I'm all in favour of collaboration at work but not that kind. I need employees collaborating with management so that what needs to be done, gets done. I need employees working alongside each other, not collaborating with each other. If that started happening, I might just as well pack my bags and go home.

'Of course you can look at it all another way and say we can't allow the children we need to have as secretaries and fitters doing all that fancy stuff when they're at school or I'll never get enough secretaries and fitters – they just won't want to do the job. You see, the major problem of education has never been: are we educating them enough? The main question is: will I have enough people prepared to come in at 8.30, five days a week for forty years, and do what they're told? When schools can tell me yes, yes, and yes again, we've got state schools worth getting excited about. You can leave all the fancy stuff, as I call it, to the private sector and our own work experience.

'So what am I saying here? I am congratulating the government's progress on the National Curriculum and testing. I am applauding the way in which market forces are creating an expansion of the private sector in education, so enabling the selection process to begin long before GCSEs at the age of sixteen. But I am offering up a cautionary note: our colleagues in the Department of Education and Science should worry less about exactly *what* the children are learning and think more carefully about *how*. At school the basic attitude to work-practice is laid down. It is there that a child will learn to respect or reject authority, it is there that a child will learn to accept or reject a set task, it is there that a child will learn time-keeping or absenteeism. And it is at school that a child will learn whether it is better to do the job himself or look to his mates for support. It is my experience that these are the basic alternatives. It is almost as if I could draw up two columns: in the one is the child who respects authority, accepts the set task, keeps good time and does the job himself, and in the other is the one rejecting authority, rejecting the set tasks, not turning up, and looking to his mates for support. It makes for two very different pictures. I don't think there can be a person who does not know which of the two he prefers. That is why we need to say very clearly; give us the educational system that will deliver accepters and not rejecters. That way we all know where we are. Here's to the nineties. Thank you.'

A New Internationalism

KEN BOOTH

History did not come to an end at the close of the 1980s, as was fashionably asserted in right-wing US circles. It went into fast forward. But Britain stands still. The official mind, traditionally nostalgic and discomforted by change, seems reluctant to think systematically about the future, or make decisive choices. Old habits of caution, incremental-ism and pragmatism are in the bloodstream and have brought on a 'hardening of the categories' which is unhealthy as we move into a new era. If Britain continues to do this, refusing to consider and adopt new thinking and policies, it will become an increasingly irrelevant factor in the international relations of the 1990s.

Trends and Transformation

The 1980s opened with yet another round of East–West tension, but closed with the breaking beyond repair of the mould that had shaped world affairs for over 40 years. 1989 became instant history as yester-day's unthinkable possibility became the next day's headline. Some of the major features of the postwar world changed overnight. A demo-cratic non-communist government was installed in Poland. The Iron Curtain was taken down in Hungary and Czechoslovakia and pluralism established. Direct elections were held in Moscow, and the Kremlin rejected the Brezhnev doctrine. Arms reduction talks made progress, after years of failure, in Vienna and Geneva. The West began to reciprocate in disarmament and economic assistance to the develop-ments in the East. Finally, the groundswell of popular discontent in Eastern Europe undermined or overthrew the communist rulers in the GDR, Bulgaria, Czechoslovakia and Romania. The breaching of the Berlin Wall was the universal symbol of the end of the first postwar era. It happened at a rate nobody had forecast, or could easily comprehend. It was naturally accompanied by much optimism, but also anxiety.

Would the Cold War order simply be replaced by new (or rather pre-1939) instabilities? Although the events in Europe were the most dramatic, they were only part of a pattern of change which had been altering the structures and processes of international relations for some years. Together, these trends will help shape the landscape of the 1990s, though its structures and even some of its players can now only be guessed at. What is predictable is that the post-postwar era will be neither static nor quiet.

The end of the Cold War. The Cold War helped define the first postwar era. Its structures and mindsets still survive, but its rationale has disappeared. The latter does not rule out temporary aberrant reactions.

The decline of bipolarity. The superpowers, especially the Soviet Union, have lost their former pre-eminence. Their international influence has declined, and with it the regimentation of their allies and associates. Their authority is overstretched even in their own geopolitical backyards.

The collapse of communism. Through the 1980s the countries of the Warsaw Treaty Organisation ran out of steam in everything except military power. Their command economies did not meet the material challenge, their political systems lacked legitimacy, and their ideology lost appeal.

The rise of new powers. Power in world affairs is becoming diffused. As the superpowers have become more normalised, so have new centres of economic and political power emerged. Japan and the FRG are economic superpowers, and commensurate political status cannot long be avoided, while 1992 promises to confirm the European Community's political as well as economic maturing.

The changing map of Europe. As Stalinism is replaced in Eastern Europe and integration proceeds in the West, the postwar division of Europe is being replaced by a more fluid map which will involve a reduced role for the superpowers, the disappearance or transformation of the alliances, the rise of new pan-European structures, and changing political and economic associations. Boundary changes are possible, including the unification of the two Germanies and the redefining of the Soviet Union.

The new significance of non-state actors. A notable feature of the 1980s was the increasingly influential role of non-state actors in determining national and international agendas. Peace organisations, opposition movements, refugees, environmental activists and ethnic groups had remarkable significance. Multinational corporations and financial organisations globalised economic activity while being relatively immune from the control of governments. Alliances and economic institutions constrained national governments. States, while still the main actors in international politics, have less independence.

The growth of interdependence. A steadily growing density of interaction between the world's economic, political, social and military actors has produced a web of complex interdependence. This creates both new strains and new possibilities by increasing mutual dependency and limiting national independence.

The declining significance of military power. Military power is not unimportant, but the decreasing political leverage of the muscle-bound superpowers underlined the increasingly restricted useability of military force, the growing economic liability of big defence spending, the irrelevance of nuclear overkill and the limited utility of large-scale projection forces.

The changing security challenge. The amelioration of the superpower relationship has reduced but not eliminated the risk of nuclear war. Dangers exist of nuclear proliferation or of a reversal of superpower trends. The reduced risk of East–West conflict has made clearer the extent to which the daily lives of people in the West are threatened by drugs, terrorism, refugees and the spread of modern weaponry to the Third World.

The changing international political economy. As the internationalisation of the world economy develops, power and status in world affairs is increasingly determined by economic success. A significant shift has been taking place in the balance of world trade towards the Pacific Basin. Although capitalism buried Stalinism, it creates casualties both at home and in the Third World.

The accelerating technological revolution. As a result of innovations in electronics and communication systems, the evolution of world society proceeds apace. This will have profound implications; multi-dimensional transparency will improve the prospects for international security, while the growth in productivity at lower employment levels may have disturbing socio-economic consequences.

The crisis of development in the Third World. Burdened by debt, environmental problems, ineffective administrative structures, ethnic divisions, and weak economies, the systems of many Third World countries are overloaded. The result will be further poverty, economic and political instability, social dislocation, and the ever-present possibility of violence.

The increased salience of environmental issues. The degradation of the physical environment is global. There is a growing consciousness of the inter-connectedness of the issues, but neither the problems nor the solutions can be national. The solutions must also be long-term, since they involve such basic issues as population growth, economic management, and the global maldistribution of wealth. The fundamental problem, exacerbating all others, is that of a world with too many people.

These overlapping trends are shaping the international landscape; old power structures will disappear, new associations will arise, complex interdependence will evolve and the post-postwar era will develop its own character. Whether it turns out to be a more or less secure era will depend on the way governments and peoples respond to the challenges. The prospects are mixed, though in the aftermath of the breaching of the Berlin Wall and the settling of several long-running wars in the Third World, it is difficult not to have more optimism than for many years. But there remain many morbid symptoms, threatening turmoil. In this momentous era in which we are now living, making a virtue of immobilism (draped in the banner of 'stability') is calculated to ensure that the Thatcher Government will be left behind by the flow of events, isolated, and decreasingly able to shape the future.

New Thinking for Old

The Iron Curtain not only divided two blocs, it also imprisoned each of them. This was most obviously the case in Eastern Europe, but the West was also behind the wire, psychologically speaking. The Iron Curtain helped detain old thinking about the game of nations and domestic politics; it legitimised static analyses and prescriptions, and discouraged alternative ideas about domestic society and international security. Reason gave way to loyalty tests. But as the Iron Curtain is dismantled materially and in the mind, we in Britain have also a new opportunity to be liberated. We have a better opportunity to see who we are, where we stand on the political map, and what are our potentialities as a medium-sized country on the western edge of Europe. So far, since no British Gorbachev has emerged to challenge society's old thinking, the impetus must come from below. There have been stirrings: in the early 1980s the peace movement helped raise the level of debate about security, while later Charter 88 helped stimulate ideas about domestic reform. A critical mass of alternative thinking has yet to form.

Old thinking about international relations is rooted in such regressive mindsets as ethnocentrism, the doctrine of political realism, ideological fundamentalism and strategic reductionism. Together, these have had a deleterious effect on international relations, resulting in narrow nationalism, pessimistic interpretations of history, the comprehending of international politics in crude power terms, the stressing of basic ideological beliefs, and the tendency to reduce relations betwen states merely to issues of military balance. In Britain such old thinking is characterised by Little Englandism, outworn notions about the role of the state and the nature of sovereignty, an exaggerated view of the success of British foreign policy, a reluctance to abandon the idea of Britain as a major power, a commitment in principle to the idea of a so-called independent nuclear deterrent, negative attitudes to Western European political integration, half-hearted commitment to international institutions, an exaggerated significance given to the 'special relationship' with the United States, an unwillingness to change what are thought to be winning ways in military policy, the expectation of new troubles to rise (German or East European nationalism) just as others (the Soviet threat) are falling, an unwillingness to think systematically about the long-term future, and neglect of the domestic and social dimension of foreign and defence policy. It is a static and self-fulfilling approach.

Much influential thinking in Britain is in the grip of such ideas. A Cold War mindset evolved which constrained the growth of creative forces. That the imprisonment of the West was never so blatant as the East, together with the belief that the collapse of communism was the result of Western rather than local efforts, will make it more difficult to bring about changes in attitude. Bulldog nationalism, Cold Warism, pro-nuclearism and exaggerated Atlanticism have been flaunted by Margaret Thatcher, but such attitudes are not confined to the Prime Minister or her party. Nevertheless a growing body of opinion rejects old thinking, and some officials are not as hostile to new ideas as they were. Unfortunately, individuals and groups in powerful positions have a stake and an expertise in the old ways at just the time when change is needed quickly. Old thinking – static, mechanistic and self-fulfilling – is not capable of comprehending and dealing with a momentous era. The future will be demanding in policy terms and will require different attitudes and skills to those displayed in the past.

The phrase 'new political thinking' was coined and given prominence by Gorbachev, and he has proved a remarkable exponent of ideas which in the early 1980s were developing behind the scenes in Moscow, as well as on the streets of the West. The latter fertilised the former. It was never, as was crudely asserted during the period of High Heseltinism, that the peace movement was the dupe (or worse) of the KGB; actually Western alternative security ideas invaded the Politburo, and so helped shape today's agenda. Nor is today's new thinking simply the old 'utopianism' discredited in the interwar years. It is the realism of the present, offering a more accurate analysis of Britain's potential and a more dynamic interpretation of the forces of change.

The central notion of new thinking about international relations is 'common security', the idea that safety in the nuclear age can only be worked out by mutual co-operation. This is related to the problem of the 'security dilemma', whereby what one state does to try to improve its security through military preparation often appears to be threatening to others, and so stimulates mistrust and arms competition. The idea of moving towards more obviously defensive military postures (non-provocative defence) has been developed to combat it, together with emphasising stabilising arms reductions and crisis prevention schemes. At the root of common security is the appreciation that security is more a political than a military phenomenon.

New thinking adopts a world society perspective rather than that of the nation state. It is not ethnocentric or ideologically fundamentalist. This does not mean the sacrificing of national interests to some vague notion of humanity, but does involve the realisation that the interests of single nations can only be furthered by taking a global view of the human interest. This is most clearly seen in ecological issues, which are increasingly part of the security problematique. New thinking requires that what has been called a 'holistic' view of security be adopted. 'National security' in the old military sense is only one dimension. Due priority should be given to the security of the international system as a whole (avoiding nuclear proliferation is more important than building symbols of national nuclear independence) and to individual security (the threat from the arms race itself is more significant than that from the Soviet Union). The security of people as well as states needs attention, and in this regard there should be more sensitivity to domestic issues.

New thinking, above all, is forward looking. It seeks to establish feasible goals and benevolent processes that enhance security not by the amassing of weaponry – peace through fear – but towards what Kenneth Boulding has called 'stable peace', namely peace based on political accommodation. In contrast to the operational assumption of old thinking – that this is the best of all possible worlds, and that nothing can go catastrophically wrong – new thinking recognises the risks but believes that if we change the rules and institutions of international relations we can over time change the way states and peoples behave towards each other. This involves being able to imagine that there is a more satisfactory future than the old war system, then identifying the steps needed to achieve it, choosing priorities, and mobilising political support to further the process. British thinking is lagging behind much of Europe; the tone of the debate on the Continent sounds quite different. Britain's international image, as personified by Mrs Thatcher, is increasingly anachronistic, a piece of flotsam from the unmourned Reagan years.

Old categories die hard, and the major differences today are not between 'East' and 'West' – which are increasingly geographical rather than political expressions – but between old and new thinkers in different countries. As world society evolves, those states that do not attempt to be part of the solution will increasingly become part of the problem; this is the role the present British Government seems bent on playing.

Bottom of a Shopping Bag

The aim of British external policy is to exert whatever influence it can to create a world in which society-wide interests can flourish, namely peace and security, economic development, environmental protection, and democracy and human rights. It is equally obvious that Britain lacks the clout to shape significant change independently. It must make definite choices and seek to exert its influence through international associations.

The key relationship for Britain is with its partners in the EC and, in the longer-term, with the other countries of Europe. Britain must finally decide whether it is 'European' and, if it is, must act accordingly. In the past no British Government has found it easy to reconcile itself with an essentially 'European' role. For the most part Europe has meant a common market, an economic convenience, rather than a grand idea. While such attitudes persist, Britain will continue to fail the test of being a 'good European', and so will play a less than full role in shaping the answers to fundamental questions about the future character of the EC, its eventual size, and its relationship with the rest of the world.

This is a decisive time in the history of Europe. The regeneration of European idealism in the West, the commercial challenge from East Asia and the United States, the decline of US hegemony, the virtual disappearance of the Soviet threat, the collapse of Stalinism in East Europe – together these require a fundamental reconsideration of the EC. Political factors are now piling on economic considerations in the shaping of the next stage of the Community's development. Necessity and ideals are driving Europe forward.

The need for the single market arose from the pressures of the international economy, and particularly the challenge expected from the industries of the Far East and North America. To meet the challenge, most EC governments believed it was necessary to move to full economic and monetary union. Then, with the collapse of the communist regimes and the growing prospect of the unification of the Germanies, the response of most EC members was to press on to deepen the Community, to provide an element of stability within the change, and for it then to act as a magnet for the reforming countries. It is not only believed to be possible to deepen the Community at the same time as widening its associates, it is believed to be essential: if the 12 are not to be diluted they must be strengthened, and the EC is the most promising foundation on which to build pan-European structures.

Even conservative EC governments accept that man cannot live by market forces alone. A growing consensus recognises the need to fill in the 'democratic deficit' at the centre of the Community decision-making by, for example, strengthening the European Parliament. At the same time all EC governments, except Britain's, support the Social Charter of Workers' Rights, the idea that unless there is a net of guaranteed social rights, to spread the benefits accrued, then the single market after 1992 will only help those regions and groups which have infrastructural and other advantages and are already doing well.

Historically, being reluctant Europeans has been the British norm. Britain was slow to join the Community in the first place, and even after it did, its relationship was, in the words of Roy Jenkins, 'semi-detached'. At present, the Prime Minister objects to moving towards full monetary union, let alone federal union, on ideological and nationalistic grounds. Support is offered to limited (economic) integration, but Thatcher's criticisms of the European Monetary System and the Social Charter are red herrings, to distract attention from her opposition to the whole 'European' venture. If the Prime Minister's attitude to her neighbours is semi-detached, how co-operative a tenant can she be expected to be in a Common European Home? Not surprisingly the original Community members have been disappointed in Britain. They looked for qualities which the dismal Britain of the 1970s and 1980s was unable to deliver. In the 1980s, with Thatcher at her most combative, the British Government drew heavily on their goodwill. As they built modern democracies and efficient economies, Britain's institutions ossified and it ate its seedcorn.

Britain would benefit from becoming a 'good European'. Economically, it is important for Britain to be influentially involved in the next stages of integration, which will involve difficult technical issues.

Integration is proceeding towards monetary union and if Britain does not constructively participate, London might well lose its position as a centre of finance. Britain is no longer so powerful that it cannot be ignored. Support in Britain is growing for joining the Exchange Rate Mechanism on the grounds that it will lead to greater financial stability, a lower level of interest rates, and will be a useful counter-inflationary mechanism.

In terms of the social and democratic development of the EC, the Thatcher Government's opposition obstructs logical and desirable ideas supported not only by conservative EC governments but also by British public opinion. The Thatcher Government cannot reasonably criticise bureaucratic domination in Brussels and at the same time oppose ideas for democratisation, or support a barrier-free EC but oppose a net of social rights to spread the benefits.

Politically, the EC will be an increasingly important international actor and will move ahead regardless of Britain. Thus, by holding back we are in danger of repeating the mistakes of the past, when we joined late, and so lost the chance to influence the developing rules and institutions. All EC governments want to preserve their national identity, but they recognise the need to integrate their economic and political behaviour. As we move beyond the Cold War, Europeans in both former blocs want (and need) to take charge of their own affairs instead of being dominated by the superpowers, who may again, jointly or separately, want to interfere. Furthermore, the EC is bound to play a key part in the transition of the Eastern European countries and in providing a setting for the probable unification of the Germanies. If Britain continues to stand alone against the decisions of the rest, the latter will simply move ahead on their own, leaving Britain to adjust later, at a heavier price. This will be the cost of subsidising what is already largely an illusion of sovereignty. Except in its most legalistic sense, talk of British sovereignty is now an irrelevant distraction, or simply a device to manipulate domestic opinion with the image of Britannia holding back foreign influence. But the economic life of the Continent and the increasing Europeanisation of decision-making in Whitehall belies the images of sovereignty. The network of interdependence densifies each day. Britannia is Canute in drag.

After the heady days of 1989 it is easy to be carried away by 'Europhoria'. The evolution of the EC and the building of wider European structures will face many difficulties as the East undergoes the travails of transition, the superpowers withdraw and the two Germanies unite. In addition, old nationalisms, reactionary politics and sheer self-interest could flourish and create an unhealthy Europe. If Europe is seen simply from the bottom of a shopping bag, or through power-political lenses, the outcome could be a rather unpleasant fat cat's market, separating a rich West from an exploited East, and also one with a military identity. To avoid this, the single market should be followed by the expansion of the EC's democratic, social, regional, environmental and international potentials. An EC beckons which is stable, prosperous, socially just and democratic; which has an effective regional policy, is environmentally sensitive, and has an industrial R&D policy comparable with any elsewhere; and which, internationally, has a constructive approach to the development and the closer association of the countries of Eastern Europe, and is open to the needs of the Third World and the creation of a more just distribution of the world's wealth. In short, a democratic *sui generis* suprastate beckons, whose influence in international politics would be based on political and economic example rather than military muscle. The precise structures of this new Europe are not yet envisaged; for the moment it is more important to pursue benevolent processes pointing in the directions indicated. Britain's choices are clear; but before it can be expected to push for the progressive Europe just indicated it must first become a more modern and internationally-minded democracy itself. Foreign policy begins at home.

British policy towards its EC partners, as well as its overall posture in international relations, has been seriously misdirected by the illusions surrounding the 'special relationship' with the United States. For too long, British governments' flirting with the United States (personified by the Reagan–Thatcher 'chemistry') has distorted accurate assessments of Britain's position in the world and the rational development of foreign policy. As time has passed, the concrete results of the relationship have decreased, while the theatre has grown.

While the US–UK relationship undoubtedly has some unique cultural and historical reverberations, in hard political terms the only thing *special* about it, as time passed, has been its unequal character. The relationship was always more important to London than to Washington, for whom more important special relationships have grown. This, together with US nationalism and domestic preoccupations, the US shift of focus from Europe, and Britain's marginalisation in the EC, will result in Whitehall featuring even less prominently in US thinking. Meanwhile, the vaunted benefits of the relationship – intelligence and defence co-operation – will wither if the Soviet threat continues to recede and disarmament progresses. Progress in START will lead to superpower pressure on Britain to reduce or eliminate Trident. In any case, this 'rent-a-rocket' system is likely to be Britain's last 'independent' nuclear deterrent. The next system, if there is one, will not be operated alone but will be in partnership with one or more European partners. In either of these cases, a major rationale for paying the price (deference) for the 'special relationship' will disappear.

As the alleged bonuses of the US–UK relationship diminish, the costs, which successive British governments have tended to ignore, will become more apparent. These consist of the illusions which have distorted Britain's ideas about its military status – at a heavy cost to the economy – and the negative impact of the relationship on Britain's image with third parties. In Western Europe, the UK's identification with Washington has led them to distrust Britain's commitment to 'Europe'. More directly, mistakes have been made as a result of the perceived need to defer to Washington. In the first half of the 1980s the way the Thatcher Government followed or failed to oppose US policy on, *inter alia*, the UN Conference on the Law of the Sea, UNESCO, Star Wars and the bombing of Tripoli, led to the 'Reagan's poodle' tag. President Bush, when he finally acted on East–West issues, moved independently of London, but he did call in the 'special relationship' in order to get the Thatcher Government to rubber-stamp his intervention in Panama.

For the future, British governments need to normalise relations with the United States. This means using any special experience with Washington to help Western European–United States relations through a time of great difficulty, as the US hegemonial role decreases, trade competition grows, and the EC's political impact increases. Between the United States and Europe, Britain has Hobson's choice; the two are of entirely different value, and the disparity will grow. Any British government which still invests faith or political capital in the 'special relationship' will be disappointed. Rejecting the opportunities to be a good European in order to secure support for the increasingly irrelevant Trident will be a decreasingly bad bargain in the 1990s. As the shared experience of World War Two fades, as the pressures of the Cold War decrease, and as the Europeanisation of British life proceeds, the gaps between Britain and the United States will widen.

British governments, alongside the United States, played a major role in the girding of the West during the early Cold War. In the unpromising 1950s Britain took initiatives to relax tension. Then between the early 1960s and early 1980s Britain became less visible on East–West issues as other European states (notably the FRG) led the West's *Ostpolitik*. In the early 1980s the Thatcher Government followed the United States in the new Cold War, but in 1984 changed from 'Iron Lady' posturing to the more mediatory approach favoured by the Foreign Office. The change was capped by Mrs Thatcher's early comment that Gorbachev was somebody with whom we could do business. It looked as though Britain might take the lead as a new detente opened. But events moved too quickly for the British Government; this was the last time it was in touch. Britain is now the most anachronistic of Western governments on East–West issues. It was even overtaken in mid-1989 by the hitherto do-nothing Bush administration.

The early Thatcher–Gorbachev relationship proved a quickly wasting asset. Thatcher used Gorbachev largely for image-buttressing purposes, while Gorbachev employed Thatcher as a Trojan horse within the suspicious Reagan White House. Once the improvement in US–Soviet relations was underway, the Thatcher link grew less important. Equally, once Cold War concerns gave way to ideas of reconstruction across Europe, London was left behind, and Moscow looked to Bonn and Paris. The firms of other countries than Britain took the lead in making commercial agreements with the East. Some in the West could indeed do business, but the British Government seemed to lack a strategy, except for that of insisting on the maintenance, as long as possible, of the vestiges of the old order – NATO, nuclear deterrence and Atlanticism.

The unfulfilled potential of Anglo-Soviet relations was matched by the government's disappointing response to the other changes in Eastern Europe. Due welcome was given to the march to democracy, but the response fell victim to Thatcherite triumphalism, the inventing of a new reason for delaying EC integration, and the old British habit of willing the ends but not the means. While British defence spending increased as the threat dramatically collapsed, there was a failure to give full assistance to Poland, whose success in overcoming the first winter of transition would be crucial to future progress. Although it was understood that the new systems in Eastern Europe would all have a bumpy time, and that success would take at least a decade, the British Government would not countenance the massive injection of support implied in the notion of a 'Marshall Plan' for East Europe, although, as a moral equivalent to the Cold War, it had much to favour it. Lacking a grand strategy for Europe, comparable with that of a Common European Home, British policy has been reactive, negative and piecemeal at a time of tumbling change and historic possibilities.

London, more than other Western capitals, has found it difficult to think in pan-European terms and to conceive a new post-Cold War order. This difficulty is probably not unrelated to fear of Britain's lower significance in such a setting. The Cold War gave Britain status: peace promises decline. As the Common European Home is being built, what price an independent nuclear deterrent, 'the special relationship', the role of forward US bases, the possession of senior commands in NATO, or high defence spending? When the currency of power is becoming the power of currency (like the Deutschmark) rather than military innovation (like the Mark II Lance), what is the value of an economy with a decimated manufacturing sector, a low level of training, poor management and a persistent tendency to high inflation?

Gorbachev helped create opportunities for better East–West relations, but Britain's policy should not be dependent on his personality. It should arise out of the objective situation. While the Soviet Union and other WTO countries should be encouraged in their steps towards democracy, the liberalisation of their economies, the reduction of their military potential, and the extension of military *glasnost*, these should not be preconditions for increased trade, joint scientific research, investment, managerial and technological assistance, and extensive food and consumer aid. There is a considerable margin of safety when it comes to winding down the Cold War military confrontation, and some of the extensive resources from this should be diverted to reconstruction. But each Eastern European country should be allowed to determine its own system, and also allowed to make mistakes.

In order to live together successfully, Britain and its partners must not treat the Eastern states as being on probation or as defeated nations to be patronised or exploited. We must also recognise the difficulties they face and not expect behaviour we could not match ourselves (a Britain which has just marked twenty years of having troops on the streets in Ulster should be especially sympathetic if Moscow deploys its troops in the capitals of unruly republics). Only on the basis of equality can a pan-European order emerge. But having recognised that business could be done with the new Soviet Union, the Thatcher Government has never seemed sure what business actually to do. This was the case when the old structures were intact, but is even more so today. It has failed to transform the static theory of nuclear deterrence into a dynamic theory of coexistence.

Coexistence on a broader scale should be a theme of British policy towards the Third World. Along with the other industrialised nations Britain has a great deal to lose from turmoil there. Britain long since ceased to be a global power in a power-political sense, but it does have global interests. Although British trade is largely European in focus, it still has important markets elsewhere. These, as well as more directly financial interests, would suffer from instability and dislocation. Britain's former imperial role also creates problems. The Commonwealth connection and the implications of the ever more complex ethnic mix at home gives certain Third World issues a salience which they would otherwise lack. The positions taken by the British Government on such issues is important both for domestic politics and for relations with other countries.

In the Third World, as elsewhere, British influence can best be exerted through international bodies. But here the Prime Minister's pride in being out of step with the other 11 of the EC or the 48 of the Commonwealth is not diplomatically productive. Nor was the 'Reagan's poodle' reputation, given the Reagan administration's position on Third

World issues. The barometer of commitment to Third World matters is usually taken to be aid. Successive British governments failed to meet UN targets, but the situation in the 1980s has been worse. Aid declined relatively, but worst of all was the tone of the Thatcher Government encapsulated in the Prime Minister's 'hand-outs' comment in 1981. If the government seemed not to have understood the predicament of the people in Britain's own less advantaged regions, it is not surprising that Third World observers believed Britain to be unsympathetic. And it was not just words, as the litmus test of South Africa showed. Despite claims to the contrary, Britain's economic situation is never so bad that it cannot get worse, but a progressive government in the 1990s would seek to channel increased amounts of foreign aid to the Third World.

In addition to deep-seated development problems, which throw themselves on to the agenda in the form of refugees, famine and instability, the Third World contains dangerous trouble-spots. It is now even less acceptable than ever to see 'regional conflicts' in terms of an East–West confrontation. British governments have been slow to recognise this and occasionally the chickens come home to roost. This is now evident in South-East Asia, where British support of US policy on Vietnam's reconstruction and intervention in Kampuchea has contributed to two diplomatically embarrassing human tragedies: the Vietnamese boat people in Hong Kong and the re-emergence of the murderous Khmer Rouge. Several future British governments will be burdened by the detritus of Empire, in the shape of Hong Kong, the Falklands and, more indirectly, South Africa. These are problems time will solve, but how it is done will have an important impact on Britain's reputation. A progressive British government will work hard to encourage the UN to build upon recent improvements, and become a more effective instrument for peaceful security and development.

Britain needs to rethink its policies towards the Third World, and decide whether relative neglect, at least passive exploitation, and geopolitical priorities should take precedence over the calls of justice and development. There was, in the 1970s, an embryonic North–South 'dialogue'. That disappeared, but with the amelioration of the East–West conflict, the crisis of development and the growing significance of global (especially environmental) issues, it could and should revive. The keynote for the latter should be the idea of holistic security, that is, the security not simply of states (governments) but of the people who live in them. A more just world order will also be a more stable one. This means more attention to economic and environmental security; for many people in the Third World, their country's indebtedness is more a threat to a reasonable quality of life than are foreign armies. Even so, there are conventional security issues that need addressing. Of these, the pursuit of arms control to stop the further proliferation of ballistic missiles and chemical weapons is particularly important. Conflict reduction requires effective nation-building. Britain can make a contribution; the support given to charities suggests that there is a well of sympathy to be tapped in the British people. A deeper EC should not be a rich man's club. In North–South relations, as the Brandt Report argued, the good and the self-interested are synonymous.

Defence Without Offence

Even before the momentous events of 1989, when the image of a WTO land-grab westwards collapsed, there were strong military and political reasons for a sweeping review of Britain's defence roles and level of effort. But avoiding fundamental choices has become an art within the defence establishment over the years. Defence has usually been treated as an accounting problem, involving the balancing of variable resources to established commitments. It is a conservative and incremental approach, with choice being avoided as long as possible: 'equal misery' between missions and arms is preferred to defence reviews. One consequence of this has been that the defence establishment has not been sensitive to the changes taking place in the international environment and is ill-prepared to adapt. Having set its face so dismissively against such alternative ideas as 'common security' and 'defensive defence' in the early 1980s, it is having to swallow hard in order to contemplate them now they are on the international agenda. Few tears would be shed in parts of Whitehall if circumstances led to the revival of the familiar bipolar world.

British defence policy faces a choice between an old and a new agenda. The former simply consists of a search to update the old framework – a 'new' Atlanticism, a 'new' NATO, and a new rationale for nuclear deterrence. The new agenda, in contrast, seeks to adjust defence policy to the emerging trends discussed earlier. But even if British defence policy were adjusted to the new security agenda, it would take several years – perhaps a decade – to be completed. The new security agenda seeks to achieve common security. This involves recognising that security is more a political than a military phenomenon, pursuing a holistic conception of security, transforming the confrontation of two alliances into a network of pan-European security structures, bringing about minimum nuclear deterrence between the superpowers at the strategic level and of a nuclear-free Europe below that level, rejecting military intervention and any out-of-area activities for NATO, moving towards significant arms restraint, rejecting heavily pro-nuclear doctrines and deep-strike operations, vigorously pursuing nuclear non-proliferation, and adopting non-provocative defence postures. Britain's military roles, alliance relationships and procurement decisions should be determined in relation to the achievement of these objectives rather than attempting to squeeze everything into the old framework.

Ironically, as the Labour Party moved towards the centre in its defence thinking in the late 1980s, the times seemed to move leftwards towards some of the party's earlier more radical positions. Although the multilateral approach to disarmament was given a boost by the INF Treaty and progress in the START and CFE talks, the results have not so far been remarkable. The INF Treaty destroyed no warheads, while military planners have sought ways of compensating for the missiles destroyed. We should not expect too much from the multilateral negotiating process. Such forums are easily overstrained, and, if progress is delayed, risk being overtaken by the pace of the weapons developers and their supporters. Already we are probably expecting more from the formal talks than they can deliver.

This multilateral approach should not be ignored, but neither should unilateral tactics. The latter have been greatly vindicated since Gorbachev came to power and used them to show sceptical Westerners that he was serious about arms reduction. This encouraged a more accommodating Western approach. In the complex times ahead, reciprocal unilateral actions may well be more useful than overloading the multilateral processes and causing disappointment. A judicious mixture of both approaches is desirable. Logically Britain should keep open the option of the unilateral scrapping of Trident, since the weapon is immoral, costly, adds nothing to Britain's security and is increasingly irrelevant. However, the question of how to get rid of it is vexingly tied up with the issue of how to win an election, and if unilateralism is rejected on the latter grounds, the most sensible course is to limit Trident warheads to no more than are held in the Polaris fleet, insist on their earliest inclusion in START, and vigorously pursue coexistence, so that weapons of mass destruction become as irrelevant in British relations with the Soviet Union as they are in British relations with the FRG.

Balance-of-power policies are archetypal old thinking. One possibility being contemplated in official circles is of Anglo-French co-operation to 'balance' Germany. In order to meet what are seen as the threats of German unification and possible 'neutralism', officials have been thinking about deepening Britain's military relationship with France. Such an approach is anachronistic. In this post-Clauswitzian era, integration not balance of power is the answer; Britain should play no part in any policy leading Germany to think it is on its own against the rest. The FRG has been the most integrated country within the Community, and the way to deal with the German 'problem', whether united or not, whether neutral or not, is to build a community and then a pan-European framework to integrate whatever state the German people desire. Neutralism, in any case, will cease to have much meaning as the EC expands, the superpowers withdraw, and Eastern Europe ceases to be more than a geographical expression.

A stable security framework is important while the situation in Eastern Europe works itself out. Thus NATO and the WTO are useful until the picture is clearer, but then they can be disbanded and replaced by a network of pan-European collective security structures. During this interregnum what matters is not the existence of the alliances but their character. In particular, appropriate military steps should accompany the political changes that are taking place. If Western leaders want to be taken seriously in their claim that they want to move beyond the Cold War, their words and actions must be in accord, as must their foreign and defence policies. It is not only inconsistent but also potentially counterproductive to react to the changing scene in the East by insisting on 'steady-as-we-go' as the basis for our own military policy. By the end of 1989 even the Bush administration recognised this, and big cuts were foreseen. The British Government, in contrast, announced an increase in spending.

We cannot expect to have prolonged political detente without military detente. Political and military agendas must go hand-in-hand, or we will repeat the experience of the 1970s, when uncontrollable military innovation degraded political efforts at detente. Military detente is necessary, but will not make progress if we only tinker with Cold War postures. Fundamental military reform should take place; and there is no better concept for it than non-provocative defence. Instead of relying on offensive military doctrines which feed the fears of the adversary, states should seek to maintain a level of deterrence against aggression but do so in an overtly defensive fashion; by eschewing offensive capabilities it is expected that the arms race will be dampened, crisis stability increased, and arms reduction encouraged. Political stability will evolve and gradually there will be more security for all at less cost. Non-provocative defence should be the philosophy around which procurement, arms control and doctrinal innovation should be organised. Furthermore, resource pressures will squeeze defence in the 1990s, so the demanding requirements of high-tech offensive systems will be unsupportable. Equally, if CFE II moves to deep cuts, NATO's present posture will not be viable; indeed it will become increasingly provocative. The ragged posture of 'flexible response' will be characterised by stretched area defence and an over-emphasis on heavy armour, nuclear first use and high-tech deep-strike systems.

The choices in addressing defence policy are clear, between an old and new agenda. A progressive government in the 1990s, addressing the latter, can safely downgrade the military factor in security and direct new resources and human potential towards overcoming those problems obstructing the achievement of a more just international order.

Second Chance

The end of the Cold War frees British society of excuses for not doing better, both at home and abroad. International circumstances have opened up which offer definite alternatives. On all major issues we can choose old or new thinking, depending upon whether we believe the game of nations is unchanging, or whether we think the trends discussed earlier indicate the possibility of a significant break with the past. Unfortunately the recent British debate about foreign affairs has been both parochial and static. Inertia, Little Englandism, a cosy foreign policy establishment, vested interest in the status quo, an inexpert House of Commons, and largely pro-government newspapers have hindered the discussion of the desirable and feasible alternatives that exist. Furthermore, until there is a higher level of public education about international affairs we cannot know what the British people really think. We know how they vote, but that is not always the same thing. Parliament is little help: who goes to *Hansard* to be informed about the outside world? Without doubt, British society is the basic problem of British foreign policy. So, as we enter a new era marked by heartwarming developments and huge challenges, the British Government sings old tunes while our partners in Europe outperform us.

A people as pragmatic as the British will adapt in the end, but at a higher price and with less influence than is necessary. The chief priority is to create a more stable (and less costly) system of peace across Europe. It is possible to envisage this in a three-stage evolution. Through the 1990s we should learn to operationalise common security. In the following ten to fifteen years we can build the institutions of the Common European Home for the wider community of nations. If this is achieved, we can then look forward to an indefinite period of stable peace, in which peace exists not because of fear but because of common satisfaction with the prevailing situation. Such an outcome is not only desirable in itself but just might release some of our energies to deal with all the economic, social, environmental and other issues the future is bound to dump on us.

The future course of international relations is packed with uncertainties. In the 1990s British politics will be hounded by external events. But how the future evolves is partly in our hands. There is an important relationship between 'image' and 'reality' in all human affairs, including international relations. Having survived the Cold War, we now have the capability and the opportunity, working with others, to rebuild the postwar world; but first we need the imagination to believe we can. We must not fear either internationalism or big ideas: otherwise old thinking will drag us back into the vicious circle of the past. We have a second chance. With vision, patience and the mobilisation of people and resources we can take steps towards the achievement of significantly greater international security and social justice. Progress in internationalism could yet be the outcome of a bloody century of ideology and nationalism.

The Swinging Pendulum

JENNY DISKI

For the last thirty years or so I've been certain that the world was going to end sooner or later – sooner, I suspected – in a nuclear fireball. Suddenly, within weeks, it seems, the news is all good. Totalitarianism looks like it's going out of style; Thatcher's in deep trouble; people are demanding that governments listen to them.

So why is it that my heart, far from singing, stops with each new blow against the forces of repression? Middle age, perhaps: the world I've grown up with is familiar and if I don't like it, at least I know it for what it is. Perhaps it's because I just don't happen to be one of nature's optimists – a trick of brain chemistry more than a careful political analysis. Maybe I just don't know how to enjoy myself.

I'd prefer those things to be true, than to have to acknowledge the voice that keeps whispering 'History' into my ear. It reminds me, that voice, that the loosening of the grip of Cold War and confrontation politics depends on the continued political existence of a single man. And that the world becomes a much more dangerous place when once-strong men have to fight for their survival. The massacre of Tiananmen Square was a result of dithering, frightened men grabbing at previously unquestioned power that was slipping away from them. I wonder, too, what those who look towards the West and demand liberty are going to think when they examine us close-to. If it's the ideal of freedom that is compelling to the people of Eastern Europe, how will they judge the quality of life as they find it in the West? By quality, I mean quality of concern, of humanity; the way in which we consider ourselves responsible for those with lesser abilities or opportunities. Thatcher is not a totalitarian leader: she has been elected three times by free people who have expressed, until now, satisfaction with the material results of her government. And the present dissatisfaction with her is quite as materialistic.

The pendulum may be swinging, but I wonder if we can ever again even pretend that it is the best interests of others that we hold dear. Hobbes looks to me like the man of the century. Samuel Smiles, all has been forgiven. I miss the days, in the sixties, when, more or less hypocritically, we voiced concern for the wellbeing of others; when officials had at least to pretend that they minded if people were homeless, discouraged and in need of the community's support. Hypocrisy has the virtue of being something of a brake on the worst that humanity can do.

I miss the days when the thought of ousting Macmillan's Tories made the heart leap that something new and hopeful might happen. I miss my heart leaping, but, perhaps it's just that, in the sixties, I didn't yet know better. The best hope I can come up with is that I hope I'm wrong.

Oiling the Machine

PETER HENNESSY

Instruments of Power

Tony Benn has a nice, dry line about the Friday when new Labour governments take power. For the freshly-appointed ministers, he says, it often appears to be the day on which socialism has arrived. All it really means is that *they've* arrived.

The reasons for the illusion are easy to see. The tyro minister is instantly taken up by the civil service machine and, as it were, borne aloft until removed by the Prime Minister or the electorate, and then brought back to earth. It's a highly seductive business. No more queueing for buses or trains. The government car pool takes care of that. It's all red leather boxes, swish private offices and deferential civil servants from now on. It's much better than real life.

For the civil service is the great prize parties inherit when their tally of seats passes the magical 326 that Friday morning – a 600,000-strong direct-labour organisation, a remarkable mixture of skills which costs £15 billion a year just to keep in being before it does anything; plus another £160 billion or so in the public expenditure pot; plus the power to influence society, the economy and international relations through the richly obscure wording the parliamentary draftsmen (civil servants too) will help you put into statutory form.

The instruments of power are crucial to the prospects of any government. Yet rare is the opposition leader or shadow cabinet that gives the problem more than a cursory glance before the great day when they line up to 'kiss hands' with the queen. The working hypothesis is that it'll be all right on the Friday night.

This delusion is prone to produce two damaging side-effects. The first temptation is to succumb to the civil service embrace, those soothing ways, those beautifully phrased briefs. The second is to declare war from day one. Too many new ministers half-remember Arthur Henderson's famous dictum that it's the first 24 hours which determine who's the boss – the minister or the department. This can lead to some absurd

[175]

macho behaviour and the taking of awful, instant decisions for the sole purpose of showing who's in charge. No one is deceived by this apart from the new minister.

Such distraction can take another form – the conviction that the senior civil service is in the ideological pocket of the outgoing rival government. It's not just returning Labour administrations that succumb to this. Churchill in October 1951 peered into the private secretaries' room at Number 10 and growled, 'drenched with socialism'. He soon changed his mind.

Mrs Thatcher has given the *impression* of politicising the senior grades of Whitehall since 1979. I think it's no more than that. If Labour treat her alleged contamination of the civil service as reality and use it as an alibi for doing the same, it will not only be unjust to the individuals affected, but it will set the public service on a sure road to eventual decline.

This is not to say that incoming Labour ministers won't need some scope to arrange structures and people to fit their priorities. They will. It can, however, be done without applying political tests to the regulars of the career civil service, as I'll explain in a moment. Labour secretaries of state *will* need a different kind of personal back-up in their departments. It's an area to which careful pre-election thought should be given.

There are two other priority issues which deserve similar treatment: the quality of public services and the efficiency of their delivery to the public; and the need to raise civil service morale in circumstances where the claims on public expenditure are unlikely to allow for generous public service pay settlements. I shall tackle each priority in turn before finishing with a treatise on past mistakes which must be avoided in the 1990s.

Ministerial Back-Up

For once it is possible to get the best of both worlds – to maintain the virtues of a permanent civil service as a piece of transferable technology from one administration to the next (with the virtues of continuity, experience and relative disinterestedness of analysis and advice which that can bring), while creating a personal support structure for new ministers which genuinely enhances their capacity to turn round policy where it matters most to them and to the government's overall strategy.

The way to do it is to adapt the traditional Whitehall private office to the point where it resembles a Paris or a Brussels *cabinet*. Such a proposal was discussed, developed and costed by a small 'Reskilling

Government' group in the mid-1980s consisting of 'Whitehall watchers' of all parties and none, with the then general secretary of the top officials' union, the First Division Association (FDA), sitting in on meetings as a kind of informal consultant.

The three key paragraphs of its report in May 1986 could, I think, be adopted wholesale by the current opposition and presented to Sir Robin Butler, Head of the Home Civil Service, as soon as the 'Douglas-Home' rules permit Neil Kinnock to approach him with his machinery of government plans in the run-up to the next general election.

They read as follows:

Using the 12-year experience [now 14] of the Prime Minister's Downing Street Policy Unit, the 13-year life of the Central Policy Review Staff [the Cabinet Office 'Think Tank'] and the special adviser experiments conducted by successive governments since 1964, a new kind of Executive Office could be designed that would blend:

- traditional private office functions
- political appointees to help ministers with constituency and party work
- experts to advise the minister on key problems high on the departmental agenda (these can be drawn equally from young high-flyers within the civil service and from capable outsiders, whether politically sympathetic or not)
- analysts capable of policy research and development on long-term issues and with live links to outside research bodies

while between them, the members of an Executive Office should be capable of briefing the minister on important but not narrowly departmental issues which reach the Cabinet and Cabinet committee agenda.

No significant additional public expenditure would be required to fund such an innovation. Some six to eight people would be needed to staff such an enhanced private office at a cost of £350,000 per Cabinet minister, a total of £7.7 million (1985–86 prices).

Executive Offices of this type could be a standard feature of Whitehall life within days of a new administration taking office. Their establishment would need neither a statute nor a change in the Civil Service Order in Council, merely a parliamentary statement by the Prime Minister and a minute adjustment in departmental votes.

If a new Labour Prime Minister wished to revive the 'Think Tank' in some form – and he would be well advised to do so – the Executive Offices of his 21 Cabinet colleagues would plug as naturally into that circuit as they would into the Number 10 Downing Street Private Office and Policy Unit. All 25 or so outfits could, especially if Labour kept its pledge to pass a Freedom of Information Act, tap the thinking and output of external 'think tanks' such as the Policy Studies Institute, the Institute for Public Policy Research, the Royal Institute of International Affairs and the Royal Institute of Public Administration in a genuine two-way exchange that was not vitiated by secrecy legislation.

If a ring fence were put around these Executive Offices in the sense that 'political' appointments would only be made within their per-imeters, the remainder of the civil service could stay non-political. If a secretary of state with a particularly complicated policy programme wished to bring in expert outsiders, the Civil Service Commission (the non-political recruitment agency invented by Gladstone) could advertise and run a competition for temporary appointments at whatever senior level the minister felt the policy problem merited.

Service to the Public

This section may strike Labour people as heresy. It may be, but it's the truth. The Thatcher years *have* seen Whitehall departments paying a high degree of sustained attention to the better delivery of services to the public, which was as welcome as it was unexpected. Labour people may think the benefit changes malicious and mean, the notion of 'opting out' for schools and hospitals pernicious. But, such political judgements apart, financial and management systems have been put in place since 1979 which will strengthen the hand of Labour ministers whatever the level of state activity and public expenditure the new Cabinet may decide upon.

For example, the ministerial information systems pioneered by Michael Heseltine at the Department of the Environment and now standard across Whitehall will enable Labour ministers to implement their programmes with more than a fighting chance of deploying only that amount of public manpower and public money the projects require. Labour governments, above all, cannot afford to squander public resources. There is always a queue of much-needed public tasks for them to be spent upon.

Equally, the 'Next Steps' programme of hiving off large chunks of central government work into freestanding Executive Agencies with, by Whitehall standards, substantial devolved powers over recruitment, pay, promotion and methods of work, holds out the prospect of great benefits for an activist Labour government. As the all-party Treasury and Civil Service Select Committee has pointed out (with the enthusi-astic endorsement of its Labour members), improved service to the customer is the test by which the new agencies will succeed or fail. And it's the customers of the benefits system and the Employment Service that Labour is in business to protect. (A well-managed state should be – should always have been – a Labour priority.) In Sweden, where such agencies have been a standard feature of government for a generation, the returning Socialist administration in 1983 implemented an impressive programme of improved service to the state customer and better value for money for the taxpayer's kroner. There is nothing anti-socialist about public service efficiency. The aim should be to surpass the Thatcher administration in this respect while restoring benefits and state pensions to the levels required for a fair and equitable society.

Civil Service Morale

One of the intended spin-offs from the 'Next Steps' programme is improved morale across the counter in the benefit office or tax establishment. It's much needed. No government will do anything but lose by the kind of demotivated, unappreciated civil service that has existed (the verb is carefully chosen) in the 1980s. There is something perverse about a set of political values which places greed on a pedestal and decries public service as a motivation. On taking office, Labour could do more – much more – than merely putting an end to the notion that a public servant is a second-class citizen, if not a drone, even if big pay awards are out for the 600,000-strong civil service.

Three actions, all cost-free, could be taken at once and all three are sure-fire morale-raisers. The drum can be banged very loudly for public servants, their indispensability and the kind of impulses that motivate them. Trades union rights can be restored at the Government Communications Headquarters *at a stroke*. No law is needed. An instruction faxed to Cheltenham by the Foreign Secretary is all that's required.

Thirdly, the right of officials to be protected against illegal or improper political instructions could be recognised and entrenched by adopting the FDA's proposed code of ethics for the civil service and by presenting them to Parliament. With a right of appeal to an independent outsider – such as the Ombudsman – for a civil servant whose conscience conflicts with an instruction from a minister or a superior (once internal redress has been tried and failed), future Ponting affairs could be avoided. It is not a charter for 'whistleblowers' or for anti-socialist officials within Whitehall. It's the kind of protection people need in a profession which involves notions of serving the public and truth-telling to Parliament as well as working for ministers. A new Labour Prime Minister could have such a measure in place inside a week. He would appear as just as he was statesmanlike. It would not cost a penny. It would be worth doing if it cost a million. It should be done without hesitation.

Mistakes of the Past

The Attlee Government, Stafford Cripps apart, gave insufficient attention to the government machine it inherited. They had seen how well an outsider-enriched Whitehall had worked during the war when they served in the coalition. They failed to foresee the return to an inadequate business-as-usual once the gifted temporaries returned to their outside jobs after 1945.

Harold Wilson in 1963–64 gave the civil service too much attention of the wrong kind. Creating new ministries and rushing officials and furniture from one end of Whitehall to the other was a poor substitute for thinking what the machine was really for. The Fulton Committee on the Civil Service had much of value to say about the better management of government business, improved methods of policy-making and more open government. But Wilson had lost interest in the non-cosmetic aspects of Whitehall reform by the time he left office in 1970. The Wilson and Callaghan administrations of 1974–79 were too preoccupied by crisis management with a nil or a negligible majority to give such machinery of government matters serious attention.

History, however, has two hard lessons for would-be Prime Ministers. Those who enter Number 10 in difficult times and want to achieve demanding policy goals must give the instrument of government careful thought in advance and stick with it once they have arrived, however intrusive competing pressures. Above all Neil Kinnock must remember his fellow Welshman, David Lloyd George. When *he* took over in a mother-and-father of a crisis in the middle of a world war, his first acts were to create a War Cabinet, a Cabinet Secretariat to service it and a Prime Minister's Secretariat to service him. He had his priorities right. Machinery of government is too important a matter for the back of an envelope in the car between kissing hands at the palace and talking to the cameras outside Number 10. It is the instrument indispensable to the effective use of power. Lloyd George knew it and so did Aneurin Bevan when he arrived at the Ministry of Health in 1945 never having held office before. Let's hope their lineal successor knows it too.

POLITICS

The End of History

JOHN LLOYD

The End of History has had a bad press in the UK, but it's hard to see why. It seems a useful notion for our times as long as it's taken – as Fukuyama, its author, says he wished it to be taken – as a tongue-in-cheek metaphor.

It does not mean that a great many terrible and wonderful ideas and movements have ceased to exist, or will cease to exist. It does mean that none is presently visible which presents a challenge to a liberal polity married to free markets ('liberal' and 'free' are relative concepts: indeed, their relativity is what makes end-of-history politics) on a universal front. In so far as that is the core of the argument, it seems, as my colleague Edward Mortimer remarked in *Marxism Today*, almost obvious.

Much of the criticism has been directed at regretting the 'triumphalism' of the notion: triumphalism is of course impolite, but the vehemence with which Western commentators insist that communism is dead is pale beside that with which East European dissidents and indeed East European ex-communists or even 'reform communists' (pre-ex-communists) say it. At the 45th Congress of Comecon in Sofia in January, for example, Marian Calfa, the Czechoslovak Prime Minister and then a senior member of the Communist Party, said in so many words that 40 years of Soviet-imposed socialist planning had ruined his country's wealthy, technically advanced pre-war economy – which was of course a capitalist one.

So history, in the sense of a clash of universal ideologies, has ended, at least for the moment: it may start again sometime, but it is presently difficult to see how. Islamic fundamentalism, though dramatic in its ability to inspire loyalty and terrifying in its ability to legitimise oppression, does not offer a universal organising force, not least because it contains no prescription for economic organisation, as communism certainly – and initially successfully – did. Catholicism has in the past decade succeeded in throwing back Stalin's jibe about the Pope's lack of divisions in the teeth of his successors, but while it undergoes a renaissance in parts of Eastern Europe it decays in those countries where it has been freely practised for centuries.

Nationalism is by definition limited to each country, and even within them it now runs up against limits imposed by the internationalising force of liberal capitalism. For example, in so far as Yugoslavia wishes to become a market-driven, pluralist society, which its current government says it does, it will have to deal with the Serbian nationalism which, under the leadership of the Serbian President Slobodan Milosevic, alarmed not only the ethnic Albanians of Kosovo who were its focus, but the Croats and Slovenes who felt distaste for its cruder manifestations, thinking it gave the country they wished to be seen as Western a bad name.

Similarly, one of the first acts of the new Bulgarian leadership which replaced the Todor Zhivkov at the end of 1989 was to restore civil rights to the ethnic Turkish minority whom Zhivkov had made the object of an assimilationist drive: the act was an indispensable part of attracting foreign capital and seeking to pass to a pluralist system. (Being minimally decent to the Turks may not, of course, be very popular with many Bulgarians, and Milosevic's reassertion of Serbian pride *was* very popular; but what the people want in these respects is sometimes another matter.) Thus even Balkan nationalism, that seductive demon of the late nineteenth and early twentieth centuries, is somewhat tamed by the lure and criteria of political and economic choice.

So the East Europeans are largely mightily glad to see the End of History, and hope it lasts a thousand thousand years: but what about we who, to judge by the critique, still in many cases want it to continue?

History Woman

A fraction of the British Left attempted to end history in the early 1980s, under the banner of the SDP. With the most active tide in the Labour Party running strongly for a reassertion of the class struggle, it affirmed the ridiculousness of such a project and said that the violent swings of the political pendulum were the main cause of an economically lagging Britain. The development of the market and private ownership was irreversible, they said: to continue a struggle over it was not to fulfil the laws of history, but to distort them. Of course politics would continue over the relativities of freedom and of liberality – there would be arguments of principle but the principles would derive from moral stances on the same general ground. It was, of course, non-utopian and gradualist, and determinedly so, because many of the positions which it opposed, then officially adopted by the Labour Party, were either utopian (unilateral disarmament) or were logically achievable only by something like a revolution (widespread nationalisation). The Labour Party of the early 1980s was a most curious political phenomenon: its leading figures, many of them social democrats (as opposed to Social Democrats) performed in a rather trance-like way their parliamentary business while formally declaring allegiance to mounds of unachievable horrors (which they knew were horrible and unachievable) while at the same time battling to keep their constituency parties out of the hands of the far Left. A careful narrative of how that was transformed into the contemporary Labour Party, which has adopted nearly all of the positions of the Social Democrats and, by adoption, killed them, has yet to be written: a central place has to be granted to the unique political talent of Neil Kinnock.

Mrs Thatcher, who assisted the social democratisation of Labour by destroying much of British syndicalism, also necessarily destroyed much of her own popular appeal thereby. It was a sub-theme of the December 1989–February 1990 ambulance dispute that the Health Secretary, Kenneth Clarke, has attempted to cast the National Union of Public Employees as the same organisation which turned the sick away from hospital gates a decade before – but consistently failed, breaking on the rock-like civility and concern of Roger Poole, the main union negotiator, and the evident determination of his and other unions and of the members themselves to uphold civilised behaviour. Whereas in the seventies the pursuit of class aims was a solvent for every other concern, now primacy is given to the decencies of public provision. It was the kind of struggle many miners had wished to wage in 1984/85, and had been prevented from by the brilliant class war waged by the miners' union leadership, which ultimately meant Arthur Scargill, the country's foremost History Man. Mrs Thatcher may have helped create Roger Poole, but she needed Arthur Scargill and, for that matter, General Galtieri (which is not at all to say she sought them, or 'set them up'). She, too, is a History Woman, though she chose the right side.

It is worth noting, as an aside, that these choices were made nearly everywhere. The French socialists smothered communism in their embrace in the early eighties, but also put paid to their own theories of refashioning their country's structure of ownership. The Italian Communist Party, leader of the Italian Left, progressed in a stately and overrated fashion from a sophisticated and ambiguous revolutionism to social democracy under Enrico Berlinguer, who used the destruction of the Chilean Left to jolt his party out of utopianism. The German Social Democrats killed history at Bad Godesburg and in doing so readied their country, thirty years later, for a reunification with the German Democratic Republic which may be generally accepted as non-alarming. The Spanish socialists, it seemed, barely paused in seizing the point that the overdue modernisation of their country could only be done quickly by European integration and international capital. British Labour lagged, cursed with a terrible insularity which afflicts it still, but it did change, and convincingly.

Yet it seems that the liberating effects of the road it has chosen have yet to be fully felt within British Labour. End-of-History politics, escaped from ideology, are tremendously free compared with History politics. As Vaclav Havel has noted, the communist leaderships, intent on suppressing everyone, suppressed themselves most of all, ultimately rendering themselves incapable of even understanding how detested they were and taking evasive action. They were wholly trapped inside a politics which demanded that they nail their peoples to the wheel of history and whip it forward, come what may. The sense of liberation felt by their successors is everywhere evident, and sometimes leads them to do crazy things: Havel himself, the artist-as-hero turned President, let out 20,000 prisoners a week after taking the oath of office, most of whom were in prison for ordinary crimes rather than for political offences, and the citizens of his country, many of whom have things to lose, were not impressed. Of course these successors inherit economies which have been pillaged for years by regimes so scared of their masses that they put nearly all their resources into consumption, neglecting investment to keep the workers quiescent (and they were right: look what happened to the man of fiscal prudence – Nicolae Ceausescu): but they are also free to tackle these catastrophes with rational instruments.

The use of rational instruments is the key matter. When politics loses ideology it is free to be clever – or rather it is compelled to be. The Conservatives cottoned on to this in the seventies, with the burgeoning of think tanks which took the knife to the rickety edifice of British corporatism (though they have not been able to propose anything other than greed, which certainly has the virtue of reliability, to address the relative sluggishness of the British economy). Labour belatedly established the Institute of Public Policy Research, which under the leadership of James Cornford will clearly be a low-key and careful institution, eschewing the grand gesture. That is not to everyone's taste, but it is probably the most rational choice, and if it really can produce a reasonable antidote to London's traffic problems (one of its first projects) it will earn well-merited gratitude.

However, the sallies in this direction are still rather timid. British Labour seems gripped by a kind of stasis born of nervousness and lack of confidence in its own success. Since it has got to a position of consistent leads in the polls by becoming less threatening and being able, through the talents of many on its front bench, to bite the heels of a floundering government, the view transmitted from the top is: keep discipline, maintain an even step and no talking. This is a perfectly understandable response after years in which it sometimes seemed as though everyone was speaking rubbish in all directions at once, and when the Conservatives are going through a period during which, as the papers say, carefully coded disloyal speeches are made almost every weekend. However, it is rather dull, and perhaps self-defeating.

Paper Policy Castles

Most people will readily grasp that End-of-History politics are complex and thus highly specialised. The end of ideology releases people who had hitherto been forced to participate in politics, or at least give minimal obeisance to them. They will clearly wish political solutions to be worked out for their approval, and these cannot be other than sophisticated, since the interests to be harmonised and the series of local, national and international interactions which must now be calibrated form a dense network round every issue, from defence to abortion. The political party which can marshal the best and the brightest ideas on this and other subjects not only may convince the public that it is best placed to address the problem in power, but it also gives itself self-confidence and takes itself off the defensive. It risks, of course, being thought of as too clever by half, or as dropping clangers, or as forgetting the 'real people' who are never intellectuals. The 'real people' was and is too often doublespeak for those who could be marshalled behind some piece of simple populism, and we must trust these numbers are declining.

In simple terms, it may benefit Labour to try to become again the Clever Party – a title it lost perhaps two decades ago. In so doing, it could make up in intellectual excitement what it has lost in ideological frenzy. It has, of course, formidable internal control mechanisms to stop this happening. Bryan Gould tried on the mantle of the Left's Keith Joseph, but in spite of his obvious cleverness (or because of it) got burned. Those who are really interested in ideas, like Gordon Brown and Tony Blair, often seem constrained not to look as if they are – though the latter bravely translated his concern for civil liberties into an end for party support for the closed shop. Few among the best and the brightest, except Robin Cook and John Cunningham, have taken up the cause of proportional representation, even though the argument against it is so intellectually shabby, consisting mainly in holding that 'if we put that up, it would look as though we think we can't win' – a posture which, once enough people outside the party grasp its full timidity, would seem bound to ensure what it is designed to prevent. The

Liberals, and even more the SDP, struggling for visibility, have not had the energy left over to play intellectual gadfly as once they did.

This means a bit of organisation, an opening up of policy-making to streams of thought. Labour's apparat is hugely wary of this, remembering the teams of demented academics who sat round tables with often no less demented MPs building paper policy castles deep into the night a few years ago, none of which were ever translated into practical politics. Now, however, much of the dementia has gone and the exercise might prove much more fruitful, even if the same people were on the committees, since many of them are politically unrecognisable as their old selves. Such endeavours lack the thrill of storming the palace: but the old Fabians found great joy in rigour and detail, and the new Fabians could again.

Credit for Mrs Thatcher

TERRY JONES

Some of the achievements of Mrs Thatcher's ten years in office are, even now, barely recognised. I think it is disgraceful, for example, that Mrs T is given so little credit for stamping out the disgusting – not to say dangerous – practice of eating partially cooked or even sometimes *raw* eggs (as in foreign confections such as omelettes and mayonnaise). And yet it is the emphasis which she has placed on commercial gain over and above public safety that has enabled so many of our great egg-producing companies to continue to flourish despite the endemic problem of salmonella contamination. It is also Mrs Thatcher's unselfish determination that free enterprise should not be held back by unwelcome exposure to public scrutiny that has allowed the industry to develop some of its most cost-effective techniques, such as feeding dead and diseased hens to healthy ones.

Similarly is it right that Mrs T should be denied the credit she is due for weaning an entire generation off drinking tap water? Those who wish merely to carp and niggle may pretend that it is hardly Margaret Thatcher's responsibility if people as far away as Cornwall are poisoned by their water or if Londoners wake up one day to find theirs full of worms. And yet if it were not for Mrs Thatcher's insistence that the 12 water businesses of England and Wales be made economically healthy, the Lowermoor plant would have had someone on duty on the day the aluminium sulphate was dumped into the wrong tank. What's more, if the government hadn't encouraged South West Water (if only by example) to break the 1983 water strike, keys would never have been handed out to the contractors, and the contractors wouldn't have been able to get in when no one was on duty in the first place.

Those who wish to cavil will also probably claim that Margaret Thatcher cannot be given all the credit for our record levels of radioactivity both at sea and on land. But even here, I believe, they are being unfair to her. The Irish Sea and the Cumbrian coast may have been polluted before Mrs T came to power, but it was she who refused to let that fact blunt her enthusiasm for the nuclear industry. In the same way, she may not have been personally responsible for the Chernobyl affair, or for the fact that fallout from Chernobyl has made the hills of Wales and Scotland so radioactive that over 700 farms still cannot sell their meat for human consumption, but it was she who – a mere three years later – was still stoutly defending nuclear power as the most environmentally sound source of energy we have.

When it comes to the greenhouse effect, those who wish to belittle Mrs Thatcher's contribution will doubtless point to her many public utterances on the subject – particularly her extraordinary appearance at the UN in November of 1989, when she pledged £5 million to set up a centre for predicting climatic change and £100 million to help preserve the tropical rainforests. But they do her a grave disservice, for whatever Mrs T was saying in public, she was, in reality, doing all she could to protect our production of carbon dioxide. She has never wavered in her determination to run down public transport and encourage road traffic – which accounts for almost 20% of all Britain's CO_2 emissions. During her period of office, traffic increased by over 27%, and the Department of Transport now predicts a further increase by the year 2005 of between 83% and 142%, and proposes to encourage this increase by pledging £6 billion to building new roads! What's more, even as Mrs T was making her statement in New York, her representatives at the 72-nation conference in the Netherlands were blocking a proposal to freeze carbon dioxide emissions by the year 2000. So Mrs T has nothing to be ashamed of in her record of defending our CO_2 production.

And so it goes on. The sneerers and jeerers may try to play down Mrs Thatcher's role in the accomplishments of the last ten years, but her hand has been constantly on the tiller, guiding the ship of state through the stormy seas.

Indeed, even some of the most newsworthy events of recent times – Zeebrugge, King's Cross and Clapham – may all be traced back ultimately to one of her enthusiasms – that public transport should exist first and foremost to make a profit and only secondarily to move people around from A to B in comfort and safety.

So there we are: after ten years of Mrs Thatcher we can't eat eggs and we can't drink tap water. We can't eat a lot of Welsh or Scottish lamb because it's radioactive – as is much of the milk supply, 20 miles of Cumbrian coast and the Irish Sea. We can't eat beef that may be contaminated with BSE and cheese that may be full of lysteria. There is a hole in the ozone layer. The atmosphere is overheating. Most beaches are unfit for swimming. London is crammed with people reduced to begging or living in cardboard boxes, while the streets themselves are ankle-deep in litter, the pavements are blocked by plastic bagfuls of uncollected rubbish and the roads are full of potholes. There are fires on the underground, crashes on the railways and disasters on the ferries. There are millions out of work, the poor have no safety net and more young people than ever before commit suicide. After ten years of Mrs Thatcher, the government now openly censors the BBC and tells our teachers what they can and what they cannot teach our children. After ten years of Mrs Thatcher, government in this country is more authoritarian, more centralised and more secretive. The government gags its civil servants who try to blow the whistle on abuses of power, gags scientists who try to reveal dangers to the public (such as the BSE scandal) and even gags doctors and nurses who speak openly about what is happening in our hospitals.

Ten years of Mrs Thatcher has wiped out the democratically elected metropolitan councils and effectively taken away most of the powers of local government. Oh yes – and ten years of Mrs Thatcher has wiped out the British film industry!

So what is the alternative?

Since this book is full of sensible ideas, I thought I would offer up a rather less practical suggestion.

I would first like to point out that all these startling achievements over the last decade have been made without an armed struggle and without any seizing of power by force (apart from abolishing the elected metropolitan councils). They have all taken place in a modern Western democracy. My question is: is there any point in having a democracy when it can elect and can keep on electing such a ludicrous government as we have had for the last ten years?

If the Tory Party machine can sell someone as unattractive as Mrs Thatcher, and if she can sell a policy as ludicrous as the idea that giving greed its head is the only way to ensure the welfare of the people, then what is our democracy worth?

Modern means of communication now make the manipulation of public opinion possible on a scale that even Goebbels would have found unimaginable. Thus in a modern Western democracy access to or control of the media, especially the TV and the popular press, is the key to power. Policies and politicians are rapidly being reduced to commodities to be sold like lager. Real politics goes out of the window and the image-makers take over. It all follows with the inevitability of the night's TV programmes. Once the Tory Party brought in Saatchi and Saatchi, the Labour Party had to follow suit or go down the pan. And there is nothing we can do about this situation. We can't abolish TV. So maybe we need to adapt our democracy to this changed world. And maybe we can learn something from the past.

Six hundred years ago, the definition of a tyrant proposed by certain Italian jurists like Bartolus of Sassoferato and Coluccio Salutati (and, incidentally, adopted by our own Geoffrey Chaucer) went something like this: it was supposed that a king had the right to rule only as long as he was acting in the interests of his people. As soon as he started acting purely in his own interests he was deemed to have become a tyrant and to have forfeited the right to rule.

Now a king who wields power because his father was king, they reckoned, has a 50% chance of being the right sort of ruler. On the other hand, a king who gains power because he has actively sought power is almost certain to be acting in his own interests and therefore is 99% certain to be the wrong sort of ruler. It was therefore preferable, they argued, to make do with an inherited monarch, with an even chance of his being a decent ruler, and to concentrate not on how he achieves power but on how to influence him for the best. Thus the education of the young prince was regarded as of utmost importance and, when he assumed power, the choice of the king's council became paramount. This is why every socially concerned writer, from Dante to Chaucer, wrote a Book of Rules for Princes. It was their social duty.

According to this medieval theory of kingship, then, those who sought power were automatically ruled out, and the political focus was concentrated on methods of educating, influencing and gaining access to the ruler, who was selected by the relatively arbitrary method of succession.

In some ways this was more advanced than what happens today.

Nowadays, we are allowed to choose once every five years between one set of power-seeking politicians and another. The voter has precious little control over the choice of candidates (although Labour has begun to make some efforts in this direction). Once those who have sought power are in power they have virtual carte blanche to do as they like, and to bulldoze through demonstrably unpopular policies (such as the abolition of the GLC and the privatisation of water).

Clearly the medieval ideal I have outlined didn't actually work, since by the next century Italy itself was overrun with tyrants, and Machiavelli had come up with his own Book of Rules for Princes which was, in fact, a Handbook for Tyrants. But maybe the concepts of avoiding giving power to those who seek power and of focusing political activity on the access of ordinary people to those in power are concepts that we should try to absorb into our democracy.

So, as this is a book of alternatives, here's my suggestion for an alternative democracy. How about abolishing elected governments as such, and make serving in the government more like jury service? Once a year 12 people could be randomly selected from the electoral register, and they would be given the power that we now invest in professional, self-serving politicians. We are happy to give a randomly selected jury power over the life or death of individuals, so why not give a similarly randomly selected panel power over the nation? The rest of us could carry on voting for the professional politicians who would initiate policies, who would advise and who would canvass ideas, but they would be denied ultimate power. Ultimate power would lie with the jury of 12 randomly selected good men and true.

For my part, I would sooner trust myself and the nation to the good sense of a randomly selected jury (such as the one that freed Clive Ponting) than any set of professional power-seekers who have made Britain the place it has become in the last ten years.

The Divided Inheritance

PETER CLARKE

Demythologising Labour's Past

History, it has been said, is past politics. But very often it is present politics too. The quest for a useable past is common to the most diverse political tendencies. It can, to be sure, sometimes lead to results which are simultaneously a source of inspiration to believers who feel themselves gripped by a self-propelled historical current, and a source of mirth to sceptics who find themselves affronted by a self-serving historical construct. History, then, needs to be recognised for its dangers and temptations. True enough, the past may bring a misleading sense of psychological reassurance from the notion that we are not alone; but this does not nullify history's ability to offer a bracing measure of intellectual perspective when we are stripped of the illusion that no one has been here before.

The Labour Party is as old as the twentieth century, and until the last quarter of that century it was sustained by an inspirational view of the past. This rested not on detailed historical research but on broad trends, boldly extrapolated by inference. Had not democracy gradually replaced oligarchy in Britain? Had not the working class inexorably challenged the dominance of the middle class? Had not socialism irresistibly superseded liberalism? What was the history of the Labour Party but a series of variations – albeit often ineptly executed – upon these basic themes? This outlook was made tenable by Labour's steady advance towards power in the first half of the twentieth century, supporting the claim that it might become the natural party of government. And it was made tolerable by the fact that it was not, for the most part, asserted arrogantly from a position of overweening strength but more often defiantly from a sense of only half-stilled inner insecurity.

The Labour Party's confidence in its historic destiny has continually been undermined by actual historical experience, as I shall hope to demonstrate. Over the last generation historians have recaptured the institutional and electoral frailty of Labour's position. Its claim has been that of the hegemonic party of the Left in Britain; its experience, by contrast, has been that of a party which has only succeeded when there has been an ideological mobilisation of a much wider kind – one which can aptly be called a popular front of the mind. There never was a golden age when the Labour Party surged forward on a tide of socialism. Instead, every significant gain has been paid for with some dilution of socialist principle and conversely the party has paid for its spasms of purist self-indulgence with crushing electoral setbacks. The periods of constructive achievement for Labour have been those in which its own efforts were part of a deeper groundswell against Conservatism such as periodically occur in even this most conservative of countries.

The foundation of the Labour Party in 1900 (under the name Labour Representation Committee) was an essentially defensive move, engineered by the trades union movement as the only available means of protecting its vital interests from both a legal attack on its activities and an ideological assault on its legitimacy. The franchise was already sufficiently broad to permit the growth of a major working-class party. What was lacking was the necessary political drive and consciousness. Had a significant proportion of the working-class electorate wanted a socialist party, the Independent Labour Party, as set up in 1893, would have made more ground. But its electoral experience was highly unpromising. The chastened ILP was therefore ready by 1900 to make its terms for accommodation within the LRC, an organisation dominated by the trades unions, and determined accordingly to exercise its primary role as a trades-union pressure group.

Moreover, though the new party was established in recognition of the incapacity of the Liberal Party to serve as a channel for labour representation, it quickly settled for a loosely defined entente with Liberalism rather than sectarian antagonism. Contemporaries called it a 'progressive alliance' between Liberals and Labour, and it provided the framework for the most decisive and prolonged eclipse that the Conservatives have suffered in their long history. For nearly ten years (1905–15) the Conservatives were excluded from office, losing three general elections in a row; and they were forced to watch a Liberal Government, reinforced by the support of 40 Labour MPs, seize the political initiative. Clearly this could not have been engineered without a large measure of practical consensus on the moderate Left. The development of a New Liberalism, which gave a wholly new degree of attention to economic and social issues, was a precondition for winning Labour support. As the leading New Liberal thinker L. T. Hobhouse put it, the task of liberalism in the nineteenth century may have been the winning of political democracy, but in the twentieth century its task was the achievement of social democracy.

Collectivist measures of social reform such as old age pensions and national insurance were thus conceived as at once a fulfilment of the Liberal goal of the common good and a practical concession to Labour. This happy coincidence of sectional interest with social justice may seem rather glib today, partly because the success of a strategy of correcting their disadvantages has made trades unionists no longer axiomatically a disadvantaged group. Likewise the New Liberals' qualms about the imposition of statist measures from on high – which was what distinguished them from the Fabians – may strike a chord today; but their only practical safeguard then was the hope that democratic collectivism, as an organic expression of self-government, could avoid these dangers so long as it was implemented through parliamentary means. No doubt we are wiser now about the deficiencies in this prospectus. At the time, however, an ideological conjuncture meshed traditional radical concerns about privilege with immediate economic issues which Labour naturally stressed. Providing the perfect foil, the House of Lords in 1909 united the entire cantankerous army of progressives behind Lloyd George's 'People's Budget', by using its powers to reject it. These events are worth recalling as indicating how, for once, the Conservatives could become the victims of a concerted movement among opponents whose identity as liberals or socialists was subsumed by a sense of common purpose.

The Progressive Dilemma

The progressive movement of the Edwardian period left stronger residual traces than have often been recognised, as becomes apparent if we scratch the surface of interwar politics. The fratricidal quarrels between the partisans of Asquith and Lloyd George, the Labour Party's swift rise to prominence during World War One, and the messy three-party politics of the 1920s, present a different sort of picture altogether. The moderate Left lost its sense of unity, its sense of direction – and, very often, simply its sense. The net gainers, of course, were the Conservatives, who found themselves out of office for less than three out of thirty years from 1915 to 1945. Yet the common ground between Liberals and Labour during much of this period was extensive. There were, of course, those socialists who took a mechanistic view of the class struggle and could only see liberalism as an ingenious defence of bourgeois interests. Likewise, there were plenty of old-fashioned Liberals ready to lend verisimilitude to this picture, especially when activated by fears of the red menace. But for many disinherited progressives, there was an awkward choice to be made between the Liberal and Labour

Parties; and if some found themselves on one side of the line, and some on the other, it was often with the feelings of being faced with an unnecessary dilemma.

This dilemma was the product of two conflicting pressures. When we look at the broad measure of agreement on political goals between Liberals and Labour in the 1920s, we can hardly escape an impression of ideological convergence. Yet when we see the way Labour's struggle for governmental credibility led it to make the destruction of the Liberal Party its immediate priority, we cannot ignore the reality of tactical divergence. Labour's bloodymindedness exasperated many of its sympathisers among progressive Liberals who saw only the squandered opportunites for co-operation – in tackling unemployment, for example. Yet it cannot be denied that Labour succeeded in establishing its own credentials as a mature political party in the process, laying claim to a governmental role which had once been the forte of Liberalism.

To some extent, Ramsay MacDonald and Lloyd George were fighting to capture the same ground, and their awareness of the fact brought them into sharper conflict than if their respective political territory had been more sharply demarcated. It is a familiar paradox on the Left, that the most intractable hostility often subsists precisely between those who appear to have the closest affinities but see themselves as competing for the same space. This was not, however, simply a zero-sum game in which Labour stood to benefit exclusively at the Liberals' expense. The fact is that each party reached out – beyond a contested sector to which they laid rival claims – to a hinterland of support which was not readily available to the other. This can be seen in class terms, as a Labour–Conservative contest among working-class voters and a Liberal–Conservative contest among middle-class voters. It can also be seen in ideological terms, as the justification of substantially similar policies from socialist or from liberal premises. Either way, it surely indicates a potentially complementary strategy for maximising anti-Conservative support, rather than the necessity of fighting to the bitter end.

By the 1920s, however, the tactical competition which prevailed was reinforced by the imperatives of the British electoral system. Before World War One, the penalties facing the defeat of a minor party chiefly concerned Labour, but were largely notional at that. For in return for limiting the scale of its electoral ambitions, Labour secured an immediate bridgehead of 40 seats in Parliament, underpinned by the co-operation of the Liberal Party in giving Labour candidates a clear run againt the Tories. If electoral co-operation were to be replaced by competition, it was not hard for anyone to foresee the results: damage to the Liberal Party would have been one, and the virtual annihilation of the parliamentary Labour Party another. Thus, sentiment aside, the first-past-the-post system served as a discipline which helped keep the progressive alliance together, and advocates of proportional representation lacked an equally unsentimental argument from self-interest. By 1917–18, however, when the electoral system was being reformed under the pressures created by war, women's suffrage and Labour's new-found will to power, the adoption of some scheme of proportional representation, or at least the alternative vote, seemed a likely outcome. As it turned out, this chance to remodel the voting system was let slip, and the 1918 Reform Act simply expanded the franchise. Hence the relations between the Liberal and Labour Parties were subsequently governed by the logic of first-past-the-post.

The full impact of the electoral system upon the British conception of a political party is seldom appreciated. It is a common argument against proportional representation that because no one party is likely to win an outright majority, it entails a process of coalition-building, with a consequent and undesirable need for principles to be compromised. But all that is really implied by the proportional representation of different tendencies in Parliament is that the coalition-building and principle-compromising take place *after* a general election rather than before it, which is what the present system requires. For it cannot seriously be maintained that a two-party system can adequately represent differences of political principle. In this sense the Labour Party cannot be said to be founded on principle: it cannot be if it is to do its job of mobilising an anti-Conservative coalition in support of a compromise programme, and failure to recognise this fact is a product of muddled thinking. But acknowledging the implications may help resolve a dilemma which has confronted the moderate Left in Britain for most of this century.

The problem was never more feelingly indicated than by Hobhouse in 1924[1], following the disappointing performance of the first Labour Government. As an old supporter of Campbell-Bannerman, he was not chiefly troubled by the eclipse of the Liberal Party itself. He was clear that 'moderate Labour – Labour in office – has on the whole represented essential Liberalism, not without mistakes and defects, but *better* than the organised party since C.B.'s death'. Unperturbed by the socialist bogey, he argued for 'a distinctive kind of socialism being one based not on the Trade Unions but on the community & social service. The constitution of the Labour party binds it tight to the Trade Unions & their sectional selfishness, a most serious defect.' Hence the continued relevance of a Liberal Party which might be ready to take such a stance. Hence, too, Hobhouse's reiterated belief that 'if we divided parties by true principles', there was little to separate 'ordinary Labour' from 'Good Liberal'. Such sentiments have often been echoed by liberals and social democrats who find themselves on different sides of the arbitrary fracture lines of British politics and could agree on a more rational realignment on the Left. In its absence, there has been an intermittent dialogue across party lines, mainly about ad hoc efforts to check and chastise the common Conservative enemy.

Like proportional representation, the idea of a popular front is often categorised as an alien import, from continental Europe, and it is true that it has had little success as an institutional project. Yet the various moves in this direction in the 1930s, faced with the Conservative preponderance in the National Government, did not simply ape comparable initiatives in Spain or France; they also drew deeply on the ingrained assumptions and values of an indigenous progressive tradition. Once more, the imperatives of party politics, especially those of the Labour Party machine under Herbert Morrison, led to tactical divergence despite the impressive ideological convergence on both domestic and international issues among opponents of the National Government.

It was only in 1940 that the urgency of the war crisis brought a change of government that was little less than a political revolution. Churchill may have stood as the Conservative head of the new coalition government, but its whole thrust was a negation of the outlook of the party on which he was promptly foisted as leader. Hugh Dalton slipped into calling it 'this Churchill–Labour Government'[2]. In making the immediate future safe for liberalism and social democracy, against the external threat of fascism, it was a posthumous triumph for the popular front ideas which had earlier been thwarted. 1940 has often been hailed as a crucial date in the evolution of social policy towards the welfare state; it must be recognised too as marking the turn of the tide from a reliance on market forces in favour of the managed economy, i.e. a government commitment to maintain high levels of employment. Keynes's own comment was double-edged: 'It is, it seems, politically impossible for a capitalistic democracy to organise expenditure on the scale necessary to make the grand experiments which would prove my case – except in war conditions.'[3]

A Zero-Sum Game?

Such conditions, though historically important in validating the concept of a popular front of the mind, provide little guide to normal peacetime practice. Yet here too the constraints of our historic party system may be less adverse than one would suppose. Failing realignment, to be sure, the forces of the Left have remained divided; and, failing electoral reform, that division has prevented the non-Conservative parties from maximising their parliamentary representation. But given this handicap, there has been compensation for the Left in the way the system has functioned over time. For it is arguable that Labour's own electoral performance has never been impaired by the periodic success of the Liberals in retaining or reviving their support. Indeed, there is a strong case that, for over half a century, Conservative electoral success has varied inversely with the level of Liberal support.

The strong Liberal poll in 1923 helped install the first Labour Government, and the collapse of the Liberal vote in the following year gave the Conservatives a sweeping majority. Again, the Liberal revival of 1929, although it won them few seats, had the effect of almost doubling Labour's parliamentary strength and putting it within inches of an absolute majority. Conversely, the way Liberal support plummeted in the 1930s made it almost impossible for Labour to break back; in 1935 a Labour poll as high as that of 1929 brought it 130 fewer seats – because it was now in a two-party race. The modest Liberal recovery in 1945 was a precondition of rather than an impediment to Labour's landslide victory; it was, by contrast, when the Liberal vote was almost squeezed out of sight in 1951 that Labour lost the general election (even though scoring a slightly higher overall total than the Tories). The classic two-party system of the 1950s was one marked by Conservative hegemony. Only when the surge of Liberal recovery had taken the party's support back above 10% in 1964 did Labour sneak back into power. The Liberals' decline to 7.5% in 1970 was accompanied by a Conservative victory. The remarkable Liberal performance in February 1974, touching nearly 20% of the poll, was both an object lesson in the unfairness of the representative system and an indispensable aid to an unpopular Labour Party in seizing power from an equally unpopular Conservative Party. The marked drop in the Liberal vote in 1979 did not, of course, help Labour but coincided with the start of the Thatcher era.

The tendency throughout most of the century has therefore been for Liberals and Labour to rise and fall, not so much at each others' expense as at that of Conservatism. If this is correct, Labour's frequent irritable charges that Liberal candidates have split the anti-Conservative vote must have been misconceived; instead the Tories have been on the right track in warning that a high Liberal vote would help let in the socialists.

But what about the 1980s? The general elections of 1983 and 1987 both saw a third-party vote (for the Alliance) well in excess of 20% for the first time since the 1920s. Unlike 1923 or 1929, when a Labour Government was in each case the result, the Conservatives appear to have thrived upon the divided state of the opposition. Indeed it has been a common Labour taunt that the SDP in particular was responsible for Thatcher's success. I think there may be a measure of truth in this – though not in the sense usually intended.

The tactic of simply blaming the Alliance for fatally dividing the anti-Conservative vote is a piece of know-nothing Labourism with an established pedigree. It was already being deployed against the Liberals in the 1920s, as Keynes had good reason to notice. 'I do not wish to live under a Conservative Government for the next twenty years,' he confessed in 1926[4]. 'I believe that the progressive forces of the country are hopelessly divided between the Liberal Party and the Labour Party.' Yet he rejected the 'conventional retort by Labour orators' that the remedy was to join them, if only 'because the progressive cause in the constituencies would be weakened, and not strengthened, by the disappearance of the Liberal Party'. It was, in short, a fallacy to suppose that Liberal supporters constituted a block vote which could be switched into supporting a party which they had their own good reasons for not having supported in the first place. Part of the reason for this fallacy may lie in Labour's deep-seated failure to appreciate that it does not hold the copyright on anti-Conservative politics, nor does it possess an inalienable proprietory right to the votes that go therewith. This misplaced sense of ownership explains the indignant reflex with which Labour greeted the rise of the Alliance: 'We was robbed!'

The assumption that other opposition parties are simply trespassers, with no rights of their own, and liable to prosecution as soon as they can be apprehended, has never made Labour's machine politicians endearing. But a party boss like Herbert Morrison, with a historical tide flowing his way, felt himself vindicated in having dismissed the popular front rhetoric of the late 1930s when, by 1945, he was able to present the Labour Pary as in itself a surrogate popular front. Whether Labour's appeal can be broadened in the early 1990s in an analogous way, so as to make it the residuary legatee of the support that previously fed into the Alliance, remains to be seen. What is surely clear, however, is that the bulk of the Alliance vote in 1983 – and even in 1987 – was simply not accessible to the Labour Party as it then stood. The proposition that, but for the SDP stealing all those votes, an unreconstructed Labour Party would have basked in electoral favour, in retrospect seems incredible.

If the SDP temporarily cornered a substantial section of the Labour vote, it was because this support had been alienated by Labour itself. If this was a symptom of Labour's crisis, so were the very existence of the SDP and the unprecedented voting trends of the 1980s. Though talk of mould-breaking has now gone sharply out of fashion, the evidence of the 1980s indicates unique stresses on the two-party system, which made the electoral outcomes highly unpredictable. It is arguable that the only chance of dislodging the Thatcher Government came and went in the early 1980s with the rise and fall of the Alliance as a major electoral threat. As things turned out, the triumph of Thatcherism, with parliamentary majorities in three figures, was achieved on a remarkably small, if consistent, share of the vote – little more than 42%. Thus it depended upon the existence of a third party with a level of support that fell fortuitously into a particular range: at once insufficiently high to do itself much good and sufficiently high to lower the threshold of success for a major party. A more traditional, broadly based Conservative appeal might not have needed this peculiar chain of circumstances. But the success of Thatcherism, more narrowly conceived, was the product of a political gamble in which the lady walked off with the SDP's chips.

Fabian or Asquithian

It is not worth complaining about the way this happened; obviously the point is to learn from it. Unfortunately, there are powerful figures in the Labour Party who have been ready to learn only the narrowest lesson. Their position is, in effect, that Labour should seek to emulate Thatcher in forming an unrepresentative government; it should hope to snatch a freak victory on a thin popular vote under a perverse electoral system, and then claim a mandate for its policies as she has done. Such hardfaced electoral *realpolitik* is so unappealing as to become self-defeating in a campaign to win over uncommitted voters; and, if only for this reason, one must hope that this sort of bunker mentality has had its day. A more constructive lesson is surely that Thatcherism on the wane is a creed without stamina or reserves. Electorally, it has never won enough ground to be confident of containing its losses in hard times; any slippage of its own support could prove fatal, as could a more effective redistribution of opposition support. Ideologically, too, it is becoming clear that Thatcherite values command only the most super-ficial assent within society at large; the opportunity of translating such latent attitudes into votes against her thus awaits a suitable political initiative. My own hunch – strengthened by the Lawson affair – is that when the end comes it may be relatively sudden, with a snowballing spiral of disintegration, and a wild mood of desperation among an unloveable clique who have drunk greedily on easy success. Once the Thatcherites have shot their bolt, they may well shoot their pianist.

We must indeed hope that Thatcher survives to lead the Conserva-tives in the next general election; no one else could so unite the opposition. But agreement on the desirability of her downfall is one thing; accomplishing this feat is another. How can it be done? History provides no general injunctions, still less useful blueprints for political campaigns. But one precept emerges from a consideration of the ideological convergence and tactical divergence which has characterised the experience of the moderate Left in Britain during this century. This is that while a particular political position may be a matter of principle – and therefore not amenable to negotiation or browbeating – it may not be sensible to ascribe a similar stringency to *party* support. It is the purist and the fanatic who act regardless of the consequences; as Max Weber argued, politics, by contrast, requires an ethic of responsibility, which licenses a legitimate opportunism. Thus it may be expedient for opponents of the Thatcher Government to adopt tactics which can be called, according to our differing tastes and traditions, either Fabian or Asquithian: to wait and see before deciding how to strike most effectively. It may be that the spontaneous efforts of the opposition parties will mesh together in producing the desired result; but if some unofficial initiatives in co-ordination seemed tactically advantageous they should certainly be organised. In any case, if precedents can encourage us here, a popular front of the mind will prove to be the most fruitful medium in which the establishment of a non-Conservative government can be given the ideological credibility which is a condition of success.

The Devil and the Deep Blue Sea

JOHN RENTOUL

'People now do not know where they are historically and in which direction to move. This makes the situation very unstable and has a debilitating effect on the economy.' Leonid Volkov, a founder of the USSR Social-Democratic Association, *Samizdat* No. 6, September 1989

It is risky to predict the outcome of the next election in any circumstances, but to put your prediction in print is asking for trouble. Especially in a book. Yet it is important to have a hard-headed look at the political possibilities of the 1990s in order to judge 'where we are historically' so that we know in which direction to move.

So what can be said about the next election that will stand the test of time? What kinds of judgements can be made about our political history while it is still happening? I believe there are four facts which are likely to hold true over the next few years.

Four Facts

First, the time has come and gone for the mould-breakers. The Alliance, Liberal Democrat, SDP, 'third force' is finished. There's little profit in weighing explanations and apportioning blame, but with the benefit of hindsight we can see that the Alliance seized neither its main chance in 1983 nor its last chance in 1987. It all seems like a tragic waste of time, effort and money, but there it is.

Second, we have not seen the last of the Green Party. The success of the Liberals in the 1970s and the Alliance in the 1980s was never simply a 'protest vote'. But it did include a category of voters who were disaffected with the whole of 'the old political set-up'. The Greens are

[205]

now the exclusive franchise holders of that abstract desire for a 'new sort of politics'.

However, at a critical moment in the Green Party's history, after its success in the European elections in 1989, it chose to go down the low-profile road of principle rather than the high-profile road of electing a single leader and exploiting media interest with publicity gimmicks. As a result, the Greens may do well in by-elections in the South, but in the next general election are unlikely to win anything like the 15% they won in the last Euro-election. With the voters under pressure either to re-elect or turn out the government, the Greens will do well to achieve half that figure. So, although there will be a 'green factor' in the next election, the Green Party isn't it.

Third, Thatcherism has failed politically. This is a rather stark way of putting it. But whatever changes Mrs Thatcher's governments may have wrought on the physical fabric of the nation, they have left its mental furniture surprisingly untouched. The British electorate remains, after more than a decade of what has been called 'Mrs Thatcher's Revolution', fundamentally social democratic. I shall return to the exact nature of these social democratic values in a moment; what matters here is that they are not the same as Mrs Thatcher's.

The electorate, always ideologically hostile to Mrs Thatcher, voted for her in small and diminishing proportions. She owes her election victories to the incompetence of her opponents, who ensured a divided opposition, and to an astute strategy of concentrating economic growth where it did most good electorally. Neither factor applies this time round.

At the next election, the decline of Thatcherism is likely to continue. A Thatcherite Tory Party could pick up a few votes from the wreckage of the Alliance, but what it picks up on the Alliance roundabout it is likely to lose on the economy's swings. No economic forecast predicts that the economy will be as electorally favourable for the government in 1991–92 as it was in 1987.

What is more, Mrs Thatcher herself, however good a politician in the narrow sense of that word, is clearly on the way out. Nigel Lawson's resignation and Sir Anthony Meyer's leadership challenge broke the Tory Party's Trappist vow against discussing her right to lead, with the real candidates for the succession outdoing each other in coded condemnations of Thatcherism. As Labour MP Tony Banks so memorably heckled after she retracted ('by popular acclaim') her notice of intention to retire after the next election: 'Hobble, hobble, quack, quack.'

And the fourth fact is that the Labour Party will be the main beneficiary of the first three facts. If one of the reasons Mrs Thatcher's failure had been so well concealed was the even greater political failure of the Labour Party, that has now changed.

As far as the direction of the Labour Party's history goes, 1989 was a sharp bend taken at speed. The change in people's perceptions of the Labour Party during the year of its policy review seems to have been dramatic: probably as great as the change during the whole of the period between 1983 and 1989.

In just a few months between the spring and autumn of 1989 Gallup polls showed huge swings in Labour's favour on three vital questions:

- 'Labour has become too extreme': 20% swing to 'disagree'
- 'Labour Party leadership is poor now': 21% swing to 'disagree'
- Is Labour 'united or divided at the present time?': 32% swing to 'united'

And for the first time since the mid-1970s, Labour began to close the gap on economic competence, with a majority (at last) telling Gallup that they thought they and their families would be 'better off under a Labour government'.

As for the 'green factor', Gallup polls show Labour well placed to benefit. In September 1989, a 51% to 28% majority believed 'Labour genuinely cares for the environment', 45% thought Labour would spend more on protecting the environment (5% said less, 39% the same), while 78% believed the government was 'not doing enough to protect the environment' and 50% said they were 'concerned enough about the environment to consider voting for another party at a general election'.

The Devil and the Deep Blue Sea

To go back over recent history a little, it appeared after the 1987 election that the opposition parties, in particular Labour, faced a stark choice between two options – the Devil option and the Deep Blue Sea option. Either Labour had to deal with the Devil, in the shape of the Alliance parties (most obviously by conceding electoral reform in return for a pact), or it had to dive into the Deep Blue Sea and emerge so dramatically changed that it could win over the Alliance's voters itself. It was generally thought that such a transformation was too ambitious, and that if it were attempted the electorate wouldn't believe the conversion anyway. On that view, the first option was easier. But, as history has unfolded, it became clear to those sceptics who thought the Labour Party was merely putting its toe in the water of revisionism that the party has taken the plunge into the sea with surprisingly little fuss. After all, why make a pact with the Devil when you can steal all his best tunes?

Nevertheless, it is unlikely that Labour will win an overall majority at the next election. For that to happen, Labour needs an 8% swing, larger than any it has achieved since 1945. An 8% swing means its vote has to go up eight points from 31.5% in 1987 to 39.5% and the Tory vote has to fall from 43% to 35%. If the Tory vote doesn't fall that far, Labour has to compensate by winning extra votes itself. If the Tories stay on 43%, Labour will have to pick up 16 points from the Alliance to push its vote up to 47.5%: which would mean winning an extra vote for every two votes it won in 1987.

And despite the conventional wisdom, the best academic evidence is that the electorate has not actually become more volatile over the postwar period. Of course, because so many former Alliance voters are looking for a new home, and because they are easier for Labour to attract than straight converts from the Tories, Labour *can* achieve a larger-than-average swing at the next election. But from the depths of 'no compromise with the electorate' in 1983 to the 'best-ever' campaign in 1987, Labour achieved a swing of only 1.6%. Next time the swing will be greater than that, but it is unlikely to be of 1945 proportions.

So it is more likely that Labour will run the Conservatives close, both parties winning a percentage of the vote in the low 40s. The Liberal Democrats, Greens and nationalists would be fighting for a pool of 'non-conventional' votes, at most 20%. (Again, with the benefit of hindsight, it seems that the Scottish National Party took a wrong turning at *its* historic crossroads, after the Govan by-election, by refusing to take part in the Scottish Constitutional Convention.)

In terms of seats, this suggests the Conservatives would be within 20 seats either way of an overall majority. So the best anti-Thatcherites can hope for is a minority Labour government. Hence the need for a 'popular front'.

To return to the Devil and the Deep Blue Sea dilemma, there is still a case for the Labour Party, despite having chosen the Deep Blue Sea option, to show a little sympathy for the Devil. The idea of a pact with its political rivals is out of the question, but there is a case for Labour reaching a limited understanding with them and perhaps more importantly their followers. In a hung Parliament, Labour could need the support of the Northern Irish SDLP, the Liberal Democrats, the nationalists, and, if they have any MPs, the Social Democrats and the Greens. The only way a new government could make progress would be for it to govern in a pluralist fashion. That does not necessarily mean a formal coalition, but would require the Labour Party in particular to govern on behalf of a broad consensus about the alternative to Thatcherism, rather than setting out its programme and defying smaller parties to vote it down.

The basis of that consensus already exists, in the social democratic values of the majority of the electorate. The aim of this book and the 'popular front of the mind' is, I hope, to help shape it and give it a voice.

Popular Consensus

I have now twice described the consensus values of the British electorate as 'social democratic'. Before I am misinterpreted, I had better explain what I mean. I only used the term in order to cheer up any erstwhile followers of Dr David Owen who might be reading. They may be a little depressed politically, so it is worth reminding them that, although the Social Democratic Party was a big mistake, social democracy was right all along. Again with the benefit of hindsight, it seems that those who called themselves social democrats in the Labour Party's crisis of 1981 were more right (about policy) than those who called themselves Bennites.

I would have used the word 'collectivist', but that would probably have left me open to even greater misinterpretation. What I mean is that in the ideological battle fought by Mrs Thatcher for individualism against collectivism, the vast majority of the British people are not on her side. Even of the minority who voted for her, many did so despite her values, not because of them. Thatcherite individualism may have dominated Westminster, the machinery of government and the media to the exclusion of all else for the past decade, but it has never been popular out in the real world. Out there the opposed values of collectivism have survived, and this is the territory on which 'The Alternative' has to be built.

The core of Thatcherism is captured in a few recurrent phrases: 'There is no such thing as society', 'On your bike', and 'You can't buck the market'. Thatcherism is philosophically hostile to the idea that people are entitled to be looked after by society as a whole simply by virtue of being members of that society. The philosophy of individualism regards 'society' as an abstract concept, comprising the network of contracts and obligations that 'individual men and women and families' voluntarily enter into with each other. Corrupting Adam Smith, individualists believe that 'society' (or the aggregate interests of everyone) is best served by individuals pursuing their own self-interest.

That is not what most people want or believe. They believe the opposite, that a society has a responsibility for the welfare of all its members, by virtue of the fact that they are its citizens. This is not just a question of looking after those who cannot look after themselves. It is about deciding and providing collectively the kind of society that people

[209]

want to live in, that they know they cannot obtain through their own efforts.

To take an everyday example. Bob Tyrell of the Henley Centre for Forecasting put it thus: 'Many times when you leave people to behave in an individualistic fashion, they will do things which aren't necessarily what they would like to do if there were some sort of collective co-ordination. For example, more and more people are driving their cars into London, and yet, when you ask people would they accept radical measures to limit the amount of access of cars to London, overwhelming numbers would accept really extreme measures – such as total bans on certain days.'

All the triumphs of Thatcherite individualism turn out to be sleights of hand on closer examination. Take council house sales, at first sight one of the most successful policies of Thatcherism. It has always been popular. A Gallup poll in 1967 found exactly the same level of support for the policy (74%) as in 1979. But people also overwhelmingly support the need for local councils to build more houses to replace the ones they sell. Those who have bought their council houses are generally glad to have done so, but often worried about where their children are going to live, given that they cannot afford to buy and the council may no longer be able to house them. Those who have *not* bought council houses don't tend to feel strongly about the issue either way, but don't see why individuals should be prevented from buying council houses simply because the government won't let local councils replace the houses they sell. If councils were allowed to do so, then, far from being evidence of popular individualism, council house sales would be an excellent example of the 'enabling state' providing collective access to the goal of home ownership. Instead, the whole exercise becomes one of robbing Peter to pay Paul, and, while the British public never made the Labour Party's mistake of blaming Paul, neither did it approve of the robber-government.

Thatcherism's attempts to promote private health care and private education have similarly failed to persuade the British voters from their attachment to the principle of collective provision. But one of the reasons why 'collectivism' is an unsatisfactory word to describe the values of the majority is that it carries the hint of coercion, and one of the striking features of British popular collectivism is its absolute distaste for requiring individuals to do things for the collective good. What people support is 'enabling' or optional collective provision. So the idea of prohibiting council tenants from buying, or of banning private health care or education, has never been popular.

Call it enabling collectivism, or social democracy, or democratic socialism, what a majority of the people want is a meritocratic society in which government takes responsibility for narrowing the disparities of income and wealth, without using coercive state power. At the beginning of Mrs Thatcher's premiership 59% of people thought 'income and wealth should be redistributed towards ordinary working people', and towards the end, in 1987, 58% still agreed. Asked a direct question by MORI two years later, a majority preferred 'a country which emphasises the social and collective provision of welfare' (54%) to 'a country where the individual is encouraged to look after himself' (37%).

Harold Wilson was right about one thing. The Labour Party *is* the natural party of government in Britain. Historically, its values, its commitment to social justice, especially in the form of the postwar welfare state, and its apologetic and confused egalitarianism, are closer to the values of the British people than are those of any other party. However, 'natural' does not mean 'divinely ordained' and so for a decade and more an extremely unnatural Prime Minister has held power.

Polls and Policies

As history speeds up towards the end of this period, the Labour Party is going to need all the help it can get in translating these values into government. Learning to love opinion polls was a vital step. Opinion polls are a useful, indeed democratic, instrument. But it is no use simply looking at opinion polls and deciding to say what they say. In constructing the alternative to Thatcherism, the values revealed by opinion polls are only the starting point. Part of politics is leadership, and those values have to be interpreted in relation to the direction in which our society is heading.

Hence the need to know 'where we are historically and in which direction to move'. Luckily the tides of history, and of public opinion, are all moving against Thatcherism. On social justice, more democracy, a more united Europe and the environment, the Thatcherite Conservative Party is deeply uncomfortable, while between them the opposition parties (Labour, Liberals, SDP and Greens) credibly account for the whole platform.

Opinion polls show all these tides are flowing, in the sense that young people are much more enthusiastic about them. If the Labour Party could follow the fashion for name-changing that is sweeping the communist world, and rename itself the Green European Labour Party (or GEL for short), it would be home and dry. Although, just to make certain, it might want to put in the word 'Democratic' as well. The demand for greater democracy, for 'giving people a say', is already strong but frustrated in the United Kingdom. In the 11 years to 1989, Gallup found significant falls in the proportion of people feeling they had enough say in 'the way the government runs the country', in 'conditions of work', in 'policies pursued by employers' and in 'the way newspapers present the news'.

The Labour Party needs to be more convincing in its commitment to spread democracy upwards to the European Community and downwards to the regions (and throughout society). The Green Party notion of a 'federal Europe of the regions' could have been mocked as a fairytale, both archaic and imaginary, only very recently. The Scottish National Party slogan, 'independence within Europe', *was* much mocked (until Labour came up with the utterly ludicrous 'independence within the UK'). But now both could actually fit with a realisable dream of a more united Europe which succeeds in controlling resurgent nationalisms.

But the 'popular front of the mind' is not a party political project. It is an attempt to shift the centre of gravity of politics back to collectivism, to realign British politics with the European democratic contest between social democracy and Christian democracy.

Looking ahead, this two-party system (Christian democracy versus social democracy) is likely to become Europe-wide. The European Parliament is already divided along these lines. And the problem of the lack of democratic accountability of the European Community's institutions, especially the Commission (the so-called 'democratic deficit'), could eventually be solved by some kind of democratic mandate from the whole 200-million strong electorate of the EC. Whether this is through the European Parliament or some kind of 'presidential' election, the choice will undoubtedly be between Christian democracy (which in this country would by then probably be represented by Heseltinian Toryism) and social democracy.

But this choice is no longer limited to Western Europe. The democratic forces which are emerging in Eastern Europe are already divided between nascent Christian democrats and embryo social democrats. In Poland, Solidarity is divided between those who want to throw off all vestiges of state planning in favour of the free market, and those who want to restrain the free market in the name of social justice (after all, Solidarity is a trade union).

Which brings us back to Leonid Volkov, whose words I quoted at the start of this chapter. His attempt to refound 'social democracy' in the Soviet Union is one of the many ways in which the tradition of social democracy is being reforged across Eastern Europe. By the party in Hungary (which has changed its name and its ideology), and by the people in East Germany (who booed West German Christian Democrat

Chancellor Helmut Kohl, and make it clear they see a difference between 'freedom' and 'Western capitalism').

There is very limited evidence on the nature of ordinary people's political values in Eastern Europe, but what there is suggests they are egalitarian and social democratic. As far as I know, the only detailed survey work has been done in Hungary in 1985–87, as part of the International Social Survey programme (published in the British Social Attitudes series in 1989). Although some post-communist politicians may be enthusiastic free-marketeers, 78% of ordinary Hungarians support a guaranteed minimum income (against a West European average of about 50% and only 21% in the United States). A similar proportion, 77%, in Hungary think it is the government's responsibility to reduce income differences between people – about the same as in Italy and higher than the West European average, which is around the 63% found in Britain.

While Dr Volkov in the USSR was reporting uncertainty about the direction of history after the end of Stalinism, in the USA Francis Fukuyama declared the 'end of history' with the global triumph of Western liberalism. No doubt in Europe Christian democracy will be strengthened by 'told you so' triumphalism over the collapse of communism. No doubt also that nationalism and religion will, as Fukuyama suggested, attempt to fill the vacuum left by Marxism. But Fukuyama's analysis is simple and Americanocentric in its implied triumph of the political Right: viewed from Europe, the events in the East also strengthen the non-Marxist Left. Its opponents are deprived of a powerful weapon: the threat from the Evil Empire.

Despite Dr Volkov's report of the Soviet people's uncertainty about the *direction* of history, his attempt to revive a tradition of social democracy in the Soviet Union induces a strong sense that history is not at an end. And a strong sense that Thatcherism is out of date.

Making Sense of It

JEREMY SEABROOK

When I look back now on my upbringing and education, I am incredulous that what then appeared so opaque and mysterious should now be so obvious to me. To have grown up in a working-class community with a contempt for manual labour seemed, at the time, a daring and original response, a sign of superior intelligence. It is clear now that this was merely a reflection of a growing division of labour which no longer required so many people in the production of leather and boots and shoes, which was the staple industry of my home town.

Revulsion against manual labour is something which the vast majority of the working class had always felt; but in the fifties such feelings first became permissible for a minority of us, and space was provided in which to express them. What a curious mutation of the multiple snobberies of British society, to be divided by class from individuals in the same family! Of course, our education encouraged us to believe that it all stemmed from our superior merit, this deliverance from the necessity of factory work. It was flattering to be told that we had deserved to be plucked out of the mass of the people, and to be heaped with favours. Nothing is more calculated to blind people to what is really happening to them than to have them believe that their good fortune is a reward for their moral or intellectual worth. We thought we were the actors and agents of our own improvement.

By the time I was about 13, I was aware of a feeling of lofty irritation towards the men who came home from the factory each day on their bikes, with the feral smell of animal hides that clung to their clothes and pervaded the streets where we lived. They seemed to me inarticulate, their lives joyless, with their allotments of runner beans and dahlias full of earwigs, their games of darts and dour philosophy that nothing was ever done without trouble except letting the fire go out. That they had left behind them at work something useful and durable did not occur to me. They needed no further justification than that they had created footwear that would protect the feet of soldiers in combat, enable the gentry to dance until dawn, draw gasps of admiration from those who recognised the latest fashion when they saw it, and set the feet of children on the straight and narrow path in their new Whitsun boots.

It became a perverse source of pride to me that I couldn't do anything practical; so that I grew to a version of maturity unable to fix a fuse, mend a radio, or manipulate a saw or chisel. My twin, who had always occupied the C-stream at secondary school, became a carpenter. He became the personification of the way of life I believed I had escaped, the victim of my snobbery and indifference. It looked like a tragic parting of the ways. In the long run, of course, he became far more successful than I did; and the real lesson of our upbringing was delayed into middle age, when the Thatcher era revealed that his version of pecuniary success was what really mattered, and all the nonsense I had filled my head with about the caring society was shown to be the delusion it was.

The expanding division of labour first liberated and then trapped me. It leads to a society in which people come to know more and more about less and less; a narrowing of specialisms goes hand in hand with an apparent broadening of horizons. To have lost any purchase on the material world, to have no role in the production of anything of use, represents a curious kind of orphaning of social purpose. In that respect I was, I suppose, a pioneer of the now far more elaborate service sector, that generator of such spectacularly vacuous, dispensable and demeaning forms of labour. If it felt at the time like a liberation, this was solely because of the disagreeable working conditions under which useful things were at that time produced. It seems to me now to have been simply another form of the ingenious and multiple impoverishments and expropriations of which the capitalist system is capable.

Nor was that the end of the story. Not only had I left the working class, but I discovered, at university and later, that this involuntary defection was a source of considerable fascination and some glamour to those who had not followed the same trajectory. By the time this moment of glory had passed, I had become a member of another briefly desirable group: as a social worker, part of the fabric of the then 'caring society', I was guaranteed a certain respect, even awe. During the sixties, people frequently said, 'A social worker? I think that's wonderful. Of course, I could never do it myself. It would upset me, I'm too sensitive. But I so admire you.' This time of approval passed even more swiftly than that granted to those with working-class antecedents. It was succeeded by the fashionable role of being a gay man in the 1970s, the last liberal moment before the onset of the dark age of Thatcher, and before the menace of AIDS thrust us from grace with even greater ignominy than our fall from either of the previously approved groups. During the eighties, to be gay, to belong to a

[216]

stigmatised social-work profession, to have any kinship with an archaic and doomed working class, meant – especially in combination – occupying one of the lowest positions in the British caste system.

If I have learned anything in this decade of instruction, it is that those who have seen labour as the sole locus of exploitation by the capitalist system have pitifully underestimated its protean, inventive and voracious capacity for using up human beings and then discarding them.

Politics Beyond the Party

SARAH BENTON

This thesis is simple. It is that national political parties cannot be made into the 'people's parties' of socialist legend[1]. The driving force of political parties is the need to be professional. This cannot be reconciled with the desire to make the party the public voice of ordinary citizens. Parties which are in the business of winning elections and forming governments, national or local, cannot also be the medium of the masses for shaping their own lives. Nor can smaller parties; their first task is to sustain their own organisation and policies. Attempts to make parties the means through which most people can be 'active citizens' are a waste of hope and energy.

Political parties are essential for exercising some control over the state. Sometimes they can devise grand strategies and policies. Efforts to make them do these things well are not wasted. But if political people are to change how society works, we need to develop the forms of community, voluntary and movement activity which speak to and for citizens *in society*. If civil society produces inequality and exploitation – of people and environment – political people must turn their energy to this great circus that lies between the state and private life.

The Unrepeatable Party

Mass political parties were created by particular circumstances which existed between about 1870 and 1920. Socialists invented them, and conservatives refined them for their own needs. Those particular circumstances included the nature of class relations, the form and size of the state and the relative homogeneity of the nation. Above all, they included the invention of a dominant socialist identity; anyone who didn't fit was backward, or an outsider.

It is easy to forget – within a conservative culture which insists on the historic essence of a British, now English, race – how recent these nation

[219]

states and national identities have been. The anti-semitism which shaped our century was attributed by Hannah Arendt to their nineteenth-century evolution[2]. When mass parties were founded, different ethnic and religious groups could be left out both physically (as in the exclusion of people from the colonies) and politically – even the enlightened Webbs talked of black people as 'non-adult' races lacking, like children, the qualities of the citizen (*New Statesman*, 1913).

Political parties were also the creatures of the nineteenth-century separation of politics and morality. At first, this was an advantage for women. Those who spoke of morality, mainly from the church, law and medical profession, inveighed against women's sexual freedom and any escape from their domestic role as a threat to the health of the nation. But the language left to social democratic parties – of wages, work and state economic intervention – could not speak to or for women, confined in the domestic sphere. Parties did not challenge the sexual conservatism advanced by the fathers of morality. A leading member of the Women's Labour League (which existed between 1906, when the Labour Party was formed, and 1918, when it was reformed) referred unselfconsciously to Labour as 'the men's party'[3]. Women were excluded from actual citizenship, despite the winning of the franchise.

The political parties then were a product of a peculiar national, class and sexual homogeneity. Only this allowed the mass of the working class to unite with some intellectuals behind the idea of using the state to bring about democracy, justice and equality.

This reached its peak in the few years after World War Two. Post-war reconstruction regenerated a party system which many[4], including George Orwell, believed had become irremediably degenerate by the war. But war meant national unity as well as high working-class aspiration, progressive state control and a deep hostility to the privileges of rank and wealth. The prestige and power of the party as a vehicle of mass aspiration passed its peak in the mid-1950s. In no Western country did it adapt with any grace to the reality of ethnic diversity. None was able to adapt to the pressure of women to become full citizens. That is, political parties hung on to the homogeneity which had allowed their growth by excluding those who challenged it. Few developed new forms to cope with the ebbing of the powers of the European nation states. All were driven by the imperatives of complex state management and mass broadcasting to become more professional.

The year 1968 presaged the end of the old political party. It was the year of a new generation. It was less deferential, uncowed by the Cold War and the sneer 'communist', unafflicted by gratitude to the welfare state that had fed and educated it, egalitarian in its instincts, impatient of bureaucracy and inventive with culture and sexuality. It is just possible that had the mass parties embraced this new generation, then their 'new politics' could have been assimilated; the party might have been transformed. But most mass left-wing parties perceived the new politics as their implacable enemy. Excluded British, French, Italian and German students went into direct action, along with gay, black, peace and Green movements, as well as dozens of specially honed grouplets. All the Labour Party got out of it was a strangulated form of this radicalism which was willing to speak the language of constitutional reform, branch takeover and conference resolution. The French Communist Party never recovered.

The parties of the centre were the next to go. The Liberals, the SDP, the Alliance and the SLD made their bid for power in the name of creating a wholly new form of politics; they would be parties of free individuals, undriven by the demands of capital and class. Not one of these pioneers could withstand the overwhelming pressure to turn professional. The conflict in the SLD has been profoundly destructive; the 'community politicians' are deeply alienated by the centralisation and media gloss demanded by professionalism; those who want an efficient party machine and good television performance are contemptuous of the 'woolly liberals'. The attempt to resolve this conflict has failed, suggesting the modern political party cannot contain both forces.

The newest parties in Western Europe, the Greens, exist through a constant negotiation of this tension between professionalism and openness. Significantly, many committed Green activists stay away from the Green Party precisely because they want to keep free of the conflict and bureaucracy which party organisation generates.

Similar trends are common throughout Western Europe and the USA. The few nations which, because of similar circumstances, produced mass political parties (such as Japan and India) found their own party systems degenerating into accusations of corruption, bureaucracy and exclusivity. Leading members of the ruling Liberal Democratic Party in Japan (and no doubt un-leading members too) were found to be in the pay of the employment company Recruit, or maintaining courtesans despite protestations about family life, or both. 'What has happened in India this week,' concluded Tony Allen Mills in the *Independent* after the 1989 election, 'is exactly what should happen in any flourishing democracy – a bunch of flaccid, lazy, arrogant, shifty, mostly crooked members of parliament have been given their marching orders by an increasingly sophisticated electorate.' That was a hopeful view.

Yet as long as we have a state, the political party is the best form we have evolved to give the state some sort of direction, to enforce some democratic accountability.

Only the party can do this because only the party acts fully in both state and civil society. Parties need to be kept alive; they need to have their tendency to become exclusive clubs constantly checked. But because parties have this unique function of holding the state to account, they can never be free of the limitations the state imposes on them. That is, branches will have to keep on with the sales of jumble and party literature, with nominating people for office, ensuring that the machinery of the state is kept ticking over. How can a political party, caught between the minutes of the last meeting and the resolutions for the next, also be a friendly, non-sectarian forum for ordinary citizens?

Can Eastern Europe Revive the Party?

And yet – what of Eastern Europe? Does this not negate the whole argument, as citizens take to the streets to insist on their right to speak their own political language and form their own parties? Their starting point is profoundly different. The Czech, Polish and East German civic groups start from an assumption that environmental protection may demand less growth, not more. The first mass political parties of the West were founded on the assumption of permanent economic growth. The new political forces so far perceive religion as their ally in the demand for cultural and political freedom – for an autonomous civil society. Their politics is a demand for freedom from the state, not for greater state action. Forty to seventy years of state socialism have eradicated the rhetoric of class conflict without which no mass-class party can be formed. And, despite their assertion of national identity, today's politics are international.

We are seeing the emergence of new political forms in the West too. Like all new forms, they are a response to what has gone before, what are now seen to be the threats. For instance, if Eastern Europe is asserting its national identities, many from the Third World are rediscovering a trans-national Muslim identity. 'O Muslims! It is time to realise that the present political order in the Muslim world has not come about by the wish of the Muslims or to their advantage. The current secular, capitalist, communist or nationalist regimes have been imposed on us by the enemies of Islam to keep us weak and divided,' proclaimed the British section of the Hizb ut-Tahrir Islamic party, which is campaigning for a united, transnational Islamic state. Ayatollah Khomeini spoke for many, quite unfanatical, Muslims when he condemned the USA as the devil that would devour them all. Islamic fundamentalism, which is becoming a potent factor in Britain and France, as well as the Soviet Union, is not the survival of a medieval form in the midst of modernity, but a contemporary reaction to that modernity[5].

Scottish and Welsh nationalism is also a reaction to the failures of the

UK nation-state. It is, as Raymond Williams said in *Towards 2000*, simply the wrong size – too small to be powerful, too large to allow for communal identities and self-management. Nationalist parties were struggling to survive – until they discovered the EC, that larger state form which can empower the smaller nation. Alternatively, it allows new transnational blocs; Peter Glotz, the influential West German social democrat, has proposed European institutions to promote European culture against the American tide, and argued that one of the EC's priorities must be a strategy for dealing with the movement to Europe of Third World people. We are trying to devise a new politics within frontiers when we don't know where the new frontiers will be.

Where does this leave us? There is one thing citizens of most countries have in common; that is the desire to create their own forms of self-management within civil society. There is a universal recognition of the necessary limits of government. The implications for socialists in the West, accustomed to their litany of demands for the government to do something, put things right, change society, are enormous.

The dangers seem equally enormous. It is equality within the state which gives us our language of a secular, egalitarian democracy. If we are seeing the assertion of essential new social identities – of ethnicity or religion, for instance – of one law for Muslims, one for Catholics and another for the rest – must we give up our secular, egalitarian language for good? Or can our preferred language, of democratic participation by all, regardless of sex and race and religion and ethnic background, become the lingua franca of the modern world?

For without some form of political organisation which transcends divisions of sex and ethnicity and religion, civil society will be at the mercy either of semi-secret brotherhoods or of the state itself. Thus, democratic citizens need urgently to add to their party commitments a new sort of 'civic forum' which is open to all who want to direct society through open political means.

Brotherhoods

First, some comments on the semi-secret brotherhoods, which might seem an arcane and anachronistic warning in a modern society, or even a lapse into late twentieth-century paranoia. In the last few years in Britain, the term has been applied (picking some at random) to trades unions (as in Cynthia Cockburn's book *The Brothers*), to freemasons (as in Stephen Knight's book, *The Brotherhood*) and to the Kray twins. Dr Kalim Siddiqui, the man leading the British campaign against Salman Rushdie, says, in an unselfconscious echo of the language of Muslim identity: 'I love the brotherhood of journalists.' In conscious irony, racist police officers describe black men as 'our coloured brethren'. The legal profession's inability to admit to miscarriages of justice describes a brotherhood.

In Scotland, the formation of the Scottish Constitutional Convention as the embryo of a new democracy has included only a handful of women amongst over 200 representatives. This is not because Scottish democrats are hostile to the participation of women (there is a special working party to explore how to encourage it); simply that, in order for its representatives to appear authoritative, they have been drawn from *society*'s dominant organisations; churches, trades unions, political parties, small firms. The presence of women in these societies is rare, of black people exceptional. Even Conservative women, the most discreetly loyal of subjects, share the view of the House of Commons, our democracy incarnate, as a fraternity club.

The point, here, is not to explain why this is so; only to remark that the exclusion of women and non-white men from the organisations of civil society *is* so. Society has an essentially club-like quality and these clubs are the largest single force acting against a secular democracy. More powerful than the state, which at least – because it is subject to political argument – proclaims a formal commitment to individual equality. When Chairman of the Conservative Party, John Selwyn Gummer could give his support, quite unremarkably, to the recruitment of more women parliamentary candidates. As a member of the synod, he stands for fundamental opposition to the admission of women to the clergy. The language of politics is our only egalitarian language.

While the first aim of a national political party is properly to win control over the state, the first aim of civic organisations must be to counter the power of clubs in society, whether these are tight-knit communities of professionals, associations of businessmen awarding each other contracts and favours, freemasonries in police or local councils, or the dominance of 'moral' debates by religious fraternities.

Some like to think that the hidden networks of influence and corruption are a Third World problem, a feature of a society where poverty is endemic and political institutions have not had the time or opportunity to become the dominant forms in society. Britain is currently spending £50 million on investigations into police misbehaviour. Televangelists in the USA, the Recruit scandal in Japan, the grip of the Mafia in southern Italy and the USA, Graham Greene's denunciation of systematic corruption in the South of France, the implication of the Swedish firm Bofors in the Indian corruption scandal – these are just a glimpse of the covert networks of patronage and protection which counteract democracy.

Networks like these are not necessarily the dominant forces in society;

but they do constantly threaten to subvert *politics* in every society. Democratic politics cannot function in closed clubs. Like terrorism, which has had a more baneful influence on democratic politics than we like to admit, influence networks function as secret brotherhoods, and while secret brotherhoods have often been the agents of political change (the precursor of Irish nationalism was the Irish Republican Brotherhood), they have rarely been the precursors of democracy. The South African Broederbond, the Muslim Brotherhood in Egypt, and the Mafia once promised much, but never mass democracy.

Speak Out for Politics

Only political involvement can get power out of the hands of such clubs and networks. But politics, in the truism, is a dirty word. Politics, believe many, is about jobs for the boys and telling lies. Why should ordinary people hold to this view? Take the Conservative Party, an organisation which in theory exists to express popular political will and yet seems, to the outsider, to have eschewed politics in favour of social pleasantries. Seasonal programmes go out inviting branch members to fashion shows and flower arranging sessions, to sherry parties and garden parties and wine and cheese parties and barbecue-at-a-big-house parties. These, organised and attended largely by fund-raising women, are the well-known face of local Conservatism. Membership overlaps significantly with the women who run and fund-raise for local charities and of course the local Conservative councillors. It's very nice, sincere and apolitical.

Less well known is the club which almost every constituency association has created. They have different names – Constitutional Club, Marlborough Club, Carlton Club – but each is for businessmen (owners and directors of firms) only, the annual membership fee is significantly higher (often starting at £100) and the perquisite is the annual dinner at which the company of a high-ranking MP, often a Cabinet minister, is guaranteed. At a more day-to-day level, these clubs ensure contacts within the local business and political community. Membership overlaps with the Rotary Club, Round Table, Chamber of Commerce, etc. In these ways, the Conservative Party is firmly part of civil society but, outside moments of crisis (as in 1977–79 when the business community galvanised itself to drive out socialism) its function is as much social and financial as political. In other words, the function of the Conservative Party is not to encourage democratic participation. It is to reinforce the cultural conservatism of society, and to provide access to the networks that matter.

It is usually assumed that Labour is quite different. Socialist parties are founded precisely because their supporters lack social influence. They can't make things happen in society.

Yet, as we have learned from (most notoriously) Newcastle and Liverpool, if not too many other Labour strongholds, Labour has no built-in protection against transmuting into a network for exchanging influence. It too can function as a brotherhood of trades unionists and councillors whose decisions on anything, from the allocation of housing to the allocation of development sites to different contractors, can owe more to networks than democracy. Tammany was a nineteenth-century secret brotherhood for subverting New York politics; it gave its name to 'Tammany Hall', the creation of social democratic parties. In other words, regardless of the idealistic purpose which creates and sustains a political party, any falling-off of that purpose means the party easily degenerates into a network of influence, often a brotherhood. (Few women have any purchase in these networks, many of whose transactions are conducted in men's clubs.) They are, by their nature, antithetical to democracy and popular power.

It is the Left's mission to make civil society and state accountable to politics. It is its mission to wrest power out of fraternities in civil society – bodies usually dubbed 'private' by a conservative state. Political parties have shown their limits in this task – not least because, in order to function, they reproduce many of those clubbish fraternities themselves. It is the mission of the Left because conservatism is sustained precisely by unaccountable fraternities in civil society. Hence the vehement attack on state intervention in management and industry (labelled 'social engineering' by Walter Goldsmith, when director of the Institute of Directors). Hence the attack of Conservative peers, driven on by Baroness Cox in the mid-1980s, on peace studies and the promotion of homosexuality, and the espousal of Christian education in schools in the name of keeping politics out of education.

So how do we reshape politics so that a myriad different communities, from a workplace to a religious faith, can shape its society and yet sustain a language of equality, tolerance and democracy? How can we insist that education, or your brand of washing powder, is accountable to political principles, without falling into the 1970s trap of thinking everything is always political? For while there are no theoretical limits to politics – it sometimes must intrude into the most intimate of relationships, or the most mundane of choices – politics with no limits of time or place becomes totalitarian. It abolishes the distinctions between state, civil society, and private life.

To begin with, we have to be ready to abolish one private/public distinction, and allow emotion and morality into our politics. Most of us take our feelings and experience as the only authentic test of truth. A typical example is a person who disbelieves all accounts of arbitrary police power until she finds her child locked up in a police cell for no reason; or the man who sneers at all propaganda about equal rights for homosexuals until he discovers his son is gay. Throughout modern history, with its separation of politics and morality, politics has foundered again and again on this conflict with authenticity. An analysis of the speeches of dominant right-wing leaders (whether a Hitler or a Thatcher) reveals clearly how fundamental is their stress on authenticity *as opposed to* politics.

Special Language

Here we come up against the paucity of a political culture which can speak only abstractly of public goods. Early socialism could evoke passionate emotion which linked the individual to the crowd. Think of the huge success of Blatchford's *Merrie England*, the importance of Bernard Shaw in the creation of that early socialist culture, the power of Robert Tressell's *The Ragged Trousered Philanthropists* in expressing personal longing and anguish. Even Marx's *Capital* is redolent of a Dickensian moral language.

This is what Eastern Europe has which we, at the moment, do not. In Poland in 1980, in Berlin in 1989, people said the same thing; we are discovering our own language for saying what we really want. (Briefly, early members of the SDP in Britain said the same thing.) How do we create the possibility for people to say what they want and feel? A political culture of soundbites and groomed interviews, of branch resolutions and exhortations roared at the crowd, of (from the Left) meaningless demands to 'Smash Thatcher', are all a grisly distortion of political integrity. And politicians learn it early. One woman on the hard trudge round constituencies trying to win a nomination for a parliamentary election said the worst thing was 'never being able to say what you really think. To lots of the questions I just wanted to say "I don't know".' Instead, prospective politicians have to *learn* the language of politics; otherwise an 'I don't know' might slip out.

People who use language dishonestly stand the lowest in public esteem. Estate agents, journalists and politicians regularly come at the bottom of 'How Do You Rate Them' league tables because they have all evolved a special language which is designed to deceive. Most people complain that political meetings are boring. This is not always because the subject of discussion is intrinsically less interesting than, say, what's on TV that night; but rather because it is discussed in a special language which conceals the individual and any authentic expression of desire or fear.

For these and more reasons, the electoral political party seems to me beyond reform as a vehicle of mass participation in politics. Professional politicians, in our electoral system at least, cannot speak with absolute honesty, for honest views on sex or black people or abortion or, indeed, the undeserving poor make as many enemies as friends.

In a modern society, which acknowledges its diversity (as early socialism would not) there cannot be one hegemonic political language. Those who yearn for it are living in a past to which we do not want to return. There are hegemonic values, of justice, equality, democracy, tolerance, which the political party must espouse, which the state can attempt to guarantee. But only by treating all people as individuals. Once we speak the language of the communities of society, as many socialists do, we must stop thinking of state intervention and state rights.

The more ambitious and confident groups in society have the alternative: trades unions willing to take on the issue of industrial democracy or safety at work; groups of the disabled and chronically sick willing to challenge the medical profession and the allocation of state health resources; residents up in arms over local planning; consumers angry about the lack of information or protection – all these have the potential to be the key political actors of the future. Already, pressure groups are distancing themselves from the close relationships they established with the Labour Party in the 1970s; the Child Poverty Action Group and CND are just two which know that their future lies in political autonomy.

This leaves a last question. If such groups are to develop a larger and more influential political role, and be the agencies for ordinary citizens who want to act on what they know about, and speak in their own language, there remains the question of where the power is to come from to challenge national and international forces; and where the policies are to come from if they are not merely to be those of local self-interest? Everyone knows of the danger that a residents' group can become the most intolerant of bodies, using its powers merely to exclude the undesirables.

That is to forget the very factor which has so changed the role of national political parties – the spread of a broadcast political culture outside the control of party leaderships. That is, an appetite for public debate during the 1980s has increased the number of broadcast political discussion programmes, and increased the audience for them. Contrary to the popular view that the mass media have depoliticised people, it seems probable that more people today are familiar with national political arguments, and people, than ever were before. Thanks to broadcasting, far more people are at least aware of what the arguments from the other side are. Every environmental group knows the acronym NIMBY and knows it means selfishness. So, although there are indeed very great risks in any argument for more power to local and community and self-help groups, there are also reasons to hope they can be countered. And if such groups were more politically assured, they would be doing in public (a good thing) what is anyway now done in private. 'Nice' areas have always been able to keep factories, roads or hypermarkets away; going public allows everyone else to join in.

That leaves the question of the political parties' relation to such new groups. The simple answer is that they will go on being the 'caucus and cadre' groups they are already in reality; but that, with newly influential community groups, they will be forced to listen to and consult with such groups. It is rare, for example, for a constituency Labour Party to invite voluntary associations for discussion; they think the needs of any special group should be taken care of by the state. Yet listening to and working with such groups is the future.

The Crisis of Opposition:
a Reappraisal

JAMES CURRAN

Margaret Thatcher is the first Prime Minister since Lord Liverpool to win three elections in a row. Her 1987 election triumph produced a landslide majority of 102 seats, the second biggest since 1945. Just as historians have advanced sweeping and synoptic explanations to account for the Conservative hegemony in late-Victorian Britain, so explanations of corresponding breadth and range would seem called for to account for the contemporary ascendancy of Thatcherism.

Three explanations have been advanced, all of which seem plausible: the electoral base of the Right expanded, while that of the Left contracted; a social revolution promoted yuppie values and weakened the culture of the Left; and the Right won the battle of ideas. In short, Conservatism is in the ascendant because it represents the expanding, dynamic and dominant forces in society.

This has become the received wisdom of contemporary political analysis (although the current problems of the Conservative Government are now causing many people to have second thoughts). It is this received wisdom which partly prompted the Labour Party to put all its policies on probation in the most far-reaching review it has ever undertaken. The review resulted in a defensive document which reluctantly incorporated some Thatcherite themes in order, it is hoped, that the party can survive the 'new times' in which we live. The same received wisdom has prompted some demoralised members of the Centre and Left to want to huddle together in electoral pacts in an alliance of expediency rather than of conviction.

I want to suggest that this received wisdom is fundamentally misleading. The ascendancy of Thatcherism reflects not the triumph of new social forces, nor the ideological ascendancy of the New Right, but a deep-seated *political* crisis of opposition. The remedy lies not in accommodating to the New Right or searching for a gerrymandering political fix through electoral pacts. The answer lies in developing a new style of politics that mobilises a new social coalition.

[231]

Shifts

The explanation for the Conservatives' electoral success with the widest currency is also the simplest: groups in which the Right is dominant (the middle class, house owners, share owners, people living in the affluent south of England) have all increased in numbers whereas groups in which the Left is dominant – trades unionists, council tenants, manual workers, city dwellers – have all shrunk. Structural change is thus viewed as a silent motor engineering a run of Conservative victories.

The trouble with this explanation is that it greatly exaggerates the extent of social change, and simplifies its implications. First, it often double-counts the same people by classifying them in different ways: for example, a new member of the middle class, a new home owner and a new shareholder can all be the same person. Secondly, it simplifies the consequences of social change. Council tenants have not automatically changed from Labour to Conservative when they have bought their council houses: many (as polling evidence demonstrates) were Conservative in the first place, while some have stayed Labour.

Two political sociologists, Anthony Heath and Sarah-K McDonald, attempted in *Political Studies* (1987) to quantify 'the net impact of social change' on the political fortunes of political parties between 1964 and 1986. Their conclusion is that it added 4% to the Conservative vote and 1% to the Alliance vote, while producing a drop of 5% in the Labour vote. Since Labour's share of the poll fell by 14% between the 1964 and 1987 general elections, their analysis suggests that structural change was responsible for little more than a third of this fall.

Yet even this calculation may overstate the significance of structural change since it ignored all countervailing social trends favouring the Left (as well as, admittedly, some minor shifts favouring the Right). During the last two decades, the growth of mass unemployment, the long-term increase in the number of public sector employees, the relative decline of their earnings during the 1980s compared with the private sector and, above all, the erosion of class deference have all potentially benefited the Labour Party.

But the more fundamental weakness of the structuralist approach is that it adopts a reductive explanation of how people vote. Changes in group membership create the potential for but do not determine changes in political allegiance. This point is perhaps best underlined by the fact that left-wing parties have prospered in numerous countries undergoing structural changes comparable to those in Britain – such as Sweden, Finland, Austria, Spain, France, Australia and Japan.

James Curran

Cultural Revolution

An alternative explanation of the Conservative ascendancy attributes it to an imperceptible cultural revolution. In its simplest version, sometimes advanced by right-wing journalists, this takes the form of claiming that class rigidities in British society have largely disappeared. In fact, a wealth of sociological research shows that class inequalities of wealth, income, health, higher educational attainment and life opportunities (in terms of *relative* mobility rates) have been remarkably constant throughout the postwar period.

A more sophisticated variant of this argument asserts that class has lost its 'tribal' meaning, and consequent hold on political life. In particular, a profound change has allegedly taken place within the working class. It has become more affluent, middle-class and individualistic. Working people increasingly do not think of themselves as working-class because their social identity is shaped more by the consumerist world of leisure than by the workplace. They are less inclined to view the world in oppositional terms because social hierarchies have become more opaque. Increased internal differentiation has also promoted sectionalism: a North Sea engineer does not perceive an identity of interest, so the argument goes, with a female part-time secretary in Harlow.

These arguments tend to exaggerate the extent of social change by invoking a mythical past of working-class collectivism. In fact, privatism, sectionalism and individualism have always been facets of working-class culture. The question at issue is whether they have become far more pronounced, and have as a consequence transformed British political life. The evidence suggests that this has not been the case. The connection between class and voting has not declined since 1970, as one might expect if class had diminished as a political force[1]. The British Election Surveys (1964–83) show that the spread of affluence has not deradicalised the working class (although there has been a marked drop of support for public ownership). Labour's problem is not simply that its heartland support in the working class has declined; support for it across the whole of society has also fallen in elections since 1970.

But the most telling evidence contradicting the decline-of-class thesis is provided by a recent national survey undertaken by Gordon Marshall and his associates at Essex University[2]. Ninety-two per cent in the survey thought of themselves as belonging to a particular social class, and for many this was an important part of their social identity. Most people also mapped and made sense of society in class terms. Above all, class position and identification emerged as important in generating different perspectives of society, different beliefs, and different voting preferences.

Although important socio-cultural changes have taken place during the last two decades, they have not been as rapid or as far-reaching as is often alleged. Their most important political consequence has been to erode automatic party loyalty, and foster a more critical, calculating approach to voting. Why this should have resulted in a series of Conservative victories is not self-evident, unless one is an uncritical adherent of the Conservative Party.

Battle of Ideas

The third explanation of the Conservative Party's success attributes it to the popularity of its ideas and policies. This seems at first sight to supply the missing answer since the Conservative Party's election victory in 1979 can be explained partly in terms of a shift of public opinion and social values between 1974 and 1979. Survey evidence confirms that there was both a surge of social conservatism and growing resistance to statist policies.

But paradoxically Thatcherism never succeeded in supplanting the core values of social democracy. Indeed, the ideological tide actually ebbed away from the Right during the course of the 1980s. Thus, far from explaining Thatcher's success, the available evidence about public attitudes merely makes it harder to explain.

The Conservative Government has sought to promote wealth creation partly by differential tax cuts for the rich and curbs on public spending. Yet when MORI asked voters in June 1988 whether they preferred a society in which the creation of wealth or caring for others is more highly rewarded, 79% gave the non-Thatcherite response.

This is consistent with evidence showing a cumulative shift towards collectivist values. For over a decade, Gallup has asked voters whether they would prefer taxes to be cut even if this meant worse services, or services to be extended even if this meant higher taxes. In 1979, voters were split evenly between these two options. Yet ten years later, those opting for better services outnumbered tax-cutters by seven to one. Even though this result should not be interpreted literally, it registers a significant revalorisation of the welfare state.

The annual surveys conducted by Social and Community Planning Research from 1983 onwards also show that most people reject the government's free-market philosophy. Around 90% have consistently supported the classic Keynesian strategy of job creation through public works, while about two-thirds have favoured dirigiste measures like price and selective import controls. In 1987, 69% (up 9% on 1983) wanted a corporatist approach in which government involved both unions and management in decisions affecting the economy. Numerous polls also show that the government's latest phase of privatisation is opposed by the large majority.

Indeed, what is striking – as John Rentoul also argues – is the extent to which social democratic values continued to enjoy consensual support during the Thatcherite era. Throughout most of the eighties, four out of five voters said that the government should spend more money to get rid of poverty, and the majority also favoured a smaller gap between rich and poor. In 1986, 80% (up 26% on 1979) said that workers should be given more say in running the places where they work.

It has been argued that the unpopularity of Thatcherite policies in the economic sphere has been offset by the populist appeal of the government's nationalism, social conservatism and authoritarianism. Yet, as Ivor Crewe has shown, nationalistic attitudes and social conservatism (on issues ranging from welfare benefits to capital punishment) weakened in the eighties[3]. Gallup reveals that majority approval for the government's uncompromising style converted into disapproval after 1983. An anti-authoritarian backlash also appears to have developed, as reflected for example in public disapproval of the government's banning of trades unions at GCHQ and attempted suppression of *Spycatcher*. Dissatisfaction with Margaret Thatcher as Prime Minister has intensified, according to Gallup, since 1983; she is now the second most unpopular premier in postwar Britain.

Crisis of Opposition

But if this assessment is correct, an enigma remains. How did the Conservative Party succeed in winning the 1987 general election, if many of its policies were unpopular, the tide of opinion was moving against it and structural change did not provide a fast-moving escalator carrying it to inevitable victory? The answer lies partly in the growth of affluence in oil-rich Britain, and the pre-election boom in 1986–87 which encouraged optimism about the future of the economy.

But the more fundamental reason was that the anti-government vote was split between two weak and little-respected parties. The government did not win the election; the opposition lost it.

The Labour Party has been on a downward electoral curve since 1951. Its electoral position sharply deteriorated after its disappointing record in office between 1974–79, followed by a shift to the left and a bitter internal civil war. Its private polling in the 1983 election (now publicly available) revealed a party not in temporary difficulties but in a profound process of decay. In 1983, Labour won a smaller share of the poll per candidate than at any time since 1906.

The election of a new leader and the adoption of more centrist policies after 1983 failed to rehabilitate the Labour Party in public esteem. Its electoral vulnerability was starkly revealed by the success of a concerted onslaught on the Labour Party initiated by the Conservative Party in October 1986 (but subsequently assisted by the Alliance) which featured the 'loony Left', Labour's unilateralism and its past economic failures. Between October 1986 and the start of the election campaign in May 1987, Labour lost a quarter of its supporters, most of whom defected to the Alliance. Numerous surveys show that Labour was widely regarded as extreme, union-dominated and untrustworthy during the 1987 election despite its professional campaign.

But the Alliance did not prove strong enough to fill the vacuum created by the Labour Party's decay. It came within two percentage points of the Labour Party in the 1983 election, and established a more homogeneous base than the old Liberal Party. But it suffered from a number of debilitating weaknesses. Much of its support still came from a footloose protest vote of people whose views were dissimilar, and whose loyalty was therefore difficult to sustain. It lacked the class base of its rivals, despite building up a significant bridgehead of support among the technical and professional middle class. As the third force in politics, it was vulnerable to the argument that a vote for it was wasted. And it failed to project a clear set of policies and strong positive identity. It consequently lagged behind the major parties in pollsters' performance ratings in all policy areas because it remained for many people something of an unknown quantity.

The Alliance exacerbated Labour's decline without being able to replace it as the major opposition party. The political crisis of the opposition thus explains why the Conservative Party dominated the politics of the eighties without being ideologically ascendant. The Conservatives won in 1987 and 1983 not because they were popular but because the opposition was weak and divided. Indeed, the Conservative Party gained a slightly smaller share of the poll in both these elections than it did in 1964 when it lost under Douglas-Home.

But there are two further dimensions of the politics of the eighties that need to be brought out since they have a bearing on the politics of the future. The first is that even if the electorate was anti-Thatcher, it was to an even greater extent anti-Labour. The underlying anti-Thatcherite consensus did not generate widespread tactical voting against the Conservative Party because many supporters of the political centre could not bring themselves to vote Labour (and the same was true in reverse of Labour supporters, though to a lesser extent).

The other point to be emphasised is that the Conservative victory was inspired partly by fear of what would happen to the economy if the Conservatives lost. According to one election poll, 56% thought that there would be an economic crisis under Labour, while another damning survey found that 49% thought it likely that they would be worse off financially under a Labour Government. In key Conservative-Labour marginal constituencies, almost twice as many people thought that the Conservatives would be better economic managers than Labour. Yet Labour was assessed more positively than the Alliance in relation to the economy in all the 1987 election surveys.

Both the deepseated division within the opposition, and distrust of its economic competence, are central problems that need to be confronted in the 1990s.

Ripple Effect

Events after 1987 have given rise to the impression that a watershed has been reached and that the Conservative Party's electoral domination is finally coming to an end. The government now looks distinctly vulnerable, principally because the economy is in deep trouble. Ten years into its administration, Britain has a record trade deficit, high inflation, falling investment and an eroding currency. Britain's much-vaunted 'economic miracle' is revealed as a mirage.

Secondly, anti-government feeling has begun to coalesce around the Labour Party. The Alliance's messy divorce damaged the centre parties, causing their ratings to plummet to single figures. In contrast, Labour's national ratings rose to around 45% in the third quarter of 1989, whereas they never rose above 40% during the previous Parliament.

These trends seemingly validate the revisionist and sectarian electoral strategy of the Labour Party. In a bid to reassure centrist opinion, it has moved further to the right than at any time in opposition during the last fifty years. And it has consistently kept its distance from and attacked the post-Alliance parties. Its reward has been to emerge triumphantly as an increasingly acceptable focus of opposition to a beleaguered government.

But the impression that the Thatcherite phase has finally run its course may prove to be mistaken. Labour's credibility as a manager of the economy has been enhanced by its move to the right, and by the government's obvious economic failure. Yet residual doubts about Labour's competence (crucially among skilled workers who formerly voted Labour) still remain. This is reflected, for instance, in the September 1989 Harris survey which revealed that the Conservative

[237]

Party still outpointed Labour by 44% to 27% as 'the party most trusted to deal with the economic crisis', despite the fact that the economy was then lurching from bad to worse under Lawson's chancellorship.

Anti-government forces are also still divided. Although the post-Alliance parties are in disarray, the emergence of the Greens as a political force has in effect added an attractive, alternative focus for anti-government protest votes. It is also conceivable that the more resilient of the centre parties, the Liberal Democrats, could stage some sort of recovery in the south of England before the next election partly at the expense of the Labour Party.

Although the political situation is undoubtedly very different from what it was before the 1987 election, people with long memories will recall that some political commentators also argued in 1986 that a scene shift had taken place in the political landscape. At the beginning of 1986, the Conservative Party lay third in the polls; and in the course of the year the Alliance declined sharply, apparently opening the way for a straight fight between Labour (which was in the lead for the first ten months of 1986) and the Conservatives in a two-party dominated contest. But in the event, the Conservatives stormed back to win a landslide victory in 1987, with the help of a timely reflation of the economy and a resurgent Alliance that split the opposition vote.

In short, it is not clear that external circumstances – though pointing much more in the direction of Conservative defeat than before – have fundamentally changed. The 'new look' Labour Party, now arguably the most conservative political force in the country, may not provide the inspirational lead needed to mobilise and unite oppositional forces under its banner.

But while we need to look for additional ways of reinforcing anti-Tory trends, it is still open to question whether the proposed ways of doing this will carry us much further forward. Thus, the most widely canvassed strategy for defeating the Conservatives at the next election is an electoral pact between the opposition parties. But, in reality, there is not the slightest prospect of a pact being signed by Labour and the Liberal Democrats before the next election because the principal politicians in both parties are strongly opposed to it. Even if this was not the case, it is doubtful whether opposition leaders could superimpose tactical unity on a non-Conservative electorate which remains divided (and a section of which is still strongly anti-Labour).

The other more promising approach is to launch campaigns that would transform the climate of public opinion and help create a 'popular front of the mind' unifying the non-Thatcherite majority. One strategy, already initiated by Charter 88, is to campaign for the democratisation of the state, including crucially the reform of our flawed electoral system. Another suggestion is to mobilise in defence of the quality of life, incorporating some of the themes advanced by the Greens. A third proposal is to campaign around the theme of citizenship, with guaranteed rights and obligations.

Each of these campaign proposals is worth supporting in the sense that they are directed at desirable objectives. Each could contribute (and, in some cases, already has contributed) to a climate of opinion hostile to the government. But they all suffer from the same drawback. They resonate more with the concerns of the professional middle class than with other strata in the community. Although the political mobilisation of the professional middle class will have a ripple effect, it is unlikely to bring into being a substantial new constituency of opposition. In particular, it is not clear that these campaigns will connect with the central preoccupations of a pivotal group: those skilled workers in the north-west, Midlands and south of England, whose conversion to voting Conservative has been central to the Conservatives' electoral success.

Turning Left with the Centre

I want to suggest a different approach. It is inspired by the experience of living recently in Stockholm. The standard of collective provision in Sweden – in terms of health, education (though not day-care facilities), pensions, public transport and welfare – is astonishingly high. Unemployment is minimal at under 2%. The incomes of around 80% of the population are compressed into a ratio of 2:1. Relations between men and women are more egalitarian than here. Above all, there are no pockets of acute poverty. Stockholm's immigrant ghetto – the equivalent of Brixton – has good housing, rolling lawns, a thronged pedestrian-only central avenue, a decent children's play area, and a very much higher level of personal affluence.

Of course, the Swedish model cannot readily be transplanted to Britain[4]. The Swedish economy is more successful and can sustain a higher level of collective provision; the working class is enrolled into very powerful trades unions with direct access to the state; the capitalist class is defensive and conciliatory; the population is small enough for interlocking networks to provide ready channels of negotiation and compromise. Sweden's culture is also more socially cohesive and egalitarian than Britain's.

But there are elements of the Swedish corporatist approach that can be adapted and allowed to develop in a British context. The British economy is deindustrialising, and our freedom of manoeuvre is contracting now that our oil production is declining. There is a pent-up demand for spending on our dilapidated public sector that cannot possibly be met in the short term. And there are groups of abandoned people living in crumbling housing estates, with boarded-up broken windows and graffiti-scarred corridors, without ready access to jobs, whose votes don't count because they are stacked up in safe inner-city seats, and whose plight is not visible to the affluent who have moved out to areas where there are good schools and amenities. At this particular juncture, it makes sense to start afresh with a new approach attuned to what is possible in the politics of the 1990s.

The Labour Party should develop a public dialogue with disaffected business and managerial interests, among others, in a search for a strategy to regenerate the British economy. As part of this process, it should involve the centre parties in informal policy discussions since they are a crucial part of the cross-class coalition that is needed to establish the consensual basis for economic recovery. For the Swedish experience underlines one thing; economic regeneration is achieved not simply through the right technical mix of policies but also through the creation of consent for the implementation of these policies. Crucially, this will mean in Britain, as in Sweden (and even more dramatically in social-democratic Finland, the Japan of northern Europe) acceptance of higher levels of investment in new manufacturing industry at the expense of consumption. This will only be achieved if a national consensus is won through the co-ordination and involvement of the principal interests in British society.

However, at the heart of the success of the Swedish corporatist approach (and it is a durable success, despite recent political difficulties) is a core of political radicalism that makes the Labour administrations under Wilson and Callaghan seem deeply conservative by comparison. Its three distinctive characteristics have been the abolition of poverty as a collective priority, advances towards co-determination at work, and a more equal distribution of income and rewards (all goals for which there is, according to opinion polls, consensual support in Britain). It is the pursuit and realisation of these objectives which has given Sweden's leadership its legitimacy; and paradoxically helped to make a market-based, predominantly capitalist economy function successfully. The implication of the Swedish model for the Labour Party is thus that it should be both more radical and less sectarian. It should be more unabashedly egalitarian and more ambitious in its commitment to reverse Britain's economic decline. But it should also be more conciliatory, more willing to work with other parties and interests in a spirit of partnership.

Sweden is, in one sense, directly comparable to Britain in that it has suffered from declining traditional industries which it has had painfully and with difficulty to replace. But Sweden differs in that it is not part of the EC. The Labour Party and its associates will need to take part in developing a European dimension to its national plan for economic recovery. This is already beginning to happen, although the French, Greek and Italian socialists have so far done most of the running.

In sum, this new approach entails not an electoral alliance undertaken for short-term political advantage but consensus building as part of a national strategy for recovery. Unlike a pre-election pact, it is something that Neil Kinnock could conceivably contemplate. Moreover, it could well prove more effective in winning votes than an electoral pact since it could convince sceptics that the Labour Party and associates are best able to safeguard the country's economic future. And more to the point, it could also ensure that Labour will actually run our affairs better than the failed administrations of the past four decades.

LANGUAGE LESSON

There are two main languages in current use:
The first consists chiefly
Of verbs, nouns, adjectives, prepositions;
The second, of gelignite,
Human organs, blood and tears.

The second language cannot be forbidden.
Although it's hateful
No simple laws can be passed
To have it dumped in the sea,
Buried in concrete, its hands cut off, its tongue clamped.
Not even by a total ban on parking,
Nor the house-arrest of all males under forty
Could it wholly be outlawed.
It's obscene, addictive, vibrant, rooted.

The first language
Cannot be abolished, either,
Though merely made of words.

Try severing a length of words.
You'll see it's like a worm,
Both halves alive
And wriggling into questions.

If the questions are ignored
Over a sufficient length of time
The first language, with alarming facility,
Mutates into the second.

Carol Rumens

ENGLAND TO HER MAKER

Hephaestus we tried to tell you
The signs were everywhere
You kept your head down

Face to the glare
Hammering bevelling punching
All that noise and smoke

No wonder you didn't hear
You were wreathed in the heat
And darkness of your craft

Never stood upright except
To hammer our silences
With ringing cries of grievance

Peculiar to your class
Eyes clearer than yours Hephaestus
Were noting the lack of new orders

We don't deny you had skills
You armed the fighting gods
Invented such curiosities

As the self-propelling tripod
The fire-breathing bronze bull
Magnificent yet not

Exactly what life's about
Any more we have microchips
We have genuine automation

Quiet machines that can reason
Unlike your rough irons
Clanking brainlessly filthily

Think of your lungs black
As the grass round here your legs
Bowed under you like pliers

. . .

You could have a job sitting down
Somewhere warm and well-lit
Where there's music plants fountains

Imagine yourself with white cuffs
Tapping a keyboard smiling
Taking cash and credit cards smiling

It's the future you can't fight the future
You can't argue with progress
Hephaestus look at it this way

Carol Rumens

After the Berlin Wall

MARTIN JACQUES

The collapse of the Eastern European regimes marks the end of an historical epoch. The communist era ushered in by the October Revolution is drawing to a close. Already of course, before the monumental events in Eastern Europe in the second half of 1989, the writing was on the wall. Gorbachev himself had already brought into question many of the assumptions which were central to the communist era. And the events in Tiananmen Square, almost on the eve of the East European revolutions, had revealed the bankruptcy of a regime which, unlike those in Europe, had once enjoyed enormous prestige and support among its people.

The end of the communist era has enormous implications for the Left, East and West. The division of Europe was also the division of the Left. The predominantly social-democratic Left of Western Europe had little in common with the communist Left of Eastern Europe and the Soviet Union. Indeed, the former viewed the latter as an embarrassment, as an alien force. The advent of Gorbachev and now the collapse of the East European regimes has ended the era of estrangement. The Berlin Wall within the Left has tumbled like the real one. For the first time since 1917, there is now a common language of the Left with ideas like democracy, markets, ecology, and social justice part of its vocabulary.

But it was not only a geographical division between the Left of East and West. It was also a political division within the West European Left, between socialist and communist parties. This already began to break down in the 1970s with the era of eurocommunism, when some communist parties explicitly endorsed the democratic values of the West in preference to the Leninist legacy of the East. The process of social-democratisation of at least the more eurocommunist CPs was under way, with the Italian CP the outstanding example as always. Indeed for some years now it has enjoyed closer relations with many West European socialist parties than it has done with the equivalent CPs.

But the historical moment ushered in by the East European revolutions has a quite new force and logic to it. If it is the end of the era of

[247]

1917, then it is also the end of the era of communist parties in the sense in which they have identified with a communist tradition and seen themselves as historically different and separate from the social-democratic tradition. The modern division of the European socialist movement into its socialist and communist wings dates back to the attitude adopted towards World War One and then subsequently the Russian Revolution. The formation of the Third International alongside the Second International cast that division in stone. But there is no longer any historical justification for it. We are witnessing the reunification of the European socialist movement, either through the social-democratisation of communist parties (the case of Italy), or through their effective disappearance (West Germany, Britain).

Demise of Utopia

But the end of communism also has a wider ideological meaning. It marks the end of a particular concept of socialism and how it might be achieved. In the Leninist view, there was a belief that it was possible to jump stages. That was why the October Revolution was seen as a possibility in the first place, even though Russia was such a backward country. And jumping stages in turn involved a powerful stress on voluntarism, that of the revolutionary party in possession of the laws of motion of history. There was also the belief that socialism could be built in one country, although only with Stalin did this become an unambiguous commitment. And underlying the notion of socialism in one country, and subsequently one bloc, was the idea that socialism could be a kind of liberated area, existing in more or less splendid isolation from a hostile capitalist world, competing with it, and slowly rolling it back. It was a world of opposites, of chalk and cheese, of autarchy rather than interpenetration.

The collapse of the Leninist project marks the end of the era of socialism in one bloc. Heaven on earth is an impossibility. A utopian dream lies in ashes. Stages cannot be jumped. Voluntarism has been cruelly exposed. Democracy cannot be suppressed in the name of class. The notion of autarchic development, of capitalist and socialist systems as opposites, of socialism as some purist clause four alternative, belong, of course, above all to the tradition of the October Revolution. But the influence of these ideas is not confined to the Leninist tradition. They can be found in the social-democratic tradition, remaining strong, for example, in parts of the Labour Party. The collapse of the Bolshevik tradition marks the demise of the socialist utopia as an alternative. The emphasis now will be on interdependence, on a world of limits, in which social progress in one country will always be constrained by the level of progress elsewhere. Old-style voluntarism is replaced by interdependence and constraint. And in parenthesis, it is worth remembering that the October Revolution was carried through by the Bolsheviks in the expectation of imminent revolutions in advanced European countries like Germany. But when they failed to materialise, this particular notion of interdependence was replaced by the autarchic commitment to socialism in one country.

But the ideological meaning of the end of the communist era goes further. It has something to say about Marxism and Marxist politics. To be a Marxist came to mean, for the most part, to identify politically in large measure with the Leninist tradition. One subscribed to the tradition of the October Revolution. In the spirit of that tradition, the label was an exclusivist one: you were a Marxist and not something else. It defined your intellectual and political being. The end of the Bolshevik tradition marks the end of that exclusivist tradition. Of course, many who might describe themselves as Marxist have already gone beyond that singularity to a more pluralistic identity, as Marxist and feminist, for example. But that process will now proceed with a new fleetness of foot. Marxism will come to take its place as one influence alongside others. The classical social-democratic tradition is suggestive of what might happen. The Second International was itself part of the Marxist tradition, drawing heavily on Marx's ideas for its inspiration. It was as legitimately Marxist as its detractors in the Third International. But its subsequent ideological evolution was essentially pluralistic rather than singular.

Looking at the future in terms of the past, there is no doubt that the socialist movement will be social-democratic rather than communist in inspiration. Gradualist notions of change have triumphed over apocalyptic ones: the end point of change is not paradise, but something which bears the hallmarks of the present. But in saying this, we must not ignore a number of important features of the social-democratic tradition itself. Firstly, it too has changed over time. After 1945, for example, it became in many countries a creature of the Cold War and bloc politics. Since the 1960s, by contrast, it has acquired a new independence under the influence of figures like Brandt and Palme.

Secondly, social democracy is itself an extremely hybrid beast. It always has been. Labourism, for example, has always been some kind of exception, standing outside much of the tradition of the Second International, and having an extremely distinctive intellectual (or anti-intellectual) history. And today, there is a striking gulf between parties like Gonzales's PSOE in Spain and Pasok in Greece, and the SPD in West Germany and the Swedish Social Democrats. The PSOE has presided over a Thatcherite modernisation of Spain with little commitment to equality or reform, while in contrast the SPD and the SAP are explicitly reformist parties, seeking to find alternative solutions to the problems of modern society.

The social-democratic tradition, therefore, is itself pluralistic and porous, diverse and dynamic. It is not one thing, but many things. The way in which the Italian Communist Party has mutated into a mainly social-democratic party is an example of this. It remains distinctive within that tradition, bringing a rich and independent theoretical heritage, the richest of any socialist party in Europe. It comes from outside – though not completely, because it inherited the main reformist traditions of the Italian labour movement – yet still sits comfortably within it.

This stress on the plurality of the social-democratic tradition needs to be combined with another. It too is a tradition in crisis. The crisis is nothing like that faced by the communist tradition, but it is nonetheless one of historic proportions. Its modern strength as a reforming movement was based on the historic circumstances of the period between the wars. Its reforming highwater mark was the Keynesian, welfare state model of the postwar period, and its social base was the industrial working class. Everywhere that model has been under pressure if not actually undermined, most of all in Britain, least of all in Sweden, while its old social constituency of support has been a rapidly contracting asset.

Learning to Live in a European Space

The failure of social democracy to generate a new model of reform is probably the most obvious sense in which it faces a crisis. The evidence of this lies not least in the experience of socialist government in the 1980s. Everywhere it has for the most part operated on the ground of the radical Right, certainly in economic policy. Nowhere has the cause of the Left and reform excited positive enthusiasm, and been able to act as some kind of social magnet. With the ever-present exception of Sweden, the Left nowhere enjoys hegemony, even if it can get elected. But the problems of the social-democratic tradition go beyond its capacity to generate a new kind of political perspective. One of the distinctive features of West European societies over the last three decades has been the constant expansion and innovation of civil society, and with that a shift in the centre of gravity of politics away from political society as such, from formal political institutions like parties, towards civil society, and new kinds of political movements, such as feminism and the Greens.

What we are observing here is the recomposition and redefinition of our political culture. Old forms of collectivity and representation are in decline or are being forced to change, in response to the rise of new kinds of political concern, embracing very different identities and collectivities, and embracing very different kinds of representation. Yet by and large the social-democratic tradition has failed to respond to these changes.

There is a crisis of the party form, and as yet no solution in sight. One indication of this problem is the failure of the new popular imperatives of collectivism that began to push the radical Right on to the defensive at the end of the 1980s – environmentalism, Europe, the end of the Cold War – to engender a popular revival of the Left. There remains a pronounced cultural gap or deficit.

Perhaps the point that most deserves emphasis, therefore, is that the terminal crisis of the communist tradition does not mean that the Western social-democratic Left can rest on its laurels in the 1990s. Perhaps this is a rather trite point, for when we get down from the lofty pedestal of ideological generalisation and take a look at the micro level, as in the case of the Labour Party, for example, it is blindingly obvious. To see the events of 1989 as the victory of the social-democratic, and the defeat of the communist, tradition is a mite too complacent and conservative. It certainly is that, but looking ahead it underestimates the crisis of the social-democratic tradition and just how much that must change in the 1990s, if it is to prosper.

Two impulses which flow directly from the events of 1989 suggest ways in which the West European Left will begin to recompose itself in the 1990s. The first is the experience of civic forums in Eastern Europe – Civic Forum in Czechoslovakia, Neues Forum in the GDR, and so forth. These represent generalised movements, combining both party and movement under one umbrella. They explode the traditional distinction between party and movement, which is an unresolved dilemma of the West European socialist tradition. They may well prove to be a passing phase, the product of a moment, but their example may leave a more permanent mark, West as well as East. The other impulse is the fallout from the communist tradition. Marxism, in its non-exclusivist, eurocommunist form, will take its place alongside other traditions in the West European social-democratic movement, now an insider rather than an outsider, rubbing shoulders with liberalism, parliamentarianism, feminism, greenery, labourism and so on.

The contours of the West European Left after the Berlin Wall will thus become even more complex and variegated. The phrase 'social-democratic' will describe only part of its nature and meaning. For social democracy is obliged to go beyond itself, to transform its being, if it is to live successfully in new times. There are three major elements to this. Firstly, it has to generate a new kind of political perspective adapted to the realities of a more flexible, post-Fordist world. Secondly, it has to adapt to the new features of political culture outlined earlier. And finally, it has to learn to live in a European space rather than the national space it currently occupies.

Notes

(in alphabetical order of contributors)

Sarah Benton

1. Two pamphlets which have recently argued that they can are 'Creating A Mass Party' by the Tribune Group (1989) and, far more ambivalently, 'A Rational Advance for the Labour Party' by John Lloyd, Chatto Counterblasts No 3, 1989.

2. Hannah Arendt, *The Origins of Totalitarianism*, Andre Deutsch, 1986

3. Christine Collette, *For Labour and for Women: The Women's Labour League 1906–18*, Manchester University Press, 1989

4. See for instance Alan Ware's refutation of this analysis for the USA in *The Breakdown of Democratic Party Organization, 1940–80*, Clarendon Press, 1985

5. See in particular the analysis from Germaine Tillan, *The Republic of Cousins*

Peter Clarke

1. L. T. Hobhouse quoted in Peter Clarke, *Liberals and Social Democrats*, Cambridge University Press, 1978

2. Hugh Dalton in Ben Pimlott (ed.), *The Second World War Diary of Hugh Dalton*, Jonathan Cape, 1986

3. J. M. Keynes in Donald Moggridge (ed.), *The Collected Works of John Maynard Keynes*, 30 vols., Macmillan, 1971–89, vol. xxiii

4. Ibid., vol ix

James Curran

1. This is hotly contested. For the principal protagonists on either side, see Bo Sarlvik and Ivor Crewe, *Decade of Dealignment*, Cambridge University Press,

1983, and Ivor Crewe, 'On the Death and Resurrection of Class Voting: Some Comments on *How Britain Votes*', *Political Studies*, 34, 1986; Anthony Heath, Roger Jowell and John Curtice, *How Britain Votes*, Pergamon, 1985, and their rejoinder 'Trendless Fluctuation: A Reply to Crewe', *Political Studies*, 35, 1987. It seems to me at least that Heath *et al.* got the better of the argument.

2. Gordon Marshall, David Rose, Howard Newby and Carolyn Vogler, *Social Class in Modern Britain*, Unwin Hyman, 1989

3. Ivor Crewe, 'Has the Electorate Become Thatcherite?' in Robert Skidelsky (ed.), *Thatcherism*, Chatto & Windus, 1988

4. The Swedish corporatist approach also has its problems, as was highlighted by political rejection of the Swedish Government's ill-considered initial counter-inflation strategy in early 1990. But Sweden's economy remains internationally competitive, unlike Britain's; and its polity is geared – again unlike Britain's – to dealing with its problems.

Patricia Hewitt

1. Pearce *et al*, *Blueprint for a Green Economy*, Earthscan, 1989

2. World Commission on Environment and Development, *Our Common Future*, Oxford University Press, 1987

3. Martin Janicke, *Environmental Charges and Change in Political Paradigm*, Forschungsstelle fur Umweltpolitik, Free University of Berlin, 1989

4. Kreisky Commission on Employment Issues in Europe, *A Programme for Full Employment in the 1990s*, Pergamon Press, 1989

5. P. Hewitt, *A Cleaner, Faster London: Road Pricing, Transport Policy and the Environment*, Institute for Public Policy Research, 1989

6. N. Ridley, *Policies Against Pollution*, Centre for Policy Studies, 1989

7. M. Persanyi *et al*, *Ecology, State, Market in a Changing Hungary*, Budapest, 1989

Paul Hirst

1. Michael Piore and Charles Sabel, *The Second Industrial Divide*, Basic Books, New York, 1984

2. Paul Hirst and Jonathan Zeitlin, *Reversing Industrial Decline?*, Berg, Oxford, 1984

Christopher Huhne

1. Organisation for Economic Co-operation and Development Economic Surveys 'France 1988/1989', Paris, March 1989

Julian Le Grand

1. Department of Health, *Working for Patients*, Cm 555, HMSO, 1989

2. R. Griffiths, *Community Care: Agenda for Action*, HMSO, 1988

3. Department of Health, *Caring for People*, Cm 849, HMSO, 1989

4. P. Hoggett, 'Post-Fordism and the welfare state', School for Advanced Urban Studies, University of Bristol, 1989

5. J. Le Grand, *The Strategy of Equality*, Allen and Unwin, 1982. R. Goodin and J. Le Grand, *Not Only the Poor: the Middle Classes and the Welfare State*, Allen and Unwin, 1987. G. Bramley, J. Le Grand and W. Low, 'How far is the poll tax a "community charge"? The implications of service usage evidence.' *Policy and Politics* No. 17, 1989

6. M. Young, 'A place for vouchers in the NHS', *Samizdat* No. 6, 1989

7. P. Hewitt, 'A way to cope with the world as it is', *Samizdat* No. 6, 1989

8. N. Barr and A. Barnes, *Strategies for Higher Education*, Aberdeen University Press, 1988

Julian Le Grand would like to acknowledge helpful comments from colleagues at the School for Advanced Urban Studies working on the Quasi-Markets Programme, and those at the London School of Economics working on the ESRC-ST/ICERD Welfare State Programme.

David Marquand

1. Albert O. Hirschman, *Shifting Involvements*, Basil Blackwell, 1983

2. Albert O. Hirschman, *Exit, Voice and Loyalty – Responses to Decline in Firms, Organizations and States*, Harvard, Cambridge, Mass., 1970

3. Charles E. Lindblom, *Politics and Markets: The World's Political Economics*, Basic Books, New York, 1977

4. Brian Barry, *The Liberal Theory of Justice*, Clarendon Press, 1985

5. W. Streeck and P. Schmitter, 'Community, Market State – and Associations? The Prospective Contribution of Interest Governance to Social Order', in W. Streeck and P. Schmitter (eds.), *Private Interest Government*, Sage, London and Beverley Hills, 1985

6. Brian Lee Crowley, 'The Limitations of the Liberalism: the Self, the Individual and the Community in Modern British Political Thought, with Special Reference to F. A. Hayek and Sidney and Beatrice Webb', London University Ph.D., 1985, pp. 218–77

7. Mary Midgley, *Beast and Man: The Roots of Human Nature*, Methuen, 1980

8. Peter Clarke, *Liberals and Social Democrats*, Cambridge University Press, 1978, esp. pp. 1–8

9. Quoted in Carole Pateman, *Participation and Democratic Theory*, Cambridge University Press, 1970

Contributors

Sarah Benton is a writer and journalist. She has been political editor of *New Statesman and Society*.

Ken Booth is professor of international politics at the University College of Wales, Aberystwyth. His books include *Strategy and Ethnocentrism*.

Melvyn Bragg edits and presents London Weekend Television's *The South Bank Show*. He is the author of many novels and screenplays, and the biography *Rich: The Life of Richard Burton*.

Peter Clarke is a fellow of St John's College, Cambridge. He recently published *The Keynesian Revolution in the Making 1924–1936*.

James Curran is professor of communications at Goldsmiths College, University of London. He is co-author of *Power Without Responsibility: the Press and Broadcasting in Britain* and former founding editor of *New Socialist*, the Labour Party's journal of ideas.

Nicholas Deakin is professor of social policy and administration at the University of Birmingham, and a frequent writer on policy issues.

Jenny Diski has published three novels: *Nothing Natural*, *Rain Forest* and *Like Mother*.

Gavin Ewart has published many books of poetry, from *Poems and Songs* in 1939 to *Selected Poems 1933–1988* (USA). He has also edited several anthologies including *The Penguin Book of Light Verse*.

Tony Flower is a co-founder of *Samizdat*, former general secretary of the Tawney Society, and director of several educational, research and design organisations.

Andrew Gamble is professor of politics at the University of Sheffield and the author of *Britain in Decline* and *The Free Economy and the Strong State*.

Peter Hennessy is a columnist on the *Independent*, and a regular broadcaster. His latest book is *Whitehall*.

Patricia Hewitt is deputy director of the Institute for Public Policy Research, and was formerly policy co-ordinator to Neil Kinnock.

Paul Hirst is professor of social theory at Birkbeck College, University of London, and is the author of *After Thatcher*.

Richard Holme is a former president of the Liberal Party, chairman of the Constitutional Reform Centre, secretary of the Parliamentary Democracy Trust and a Liberal Democrat life peer.

Christopher Huhne is economics editor and assistant editor of the *Independent on Sunday*, having been economics editor and weekly columnist on the *Guardian*.

Martin Jacques is editor of *Marxism Today*.

Terry Jones helped launch *Monty Python's Flying Circus* on an unsuspecting world in 1969 and has since directed several films, of which his latest is *Erik the Viking*. His books include *Chaucer's Knight* and *Attacks of Opinion*.

Julian Le Grand is professor of public policy at the School for Advanced Urban Studies, University of Bristol. His latest book, jointly edited, is *Market Socialism*.

John Lloyd is East European editor of the *Financial Times* and was formerly editor of the *New Statesman*.

David Marquand is professor of contemporary history and politics at Salford University, and is a leading member of the Liberal Democrats. His books include *Ramsay MacDonald* and *The Unprincipled Society*.

John Mortimer is the creator of *Rumpole of the Bailey* and author of many books and plays, including *A Voyage Round My Father*. His latest television series is *Summer's Lease*. As a barrister he has defended several important censorship cases.

Peter Nichols has written plays for stage and screen, including *A Day in the Death of Joe Egg*, *Forget-me-not Lane* and *Privates on Parade*, and an autobiography, *Feeling You're Behind*.

Ben Pimlott is professor of politics at Birkbeck College and founding editor of *Samizdat*. His books include *Hugh Dalton*, which won the Whitbread Biography Award.

Raymond Plant is professor of politics at the University of Southampton. He was a co-founder of the Socialist Philosophy Group. He has published *Hegel*; *Political Philosophy and Social Welfare*; and *Conservative Capitalism in Britain and the United States: A Critical Appraisal*. He is a columnist on *The Times*.

John Rentoul is a journalist and broadcaster with the BBC's *On the Record* programme. He is the author of *Me and Mine: The Triumph of the New Individualism?* and *The Rich Get Richer: The Growth of Inequality in Britain in the 1980s*, and was formerly deputy editor of the *New Statesman*.

Michael Rosen is a regular presenter of BBC Radio Four's children's book programme *Treasure Islands*, and the author of many books for children including *Don't Put Mustard in the Custard* and *Quick, Let's Get Out of Here*.

Carol Rumens has published several books of poetry, including *From Berlin to Heaven*, *The Greening of the Snow Beach* and the novel *Plato Park*.

Jeremy Seabrook regularly contributes articles to *New Statesman and Society*, the *Guardian* and the *Independent*. His most recent books are *The Race for Riches* and *Life and Labour in a Bombay Slum*.

Jean Seaton is co-author of *Power Without Responsibility: the Press and Broadcasting in Britain*, and joint editor of *The Media in British Politics*.

Roy Shaw was secretary-general of the Arts Council from 1975 to 1983; formerly he was professor and director of adult education at Keele University. His books include *The Arts and the People*.

Emma Tennant has written eight novels, including *The Bad Sister*, *Wild Nights* and *The House of Hospitalities*. She is the founding editor of the literary newspaper *Bananas*.

Anthony Wright is reader in British political thought at the University of Birmingham; author of several books on the politics of ideas; co-editor (with Nicholas Deakin) of *Consuming Public Services*; and prospective Labour parliamentary candidate for Cannock and Burntwood.

Michael Young founded the Consumers' Association and originated the Open University. Drafter of the 1945 Labour manifesto, he is also the author or co-author of *Family and Kinship in East London*, *The Rise of the Meritocracy* and, most recently, *The Metronomic Society*.